WIDER HORIZONS IN
CHRISTIAN ADULT EDUCATION

WIDER HORIZONS IN CHRISTIAN ADULT EDUCATION

Selected Addresses and Papers Presented in a Workshop on the Curriculum of Christian Education for Adults
Pittsburgh, Pennsylvania, June 19-30, 1961

Conducted by
THE SCHOOL OF EDUCATION
UNIVERSITY OF PITTSBURGH

with aid of a Financial Grant from LILLY ENDOWMENT, INC.

Edited
by
Lawrence C. Little

UNIVERSITY OF PITTSBURGH PRESS
1962

Library of Congress Card Number: 62-14381

© 1962, University of Pittsburgh Press

Preface

THE FIRST of a series of workshops on the Christian education of adults was held at the University of Pittsburgh in the summer of 1958. This was devoted to the task of "Charting the Future Course of Christian Adult Education in America." Among the questions dealt with were these: What new opportunities and problems are presented to adults by recent changes and current trends in American culture? How are adults affected by our culture? What kinds of adult learning will be required by our changing society in the next quarter of a century? What specific needs for continuing learning will adults have in order to live adequately under the new conditions? What should be the general objectives of adult education? What is the unique role of Christian education in accomplishing these objectives? What should be the objectives of Christian adult education, as distinguished from adult education in general? What are some of the major strengths and weaknesses of Christian adult education as carried on presently in our churches? How can adults be guided in their growth toward Christian maturity? How can the content and methods of Christian adult education be improved? What are some of the most pressing advances needed in Christian adult education today?

Two volumes of papers and reports produced in the 1958 workshop have been widely circulated among the agencies involved in the Christian education of adults in Canada and the United States. These, edited by the present writer, are *The Future Course of Christian Adult Education* (Pittsburgh: University of Pittsburgh Press, 1959), a collection of addresses, papers, and symposia presented during the workshop sessions; and *Formulating the Objectives of Christian Adult Education* (Pittsburgh: The Department of Religious Education, University of Pittsburgh, 1958), containing outlines and summaries of the reports of study and discussion groups.

Upon the conclusion of the first workshop, the participants were all agreed that the groundwork had been firmly laid for advances in the Christian education of adults but that additional study and research should be carried forward particularly in the area of the curriculum. Consequently, plans were made for a Workshop on the Curriculum of Christian Education for Adults. This was held at the University of Pittsburgh, June 19-30, 1961, supported by a financial grant from Lilly Endowment, Inc., of Indianapolis, Indiana.

The second workshop brought together a total of 103 responsible leaders in adult education from many of the denominations and councils of religious education in Canada, the United States, and several foreign countries. They included editors, publishers, curriculum writers, directors of adult work, leaders of men's and women's work, pastors, directors of religious education, professors in universities and theological seminaries, consultants from a variety of specialized fields, and graduate students engaged in research in adult education.

The group spent two weeks together, engaged in an intensive exploration of the needs of adults arising from the pressures and demands of modern life; the requirements of a curriculum of Christian education designed to serve these needs; the present status of the curriculum; changes needed in order to provide a more adequate curriculum; and some possible ways of bringing about these changes.

The first week was devoted largely to orientation and "self-education" on the part of the participants. Addresses and papers were presented by leading specialists in such fields as adult education, the philosophy of education, higher education, psychology, psychiatry, educational research and measurement, public and international affairs, character education, religious education, counseling, theology, and theological education. Study and discussion groups carefully considered these presentations from the standpoint of their possible implications for the Christian education of adults.

Following the workshop, the authors rewrote their material in the light of new learnings and insights that they had gained through this group process. The present volume contains the final version of the addresses and papers originally written for the workshop.

The second week of the workshop was devoted to intensive work by six "Task Groups," which sought to specify some "Guidelines" for the future development of the curriculum of Christian education for adults. These groups gave considered attention to six areas of special concern to curriculum makers: (1) Our Christian Heritage and Faith; (2) Personal and Societal Needs; (3) Curriculum Structure and Organization; (4) Methodology and Leadership; (5) Neglected Areas and Needed Resources; and (6) A Charter for Christian Adult Education. The reports of these Task Groups have been published in a preliminary volume, *Guidelines for the Development of a Curriculum of Christian Education for Adults* (Pittsburgh: The Department of Religious Education, University of Pittsburgh, 1961). Plans are under way to edit, revise, and expand these reports into a manual that should prove of continuing usefulness to writers and publishers of curriculum and to leaders of adult education in the churches.

The term "curriculum" is used here in its broadest sense—to include much more than printed materials. The workshop attempted to take into account both "curriculum" and "program" as these terms are used, somewhat ambiguously, in current educational literature. Within the present context, and for purposes of brevity, *curriculum* is intended to denote *the total organized provision made by the churches to guide and enrich the experience of those who take part in their activities.*

The editor wishes to record here his deep appreciation to Lilly Endowment, Inc., without whose financial aid the workshop would have been impossible; to the consultants for their able contributions to this symposium; to Dr. Marvin J. Taylor, who prepared the index; and to all the participants in the workshop for their devoted and loyal efforts in the direction of a more adequate curriculum of Christian education for adults in the churches of tomorrow.

LAWRENCE C. LITTLE

Contents

1. Trends in Religious Behavior during the Adult Years   *1*
   RAYMOND G. KUHLEN
2. Socio-cultural Factors Inhibiting Christian Adult Education   *27*
   GORDON E. JACKSON
3. Recent Developments in Curriculum Theory and Some Implications for Christian Adult Education   *44*
   RYLAND W. CRARY
4. Communication Theory and Its Implications for Christian Adult Education   *58*
   ROBERT S. CLEMMONS
5. A Theory of Christian Adult Education Methodology   *73*
   MALCOLM S. KNOWLES
6. Insights for Christian Education from Research in Adult Motivation   *88*
   WILLIAM A. KOPPE
7. Some Contemporary Lay Movements and Their Implications for Adult Education in the Churches   *104*
   LLOYD M. BERTHOLF
8. Insights for Adult Religious Education from Other Sources   *122*
   PAUL BERGEVIN
9. Challenges and Responsibilities for Christian Adults in Contemporary Public and International Issues   *136*
   DONALD C. STONE
10. Dialogic Foundations of Christian Adult Education   *153*
    REUEL L. HOWE

11. The Significance of Christian Theology for Adult
    Education   169
        ROGER HAZELTON
12. Christian Adult Education and the Ecumenical
    Movement   185
        A. WILSON CHEEK
        EVERETT M. STOWE
13. Some Reflections on the Current Status of Adult
    Curriculum Materials   199
        MARVIN J. TAYLOR
14. Pooling Our Efforts in Building a More Adequate
    Curriculum of Christian Education for Adults   216
        J. BLAINE FISTER
15. Behavioral Outcomes of the Christian Education of
    Adults   233
        PAUL B. MAVES
16. Criteria for Judging the Quality of Christian
    Education for Adults   257
        C. ELLIS NELSON
17. Measurement and Evaluation in Christian Adult
    Education: Present Status and Future Possibilities   278
        LEONARD A. SIBLEY, JR.
18. Adult Education in the Church of Tomorrow: A
    Study Outline   297
        LAWRENCE C. LITTLE
19. A Selected Bibliography   306
        LAWRENCE C. LITTLE
    Index   332

1. Trends in Religious Behavior during the Adult Years

RAYMOND G. KUHLEN

Professor of Psychology
Syracuse University

At the turn of the century the psychology of religion attracted the interest of a number of leading psychologists. Starbuck (1900) wrote extensively and provided early factual data. Hall devoted considerable space to the matter in his analysis of adolescence, and James's classic on *The Varieties of Religious Experience* is still sufficiently popular that it is available in paperback.[1] Possibly because of the general decline of interest in religion during the first third of this century (articles on religion in popular magazines dropped steadily in frequency during this period whereas articles on science increased) or because of the then new behavioristic emphasis in psychology, interest in the psychology of religion waned. The last two decades, reversing the trend, have witnessed a resurgence of research activity in this field, possibly again reflecting a general

---

[1] E. D. Starbuck, *The Psychology of Religion* (New York, 1900); G. Stanley Hall, *Adolescence: Its Psychology and Its Relations to Physiology, Anthropology, Sociology, Sex, Crime, Religion, and Education* (New York, 1904); William James, *The Varieties of Religious Experience* (New York, 1902), available in Dolphin Books and New American Library of World Literature.

cultural trend, this time in the direction of increased religious interest, or possibly reflecting the enthusiasm many psychologists have evidenced in recent years in the area of values. Whatever the reason, an increasing number of psychologists and sociologists are giving serious thought to the study of religion and an increasingly rich supply of factual evidence is becoming available.

The present paper will summarize some of the available findings, particularly as they relate to trends during the adult years. It seems reasonable to expect that the effectiveness of programs in adult religious education will depend in part on the degree to which they relate to the *known* religious interests, practices, and needs of young adults, those of middle age, and those in the later years. The summary is in no sense exhaustive. The reader who wishes a more extensive survey should consult Argyle.[2]

The Problem of Definition

A troublesome first question requires attention before we proceed to an examination of the facts themselves, namely the matter of definition. What is religion? Who is a religious person? By what behaviors is he to be identified and graded as to degree? What are the various dimensions along which varying "types" of religious persons may be arranged? Maslow points up the problem: "a person who goes to church regularly may actually be *less* religious than one who does not go at all, because (1) he goes to avoid social isolation, or (2) he goes to please his mother, or (3) religion represents for him not humbleness but a weapon of domination over others, or (4) it marks him as a member of a superior group, or (5) as in Clarence Day's father, 'It is good for the ignorant masses and I must play along,' or . . . and so on. He may in a dynamic sense be not at all religious and still behave as though he were."[3]

---

[2] M. Argyle, *Religious Behavior* (Glencoe, Ill., 1959).

[3] A. H. Maslow, *Motivation and Personality* (New York, 1954), 25.

Only if we can arrive at a satisfactory index of religiousness, can we proceed to study its correlates and the types of antecedent conditions—early training, rebellion against parents, etc.—that may have produced the present characteristics. In short, before an adequate psychology of religion can emerge, we must be able to answer in *operational terms* such questions as: How religious is this person? In what way is he religious? Failure of investigators to agree on an appropriate index has resulted in some of the inconsistencies that appear among various interpretations of research data.

If one attempts to specify types of religious behavior, three broad categories become evident: (1) the *overt* behavior of church-going, church program participation, and personal religious practices, (2) the *covert* behavior of believing, feeling, valuing, and (3) the living of the "good life" in the religious sense, independently of the degree of participation in program or ritual, or even of beliefs held. While these aspects of religious behavior (at least the first two) are likely to be related to a degree, perhaps even highly correlated, they nonetheless may show different trends with the passage of time or with increase in age, or differing degrees of relatedness at widely disparate ages, with the result that no single aspect of the behavioral complex may provide a satisfactory index of the trend. This issue will be returned to when age trend data are presented later, but here let us document the point by citing a study of college students tested in 1936 and again (the same individuals) in 1950. Over this period of time, young adults became *more* positive in their attitudes toward the reality of God, toward God as an influence on conduct, and toward the church, but became *less* positive in their attitude toward Sunday observance.

Further evidence supporting the view that trends in attendance on the part of adolescents may indeed be contrary to those reflecting interest in religion is supplied by Kuhlen and Arnold and by Jones.[4] Although it is well known that church attend-

[4] E. N. P. Nelson, "Patterns of Religious Attitude Shifts from College to Fourteen Years Later," *Psychological Monographs,* 17 (1956) ; R. G. Kuhlen and Mar-

ance falls off during the adolescent years, this evidence shows increasing interest as reflected in a desire to talk about religion, and a desire on the part of a majority of adolescents for help on religious problems and concern with the meaning of religion, even though at the same time they evidence increased dislike for conventional church services.

TABLE I

PERCENTAGE OF ADOLESCENTS CHECKING VARIOUS TYPES OF RELIGIOUS PROBLEMS [5]

Religious Problems	Age		
	12	15	18
Disliking church service	33	47	60
Getting help on religious problems	53	54	56
Wanting to know the meaning of religion	53	48	60
Conflicts of science and religion	42	50	57

An examination of *overt* religious activities suggests that they may be considered as falling in at least three categories. First are those essentially public and out-of-home activities such as attendance at church and participation in church activities, which require a certain amount of energy output, time commitment, and interaction with others. One may expect such participation to be influenced (1) by competing activities requiring time and energy such as child-rearing, occupation, and even social demands; (2) by factors that reduce energy such as illness and old age; and (3) by factors (such as "inferior" social level) that result in individuals feeling ill at ease in the church social group. Second are those activities which, while "public," involve a more restricted public (e.g., one's own family) and

tha Arnold, "Age Differences in Religious Beliefs and Problems During Adolescence," *Journal of Genetic Psychology,* 65 (1944) , 291-300; Mary C. Jones, "A Comparison of the Attitudes and Interests of Ninth-Grade Students Over Two Decades," *Journal of Educational Psychology,* 51 (1960) , 175-86.

[5] Kuhlen and Arnold, "Age Differences in Religious Beliefs and Problems During Adolescence." Note that adolescents increasingly seem to have certain religious problems regarding which they would like help, but find church services unsatisfying.

which are essentially sedentary. They include family prayer, Bible-reading, saying of devotions before meals, listening to or viewing religious programs on radio or TV. And third are those various private practices such as personal prayer and reading religious materials. It is apparent that, as compared to church attendance and program participation, the latter two types of activities are likely to be much less subject to limits on time and energy or restrictions upon social activity. Accordingly, we might look to the latter as providing more meaningful evidence regarding age differences in religious orientation.

A number of efforts have been made recently to analyze systematically, by modern statistical procedures, the second broad category of religious behavior, namely, that of believing and valuing. In order to obtain a reasonably adequate sampling of the religious attitude area, Broen assembled a variety of items dealing with the following hypothesized types: (1) stress on sin, judgment, and "thou shalt nots"; (2) desire and need for religious belief to fill a void, but lack of specific doctrine; (3) stress on the moral and ethical aspects of religion; (4) emphasis on the love and glory of God and worship of him; and (5) "spirit-filled" speaking in tongues, casting out demons, etc. Using a technique known as inverse factor analysis, he found that only two factors or dimensions were necessary to account for the significant portion of the common variance. The first factor, which was unipolar, was described as "nearness of God." Persons high on this factor tended to feel that God was very real and constantly near and accessible; that they could commune with God, "walk and talk" with him. Their religiousness seemed to consist in an emphasis upon the Deity's loving presence and guidance rather than his judgmental function.

The second factor, which is bipolar, was labelled "fundamentalism-humanitarianism." Persons high on this factor tended to see man as essentially sinful and emphasized his need for, and rightful fear of, a punishing God. Persons on the other extreme of this factor tend to see man as containing the potential for good and the tools for actuating this potential (rationality, etc.), thus having little need for much outside intervention in the form of a deity. The addition of the scores on the two scales yielded what Broen considered to be a measure of "general religiosity," and the difference between the scales (scale 1 minus scale 2) a measure of differential emphasis. As expected, Unitarians scored much lower than such groups as Lutherans and Disciples of Christ in "nearness to God," and were farther out on the humanitarian end of the scale.

Schand utilized a different approach.[6] Interviews of 142 ministers, rabbis, and priests yielded approximately twenty-four hundred ideas which were classified into 180 different conceptions of what it meant to be "religious." Later four other groups of clergymen rated each of these 180 conceptions for its importance in defining a "religious person." Factor analysis was again employed to analyze the relationships among these different conceptions. Five factors emerged, each of which might be considered as representing a different conception of the religious person. These conceptions (which constitute two fundamentalist types and three humanistic types) follow:

1. The *formalistic fundamentalist* places greater emphasis than other groups on observing the formalities of religion—the acceptance of beliefs and creeds, ritual and tradition, and their cultivation.

2. The *puritanical fundamentalist* places greater emphasis than other groups on a religious person being one who doesn't drink, gamble, smoke, or swear, who is righteous, virtuous, and moral, etc.

3. The *humanistic* type places greater emphasis upon having a spirit of brotherhood, being interested in human welfare, wanting better social and economic conditions, having sympathy and understanding, seeing truth, being mature, fair, tolerant, and ethical, etc.

4. The *theistic humanistic* individual, while adhering to human values, places greater emphasis upon faith in God, acknowledging and being conscious of God, having a personal relationship to God, and having loyalty to, and serving, God.

5. The *religious-law observing* (all of whom were of the Jewish

---

[6] W. E. Broen, Jr., "A Factor-Analytic Study of Religious Attitudes," *Journal of Abnormal and Social Psychology*, 54 (1957), 176-79; J. Schand, "A Factorial Analysis of Clergymen's Ratings of Concepts Regarding What It Means To Be Religious," *Dissertation Abstracts*, 22 (1961), 371.

faith), while stressing belief in God and humanistic values, places greater emphasis than other groups on observing religious traditions and ritual, laws and commandments, and participating in activities of one's congregation.

It was interesting that clergymen as a whole did not have a single general conception of what it means to be religious, nor did clergymen of a single denomination have the same viewpoints. Instead the holding of these various conceptions tended to cut across denominational lines.

The contribution of such statistical approaches to the definition of religion is pointed up by contrast with another recent paper in which three scales (orthodoxy, fanaticism, and importance of religion) were constructed on conceptual grounds. It turned out that the scales intercorrelated .74, .82, and .81, thus demonstrating that they were measuring essentially the same dimension even though conceptually they appeared to be different.[7] Although advances in our understanding of the psychology of religion may be anticipated even with inadequate definitions, research pointing toward the refinement of concepts and the development of scales to measure them is basic if these advances are to be optimal.

The Cultural Context of Research: Secular Trends and Subcultural Contrasts

The fact that the focus of this paper is upon adult trends in religiousness, and hence upon age differences, requires a caution that may not have occurred to readers who have previously given little attention to the matter of data on aging. The interpretation of age differences will depend very largely upon the character of cultural change that has occurred over the period of recent generations. If, for example, there has been an increasing emphasis upon religion in our culture over the years, we might expect that younger individuals will be influenced in the direction of greater religiosity, since attitudes of this sort (and

---

[7] S. Putney and R. Middleton, "Dimensions and Correlates of Religious Ideologies," *Social Forces*, 39 (1961), 285-90.

others as well) tend to be inculcated in youth. Older individuals, having grown up in a culture with less religious emphasis, will tend to be less religious, unless compensating influences associated with age itself are at work. This contrast of one age group with representatives of another age group in studies of adult age is referred to as "cross-sectional" investigation.

In other types of studies, in which the same individuals are studied at different ages (a "longitudinal" type of investigation), quite the contrary results would be expected. The increasing religious emphasis in the culture will tend to influence individuals as they grow older, with the result that they will be more religious at an older age compared to *themselves* at a younger age simply because they have kept pace with the culture, rather than having become more religious as a result of getting older.

Two sets of data demonstrate that there has been indeed a greater interest in the American culture over the past generation. In one study Dartmouth College students were tested when in college in 1940-41 and again in 1955-56, fifteen years later. They showed marked gains in religious orientation as reflected by scores on the Allport-Vernon Scale of Values. But another sample of Dartmouth students tested at the same time as the retesting of the first group were at about the same point in religious interest in 1956 as the older group was in 1955-56.[8] Obviously the gain in religious emphasis in the retested group could be attributed very largely to cultural change.

This general effect of cultural change upon age differences must be borne in mind in interpreting the data presented later. However, adult religious educators should nonetheless recognize that, regardless of the cause of the differences among age groups, reported differences are the kind with which they must deal in any particular congregational group, and thus in many respects they are the relevant data for curriculum development. When it comes to the matter of evaluation of curriculum outcomes, one must be concerned about differences that are due to

---

[8] I. E. Bender, "Changes in Religious Interest: A Retest After 15 Years," *Journal of Abnormal and Social Psychology*, 57 (1958), 41-46.

age or, possibly, to cultural change. It is easy, without appropriate controls, to conclude that a religious education program has produced certain results, which in fact have occurred simply because of general aging trends or cultural developments.

It is also important to recognize that religion may mean quite different things to people in different cultural settings. It is often difficult for individuals (such as religious educators), who probably come from middle-class backgrounds, to appreciate that their own ways of thinking and feeling about religion, or the trends they observe with age, are not general within the culture. Actually, marked differences will occur, and differential age trends might well be expected in different subcultures. While social class or ethnic differences are probably as important as any, it is probable also that there are marked rural-urban differences, and certainly (as is widely known) important differences associated with the cultures in which the two sexes are reared. Although subcultural contrasts are usually not made within single studies, the critical reader must bear in mind that the generalizations of a single study, and often of a group of studies, are likely to be limited because of the considerations just noted.

The Psychological Correlates of Religiousness

As suggested in the introduction to this paper, there has been, in the last fifteen or twenty years, a growing interest on the part of psychologists in matters of attitudes and values. Personality variables and motivational concepts have been increasingly relied upon as explanatory variables. Increasingly, religious needs and values have been recognized as being a basic part of the value system of the individual and hence related to his general personality and motivational characteristics.

In general, it may be hypothesized that an individual with a particular motivational pattern and personality will tend to seek out that environment—that occupation, that spouse, that college, that religion and church—which offers the potential of satisfying his needs and which is compatible with his personality characteristics. Research by Winch in the area of mate selection, by Pace and Stern in the area of college environments, and by Kuhlen and Dipboye in the area of occupation has tended to substantiate this hypothesis in these areas of living.[9] To the present writer's knowledge no comparable studies have been done in the area of religion. However, it is clear that people have basic needs to which religion makes important contributions. Over the years, from the pagan to the modern, religions (1) have provided answers to complex unknowns, thus satisfying a basic human need to see beyond the immediate and to find answers to perplexing problems, and (2) have provided a concept of a Supreme Being in whom one can find strength and succor. Religious beliefs tend to serve these needs.

Attendance at church and participation in the church programs satisfy, of course, a variety of other needs. Perhaps foremost are social needs, the need to be with others and to be accepted by them, to relate to meaningful social groups. There is no doubt that status needs and even needs for power can be satisfied in the church context. And it is to be hoped that sermons, discussion groups, religious education programs, and church services may provide satisfaction for needs having to do with intellectual curiosity and aesthetic experience.

Although little research has been done on the relationship of church programs to the needs of individuals, it may be appropriate to recall a study of twenty-five years ago by Kingsbury whose major findings are presented in Table II. In this investigation, members of one congregation in Chicago were queried as to why they went to church. An emphasis upon social needs is apparent in the first line of that table, for some two-thirds of those members of the congregation under thirty-five emphasized the gaining of new friends and acquaintances. But young adults also emphasized help in formulating a philosophy

---

[9] R. F. Winch, *Mate Selection* (New York, 1958); C. R. Pace and G. G. Stern, "An Approach to the Measurement of Psychological Characteristics of College Environments," *Journal of Educational Psychology*, 49 (1958), 269-77; R. G. Kuhlen and W. J. Dipboye, *Motivational and Personality Factors in the Selection of Elementary and Secondary School Teaching as a Career* (U. S. Office of Education, Cooperative Research Program, 1959).

of life, intellectual needs, and aesthetic needs in their desire for acquaintance with good music and literature. Presumably changing family roles and a desire to inculcate children with the values of the culture resulted in a greater emphasis upon the encouragement of family attendance among the older groups. An especially interesting trend, and one about which further comment will be made, involves a greater desire on the part of the young and the older groups for reassurance of the reality of a future life. However, the great increase with age in attending church "to keep alive the spirit of Christ" probably reflects the character of religious teaching a generation or two ago rather than representing a trend genuinely due to age.

TABLE II [10]

CHANGE OF REASONS FOR ATTENDING CHURCH BY AGE GROUPS
(EXPRESSED IN PERCENTAGES)

	Age			
	0-25	25-35	35-50	50+
Gain new friends and acquaintances	63 *	63	21	18
Seeking aid in formulating a philosophy of life	71	58	38	36
Some place to go besides home and work	33	24	14	9
Acquaintance with good literature and music	57	42	38	20
Challenge to self-complacency	52	24	14	11
To keep alive the spirit of Christ	29	48	62	82
Long-term habit	28 *	28	35	71
Encourage family attendance	13 *	13	48	47
Adjust religious beliefs to conditions of modern life	43	55	72	65
Reassurance regarding reality of future life	33	6	7	29
Number of cases	21	33	29	45

* In these instances, one figure was given for the "under 35" group.

Religious educators will probably agree that more extensive investigation of this type would be extremely useful in planning adult educational programs in the church context, even though

[10] Forrest A. Kingsbury, "Why Do People Go to Church?" *Religious Education,* 32 (1937), 50-54.

the procedure reveals only the consciously available reasons. Kingsbury's study, it is to be noted, involved only a very few cases, and thus his results can be taken as only suggestive at best. And, of course, it dealt with the situation in only one church a generation ago.

We turn next to religious beliefs and values as an aspect of personality, i.e., their relationships to the individual's other values. A major emphasis in recent research has involved the conceptualization of attitudes and values as dynamically generated by underlying personality trends, rather than predispositions learned from others in the culture. A well-known volume on the authoritarian personality and a more recent volume on the open and closed mind have both taken the view that one important way in which people tend to control anxiety is to seek out highly structured situations.[11] Such people are variously known as "rigid," "dogmatic," "intolerant of ambiguity," and presumably will be attracted to those faiths which have a highly structured set of beliefs and values. Catholics are probably close to one extreme in this regard; Unitarians at the other. In the authoritarian studies, the measure of rigidity or intolerance of ambiguity was developed to get at the basic underlying personality characteristics. This measure was found to be highly correlated with prejudice, as measured by a general scale of ethnocentrism. The scores on the latter test of several religious groups were found to vary in accordance with the above expectation. Of all groups studied Catholics scored highest and Unitarians lowest. The various Protestant denominations were ranked in between, with Lutherans highest and Congregationalists lowest.

A growing body of literature has demonstrated the interrelationships among rigidity, prejudice, and religiosity, and has also added occasionally other relatively uncomplimentary findings, such as a negative relationship between religiousness and humanitarianism. The latter suggests that, quite contrary to the Judeo-Christian ethic, those individuals who are most reli-

---

[11] T. W. Adorno *et al.*, *The Authoritarian Personality* (New York, 1950); M. Rokeach, *The Open and Closed Mind* (New York, 1960).

gious in the conventional sense are the least humanitarian. While these findings tend to underscore the point that religious values are related in basic and theoretically meaningful ways to other personality characteristics, other research emphasizes the importance of the particular definition of religion employed, if these relationships are to be properly interpreted. Thus Wilson showed that the relationship between anti-Semitism and religiousness is much higher if religion is defined as reflecting a utilitarian orientation toward religion (i.e., acceptance of religion *as a means*, an "extrinsic religious value") in contrast to religious conventionalism which emphasizes the *content* of religious beliefs. Related to this finding is an earlier comment by Allport that studies of religion and prejudice "have uncovered the fact that among people with strong religious sentiments race prejudice is often marked. Closer analysis indicates that the religious sentiment in these cases is blindly institutional, exclusionist, and related to self-centered values. Among people with reflective and highly differentiated sentiments race prejudice is rarely found." [12] Again, the importance of more careful refinement of the various dimensions of religiousness is evident if research findings are to be as meaningful as they should.

It perhaps should be pointed out that research relating different definitions of religion to such traits as prejudice and humanitarianism bears directly upon the types of behavioral outcomes to be desired in religious education. If it could be agreed that certain traits are desirable, and these characteristics then were found to be related to certain conceptions of religion, we might have greater insight into the type of religious teaching most likely to foster the desired outcomes.

In view of this emphasis upon the importance of human needs and personality as factors in the determination of religious beliefs, it might be hypothesized that differences in re-

---

[12] C. Kirkpatrick, "Religion and Humanitarianism: A Study of Institutional Implication," *Psychological Monographs*, 63 (1949), No. 9; W. Cody Wilson, "Extrinsic Religious Values and Prejudice," *Journal of Abnormal and Social Psychology*, 60 (1960), 286-88; G. W. Allport, *The Individual and His Religion* (New York, 1950), 59.

ligious orientations of people of different ages will reflect the motivational and personality changes that come with age. In one phase of life people may very well find basic satisfactions in certain areas of living; in other periods of life, when these satisfactions are no longer possible, they may turn to other sources of gratification. And the growing conservatism, rigidity, and dogmatism that occur with increasing adult age may be expected to appear in religious values also, and for the same kinds of reasons.

Adult Age Trends in Religious Participation

Among others, the present writer has argued that during the course of the adult years and especially in old age there is a return to religion.[13] While such a return can occur psychologically without being evident in actual church attendance or program participation, it might well be expected that participation would to some degree reflect this trend. Two studies of church attendance bear directly on this question.

The first investigation, the results of which are shown in Table III, dealt with the Catholic population in a Southern state. As the data show, there was a steady decline in church attendance until the age period of the 30's, with a gradual increase from that point on into old age. The investigator commented that the lower attendance during the 30's was very likely due to competition for time and energy of job and family rearing on one hand, and, on the other, to possible conflict between the teachings of the church and the practice of birth control on the part of young Catholics who desired to limit their family size. One might infer from this interpretation that when other pressures are great, or other avenues of gratification open, formalized religion tends to be pushed aside. When these pressures subside, or when these avenues of family

---

[13] S. L. Pressey and R. G. Kuhlen, *Psychological Development through the Life Span* (New York, 1957) ; R. G. Kuhlen, "Changing Personal Adjustment during the Adult Years," in J. E. Anderson, ed., *Psychological Aspects of Aging* (Washington, 1956) , 21-29.

and work no longer offer full potential of satisfaction, individuals may return to church. In any event, the findings in this study clearly suggest an increasing interest in religion beyond the 30's, at least for this one religious body.

TABLE III [14]

RELIGIOUS PRACTICES OF CATHOLICS IN A SOUTHERN CITY, AS SHOWN BY PERCENTAGE OF VARIOUS SEX AND AGE GROUPS WHO MADE EASTER DUTIES, ATTENDED MASS EVERY SUNDAY, AND RECEIVED MONTHLY COMMUNION

Age	Number of Cases		Percent Making Easter Duties		Percent Attending Mass Every Sunday		Percent Receiving Monthly Communion	
	M	F	M	F	M	F	M	F
10-19	835	833	91	93	91	95	63	79
20-29	930	1064	84	86	73	78	41	41
30-39	924	1063	57	69	62	75	24	38
40-49	745	717	67	83	68	83	30	48
50-59	365	372	72	82	71	82	30	47
60+	216	299	75	95	83	96	17	32

A more recent investigation, by Lazerwitz, based on a general sample of the population of the United States, revealed that church attendance remained at approximately the same level throughout the adult life span for both Protestants and Catholics, although the latter level was substantially higher than that for Protestants. The facts are shown in Table IV. Orbach has presented similar evidence, and both of these authors argue that their findings constitute negative evidence relating to the hypothesis that there is increasing religious interest with increasing adult age. They interpret their findings as showing no meaningful relationship between age and church attendance.[15]

The present writer would place quite a different interpreta-

___

[14] J. H. Fichter, "The Profile of Catholic Religious Life," *American Journal of Sociology,* 58 (1952), 145-50.

[15] B. Lazerwitz, "Some Factors Associated with Variations in Church Attendance," *Social Forces,* 39 (1961), 301-9; H. L. Orbach, "Aging and Religion: A Study of Church Attendance in the Detroit Metropolitan Area," *Geriatrics,* 16 (1961), 532-40.

TABLE IV [16]

FREQUENCY OF CHURCH ATTENDANCE ON THE PART
OF A SAMPLE OF AMERICAN ADULTS OF DIFFERENT
AGES, PROTESTANTS AND CATHOLICS, IN TERMS OF
PERCENTAGES REPORTING VARIOUS
DEGREES OF ATTENDANCE

Age	Protestants			Catholics		
	N	Regular	Never	N	Regular	Never
21-24	251	27	9	81	70	2
25-29	502	37	6	158	69	2
30-34	498	41	7	168	72	5
35-39	460	41	5	157	72	2
40-44	494	37	8	184	77	3
45-49	452	39	9	117	72	2
50-54	419	42	5	110	66	4
55-59	335	40	7	80	78	8
60-64	259	40	8	68	74	1
65+	515	40	8	147	66	8

tion upon these findings. As a matter of fact, the trends described in both investigations are quite unusual. A substantial
number of investigations reveal a decided decline with age in
almost all out-of-home activities.[17] People go to movies less frequently, play bridge away from home less frequently, go to
parties less frequently, etc. Organizational activities tend to
reach a peak in the 50's and to drop off thereafter. One can
interpret the *steady* church attendance *even into relatively late
ages* as reflecting a countertrend possibly produced by increasing motivation in this direction. Most studies, incidentally,
show church attendance to drop off in extreme old age, presumably reflecting greater physical infirmities and thus greater
difficulty in participating in even much desired activities.

This interpretation emphasizing increasing religiousness
with age is supported when one examines data relating to more
sedentary types of religious participation, those activities which
do not require expenditure of energy. As Table V shows, with

[16] Lazerwitz, "Some Factors Associated with Variations in Church Attendance,"
301-9.

[17] Pressey and Kuhlen, *Psychological Development through the Life Span,*
386 ff.

age there is increasing interest on all educational levels in listening to religious radio programs, a trend which is continued into very advanced ages, as examination of a later Table (Table X) will show.

TABLE V [18]

PERCENTAGE OF VARIOUS AGE AND
EDUCATIONAL STATUS GROUPS WHO
LISTENED TO RELIGIOUS PROGRAMS
ON RADIO

	Age		
Education	21-29	30-49	50+
College	11	14	28
High School	9	17	29
Grade School	11	25	36

Table VI shows an increasing tendency with increasing age for people to resort to prayer as a means of handling both current worries and longer term unhappiness. In both instances of sedentary religious activity it should be noted that there is a definite increase with age.

TABLE VI [19]

PERCENTAGE OF INDIVIDUALS OF VARIOUS AGES AND THE TWO
SEXES WHO MENTIONED PRAYER AS A MEANS OF HANDLING
WORRIES AND UNHAPPY PERIODS

	Age			Sex	
	21-34	35-54	55+	M	F
In handling worries	7	18	23	8	23
In handling periods of unhappiness	27	32	39	22	40
Number of cases	759	1007	681	1077	1383

[18] P. F. Lazarsfeld and P. L. Kendall, *Radio Listening in America* (New York, 1948), 136.

[19] G. Gurin, J. Veroff, and Sheila Feld, *Americans View Their Mental Health* (New York, 1960), 372, 374.

We thus conclude that even data on religious participation reflect a growing interest in religion with increasing age. However, it is obvious that more detailed investigations need to be made in order to identify some of the factors involved in current attendance, as well as in long term prediction of attendance. The different age trends on the part of Catholics in the particular parishes studied by Fichter and his interpretation constitute a case in point. Also, it is of interest that in the Lazerwitz study trends appeared among Protestants when the subjects were grouped not according to age but according to family life cycle. In this instance, support was found for the hypothesis earlier noted that as people move into middle age they tend to attend church as a means of fostering attendance on the part of their children. Thus, church attendance increased regularly for the following groups: single and under thirty-five years of age; married, under thirty-five years, no children; married, youngest children under five years; married, youngest children five years and older. There was then a drop in a final category composed of those who were over thirty-five years of age with no children at home. Perhaps it should be pointed out in this connection that participation in religious programs needs to be studied in the context of participation in other areas of living. While the Lazerwitz study emphasized that church association is only one aspect of general organizational activity, he required support from other studies, rather than from data provided by his own study, with the population under consideration. Problems of comparability of sample, methodology, etc., may exist.

Trends in Religious Beliefs and Values

We turn now to a consideration of several sets of findings relating to adult age trends in religious interests, beliefs, and concerns. First are the results of several longitudinal studies, the results of which are summarized in Tables VII-IX. In these investigations the same people were tested and then retested over periods of fourteen to eighteen years. In all three studies gains were registered over these years. In the study by Nelson the subjects investigated became more positive in their attitudes toward the church, in their attitudes toward the reality of God, and in their attitudes toward God as an influence on conduct. Surprisingly (and this point was noted earlier), these same individuals became *less* positive in their attitude toward Sunday observance over this period of time. This finding may be interpreted to mean that while people have become more religious in recent decades, this is not necessarily evidenced in their formal participation.

TABLE VII [20]

MEAN SCALE VALUES OF ATTITUDES TOWARD RELIGION OF COLLEGE STUDENTS IN 1936 AND 14 YEARS LATER.

	Number of cases	1936	1950	r
Attitude toward the church	887	8.90	9.20	.38
Attitude toward reality of God	863	8.06	8.27	.22
Attitude toward God as influence on conduct	851	8.02	8.39	.49
Attitude toward Sunday observance	893	5.92	5.25	.43

In the Bender study and in the Kelly study the young adults investigated had become more positive in their religious orientation as measured by the Allport-Vernon scale, and (in the Kelly study) by the Remmers scale. As the correlations (identified by r) in these tables show, there is a definite tendency for those individuals who are more religious at one period of time in their lives to be more religious at a later period.[21] Though

[20] Nelson, "Patterns of Religious Attitude Shifts from College to Fourteen Years Later," 3, 6, 8, 10. Elsewhere Nelson has shown that a change toward liberality of attitudes in general might be explainable in terms of cultural change. Similar data were not presented in this report. *Psychological Monographs,* 68 (1954), No. 12.

[21] For those unacquainted with statistical procedures, it should be pointed out that a correlation coefficient (r) of 1.0 would indicate, in these instances, that people were ranked exactly the same in their religious values on the two occasions. A correlation of .00 would indicate *no* relationship between their statuses at the first testing and at the second testing. The correlations actually found indicate some similarity in ranking, but far from perfect agreement on the two occasions.

not shown in the tables, it was also demonstrated that those who were more religious in *beliefs* when in college were more active in religious and civic *activities* fourteen years later. However, the correlations are sufficiently low as to reveal that marked shifts in position characterize many individuals. An important matter for further study involves the identification of the developmental events which cause these shifts.

TABLE VIII [22]

CHANGES IN RELIGIOUS ATTITUDES FROM THE TWENTIES
TO 16-18 YEARS LATER.

	1935-38	1954	r
Attitude toward church (Remmers)			
Males	9.2	10.1	.32
Females	9.3	9.8	
Religious values (Allport-Vernon)			
Males	30.	33.5	.60
Females	33.5	38.0	

TABLE IX [23]

CHANGES IN RELIGIOUS AND OTHER VALUES (ALL-PORT-VERNON SCALE) OF DARTMOUTH STUDENTS FROM COLLEGE (1939-40) TO 15 YEARS LATER (1955-56), AND COMPARISON WITH COMPARABLE COLLEGE STUDENTS IN 1956.

	Former Students			Present Students
	(1) 1939-40	(2) 1955-56	r	(3) 1956
Theoretical	28.30	30.29	.48	30.41
Economic	31.51	29.63	.53	28.21
Aesthetic	30.67	25.81	.61	28.33
Social	30.86	28.98	.20	29.17
Political	33.44	32.80	.41	32.21
Religious	25.21	32.37	.49	31.89
Number	84			66

[22] E. L. Kelly, "Consistency of the Adult Personality," *The American Psychologist*, 10 (1955), 659-81. Mean age: males, 26.7; females, 24.7. Number: males, 176; females, 192.

[23] Bender, "Changes in Religious Interest: A Retest After 15 Years."

It will be recalled (and the Bender study provides critical information) that it is difficult to determine whether the trends just commented upon are a product of age or a product of increasing religious emphasis in the general American culture. Available facts point to the latter interpretation. In Table IX it can be seen that the "former students" were more religious in 1955-56 than they were as students in 1939-40, but in 1955-56 they differed hardly at all from current students tested in 1956.

Table X provides interesting and significant information regarding attitudes toward religion in extreme old age, the oldest

TABLE X [24]

CHANGES IN RELIGIOUS ATTITUDES AND ACTIVITIES
IN LATER MATURITY

Religious Attitude Indicated	Age Period and Percentage with Given Religious Attitude						
	60-64	65-69	70-74	75-79	80-84	85-89	90+
Males							
Favorable attitudes toward religion *	38	41	42	39	53	55	40
Certain of an afterlife	71	64	69	67	72	81	100
Attend services at least once a week	45	41	46	45	50	45	20
Listen to church services regularly on radio	16	21	19	26	33	37	30
Read Bible at least once a week	25	29	33	41	48	45	30
Number of cases	74	92	118	121	63	21	10
Females							
Favorable attitudes toward religion *	51	56	57	64	69	81	94
Certain of an afterlife	83	78	86	77	91	90	100
Attend services at least once a week	60	53	52	53	56	33	45
Listen to services regularly on radio	22	27	37	30	46	59	78
Read Bible at least once a week	50	60	64	62	61	76	62
Number of cases	152	163	185	135	72	34	18

* A score of 6 or 7 on an attitude scale, obtainable only by checking most favorable statements.

[24] Ruth Cavan et al., Personal Adjustment in Old Age (Chicago, 1949).

group being in the age category of ninety and over. We have already commented on the tendency for church attendance to decline in very advanced age and for sedentary religious activity (listening to church services on the radio) to continue to increase. It will be noted here that there is an increasingly favorable attitude toward religion over the age range from sixty upward (especially among women), and that a very dramatic trend occurs in the instance of one particular belief, that of certainty of an afterlife.

Elsewhere, the present writer has interpreted this trend as reflecting one of the basic motivational trends in adult years, namely the need for a sense of significance and expansion.[25] In younger years, such needs may be satisfied primarily through family and occupation, in later years through identification with one's children. In extreme old age, when awareness that time is running out is likely to be keen, a return to religion and an increasing belief in an afterlife may reflect a means of achieving the important sense of "on-goingness." It may be argued that it is for this same reason that older people become interested in genealogy.

While this hypothesis is admittedly tentative, it does seem theoretically reasonable in terms of a motivational analysis of the life span. Even though the number of cases was small in the study described in Table X, it is nonetheless unusual that every single one of the twenty-eight individuals over ninety should express this view. The difference between this group and the younger groups, despite the small number of cases, is statistically reliable.

Another study by Clark bears on age trends in religious orientation. A sample of about ten males and ten females from each decade of life from the 20's through the 70's was administered a variety of tests, including a scale of attitudes toward religion. The correlation of this scale with age over the substantial age range involved was .25. When the interrela-

---

[25] Pressey and Kuhlen, *Psychological Development through the Life Span.*

tionships among the various measures were factor analyzed an age "factor" which included attitude toward religion was strongly evident.

Two more studies warrant comment in this consideration of adult age trends in religion, not only because of the substantive findings, but because of the striking difference in research methodology employed as compared to the studies cited so far. Typically, in studies of values and beliefs, data are collected by means of interview or printed questionnaire. In this particular instance, a procedure was employed which required that the subject respond with the first word that came to mind when various stimulus words were presented, and time of response was recorded. Since it is known that people tend to block (and thus respond more slowly) on words which represent tension areas, the findings give an objective measure of the significance of various areas of adjustment in the life of the individual, quite aside from whether he is willing or able to *report* such as being the case. The trends in Figure I, plotted from data presented in a study by Powell relating to adolescence, and from a later study by Powell and Ferraro involving single and married women teachers of different ages, show age differences in reaction time to words selected to represent the area of religion. The findings seem clearly compatible with the view that ideological adjustments represent one of the major developmental tasks of adolescence, and also reveal a trend toward increasing concern and tension in the area of religion with increasing adult age.[26]

We find, then, that in all studies examined, with the exception of those relating to church attendance, trends indicate an increased interest in and concern about religion as age increases, even into extreme old age. And reasons were advanced as to why the trend on church attendance might be interpreted

---

[26] M. Powell, "Age and Sex Differences in Degree of Conflict Within Certain Areas of Psychological Adjustment," *Psychological Monographs*, 69 (1955), No. 2; M. Powell and C. D. Ferraro, "Sources of Tension in Married and Single Teachers of Different Ages," *Journal of Educational Psychology*, 51 (1960), 92-101.

FIGURE I

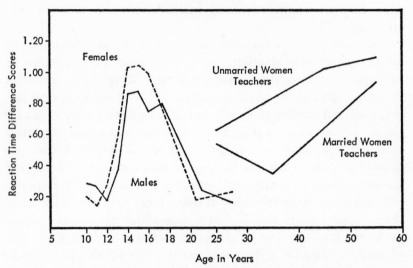

Age in Years

Age trends in tension generated by religion as reflected in mean differences between reaction time to words with religious connotations (church, God, Heaven, worship, prayer) and presumably neutral words (canary, counter, ladder, lighthouse, shadow, tower). Data for the adolescent years were plotted from Powell (1955) and for the adult years from Powell and Ferraro (1960).

as reflecting an increased interest in religion with age sufficient to counterbalance the typical fall-off in out-of-home activities that occurs as age advances.

Summary

In summary, now, what has this review of the psychology of adult religious life shown? The findings may be listed as follows:

1. It is clear from studies currently available that progress must be made in defining what is meant by religion and the religious person if advances are to be made either in our scientific understanding of adult religiosity or in the development of curriculum and methodologies in the area of adult religious education. It is especially noteworthy that the use of specialized

statistical techniques, such as factor analysis, yield important insights into the dimensions of the religious person which are not evident on the basis of a conceptual analysis alone.

2. It is apparent also that religious attitudes, beliefs, and values, as well as participation in programs, are not isolated variables in themselves, but reflect in a meaningful way the motivational patterns and the personality of the individual. These findings have important implications not only for research in religion, but make relevant to this area of human behavior the insights regarding causal variables and the means of modifying behavior which have developed from more general psychological research, especially in the area of attitudes and values.

3. The evidence seems to be clear that the nature of the satisfying religious experience will vary substantially from one point to another in time and will also vary with the age of the adult involved and with the particular subculture from which he comes. While cultural trends influence the course of age trends and age differences, we may anticipate that the more meaningful age developments will be the product of significant changes in the personality structure and need patterns of the individual. The latter will, of course, involve the interaction of the individual with his environment, and may be generated by environmental stresses encountered at different ages or by significant role changes.

4. A final conclusion relates to needed research developments. Although the available evidence makes clear the validity of the foregoing summary points, it is apparent that the research thus far has been sufficient only to mark out general trends. Much more descriptive data are needed before we are able to identify with any specificity the nature of religious development during the course of adult life, the points of special concern, the critical events, and the problems that arise of a religious nature. Nor do we have information regarding the nature of the critical background factors and current influences that serve to mold the course of religious development. Current psychological research and theory offer a rich source of

hypotheses regarding significant factors, but these hypotheses need to be tested in the context of religion. It is not unlikely that hypotheses which find support in value areas where there is less ego-involvement may not hold in an area as psychologically central in some people's lives as that of religion. Much research needs to be done also to define the relationship between the church and church programs and the needs of individuals. We know that people tend to seek out those environments which they perceive as offering the potential of satisfying their needs, but we have very little information about how people perceive churches and church programs. It is possible that some of the research methodologies now being applied to the measurement of college environments may be appropriate also to the study of church environments. This type of research, incidentally, bears directly on the question of the image of the church, and of particular churches, held by people at large.

The foregoing suggestions are only illustrative of areas that need study. It is apparent that advances in the psychology of religion and in an understanding of developmental trends have reached a point which will make possible the design of more penetrating studies than have hitherto been possible, studies which will yield basic descriptive data as well as test a variety of developmental hypotheses.

2. Socio-cultural Factors Inhibiting Christian Adult Education

GORDON E. JACKSON
Dean
Pittsburgh Theological Seminary

In a number of ways Paul Tillich has shown the correlation between religion and culture. He has put it succinctly in an essay, "Aspects of a Religious Analysis of Culture": "Religion as ultimate concern is the meaning-giving substance of culture, and culture is the totality of forms in which the basic concern of religion expresses itself. In abbreviation: religion is the substance of culture, culture is the form of religion." [1] Granted this correlation, we can expect culture not only to express the religious concern of a people but we should expect the cultural forms themselves to have their own impact and effect on the religious concern as well.

In a time of relative stability, as in the Middle Ages, cultural forms tend to freeze creative religious movement. In a time of flux, such as ours, cultural forms may harden as a protest against change, as in the Deep South where the old ways are in battle for their existence. Or there may be a violent reaction to

---

[1] Paul Tillich, *Theology of Culture* (New York, 1959), 42.

both the cultural forms and their religious substance. The Beat Generation illustrates this reaction. Jack Kerouac has insisted that the specific object of the quest of the Beat Generation is spiritual. Jack Clellon Holmes in his essay, "The Philosophy of the Beat Generation," agrees with Kerouac that it is really a religious generation.[2] At any rate, their art forms are part of their search for meaning and for expression of meaning and are atypical of our culture.

Another possibility is that the established religious symbols within a culture are empty of content, that actually a new religion is implicit, and that the cultural forms are more significantly related to the new religion than to the old forms. Will Herberg's interpretation of the contemporary American religious scene follows this line, suggesting that the new American religion is the American Way of Life.[3] Present socio-cultural patterns would seem to give some credence to this interpretation. Perhaps the majority of Americans are in the confusing position of holding on to old symbols while being at least somewhat involved in allegiance to a new religion consonant with a rather vacant humanism, a materialist secularism, and an ethic of expediency.

It is the thesis of this paper that we are involved in this last alternative and that this is the major cultural factor inhibiting Christian adult education in any fundamental sense of the term Christian. We need to look at this thesis from three perspectives: (1) the church itself as a cultural factor; (2) lack of meaning within the culture; (3) the impoverishment of the self.

The Church As a Cultural Factor

The church is both a theological and a sociological structure. Each of these structural aspects involves the church immediately in the culture.

---

[2] Jack Clellon Holmes, "The Philosophy of the Beat Generation," in Seymour Krim, ed., *The Beats* (Greenwich, Conn., 1960) , 15.

[3] Will Herberg, *Protestant, Catholic, Jew* (New York, 1955) , 287.

In its theological structure the church is seen in terms of various models: the Body of Christ, the Bride of Christ, the Temple as a residence of God, a holy priesthood, Christ's witnesses, servants of the Lord, etc. Whatever the model, the ultimate allegiance is expressed by one of the Trinitarian terms. The church stands in a line from God to the people as a mediating society of his grace. It is gathered (*ekklesia*) by God, filled with his Spirit who forms it into a new creation, and put forth (*apostoloi*) into the world for its redemption. The church is ministry. Its mission is to declare to the world the unsearchable riches of God. It is to participate in God's plan as set forth in Christ "for the fullness of time, to unite all things in him, things in heaven and things on earth." [4] Whatever the Biblical image—prophet, servant, witness, priesthood, etc.—the church is to declare the acts of God to men for their salvation.

All of this means that the church as ministry is the servant or, better, the slave of Christ. Its theological structure roots in the activity of God. His own disclosure of himself is the church's *given*. It is not the rational conclusion of a group of people, nor a clever surmise, nor a primitive projection. It is the paradox that God has met man at the edge of his existence, has met him with power to overcome his estrangement. The church is those who have been caught up in this power and commissioned to communicate it to every generation. The church like its Lord is mandated to give its life in its communication of its message of reconciliation.

It is painfully clear, however, that the church has prostituted its theological structure in favor of a hybrid one. Its God is domesticated; its power is the old middle class; its spent life is spent so often in defensive or holding-on maneuvers. Its preaching is often moralistic, peddling advice instead of announcing good news. In its worship it tends to prettify, to anesthetize by way of the aesthetic, to tranquilize by way of interlude mood music. One wonders what the liturgical renaissance really means. Does it rise out of the rich heritage of liturgy with clear

---

4 Ephesians 1:10.

theological understanding or is it further capitulation to aesthetic categories?

The architecture of the church often furthers its prostitution of its pristine theological content. While the church is a pilgrim society whose Old Testament architectural type is the tabernacle and whose New Testament type is the church-in-the-home, many an inner-city church is a gray monolithic structure whose sheer mass would seem to be further weighting down an already weighted down, hemmed in, inner-city people. The art forms used by the church do not reflect the pluralism of the neighborhood, for where is the Negro face and the laboring man? In the suburbs the cult of success provides the continuing motif. There is rarely the suggestion of a plumb line betokening the vertical comparison against which all our accomplishments must be judged. Instead of a rude cross marking suffering there is an inlaid cross with a soft light behind, thus avoiding the whole sense of the tragic. In so much of contemporary church architecture the flow of feeling is out through broad windows to beautifully kept lawns and shrubbery to continue the categories of immanence, rationality, and manageability.

While it continues to employ the old creeds and rituals, the church in its theological structure is a potpourri of Biblical and human religion. Will Herberg speaks of this new religion in America as a religion that is "progressively evacuated of content." Charles West defines human religion as the "sum total of all those reactions, ideas, and feelings whereby we human beings try to connect ourselves with God." [5] He goes on to point out the naturalness of this human activity. But this activity is far removed from Biblical Christianity where the emphasis is on the activity of God.

Confusion of salvation by God acting in Jesus Christ with salvation by human religion is a basic and overriding confusion of our time. Salvation by works, be they ever so subtle and humanitarian; salvation by moral respectability; salvation by fulfilling the American Image; salvation by overcoming of

---

[5] Charles C. West, *Outside the Camp* (New York, 1959), 81.

problems, personal, social, technical; these are all attempts to gain salvation by human effort. Human religion is concerned to have its gods under its thumb, at hand for desired results; or it projects its primitive needs on to a benign being in heaven who smiles down paternalistically. It is human action initiated to control, maneuver, make sure of God. The church, without intending it, has lost its tension with culture by capitulating to this human religion. It might appear that capitulation is too strong a word, but the Biblical point of view is that he who is not with me is against me and he who is lukewarm is to be spewed out. The one Absolute is God who will have no other gods alongside. God is not first in a series nor is his way one among several. The Biblical emphasis is exclusive and without apology.

In short, what I have been saying is that the church has veered from Biblical religion toward an emphasis on the activity of man. To whatever extent this is true, the church has become acculturated. In this situation Christian adult education suffers.

If we separate Christian education as a discipline from preaching, public worship, and the image of the manifest church, the Christian educator does not get a chance to be heard, for already the church has spoken and acted so loudly its image is set. The picture of God which the church presents to the rebel is so akin to what he is already rejecting that God is simply one more link to be broken in the fettering chain. The compliant is so dulled in sensitivity that the church in its ambiguity bothers him not at all. But that same dullness militates against any meaningful Christian education. To the vast majority, whether they be organization men, or status seekers, or comfortable Americans, the church is talking their language and there is no offense, no kick, and no education. Their kind of questions has primarily the pragmatic and moralistic answer the church is giving and, since they do not ask nor are they taught to ask the deeper question, they are satisfied. Yet they feel sometimes that something is wrong. Christian education might better be termed cultural education.

The church in its sociological structure is even more obviously a cultural factor. In its institutional form the church ideally manifests its life and mission to the world. However, when the church makes of its institutional form an end, thereby changing it from its purely functional role, it succumbs to institutionalism. As Walter Muelder has written, "This perversion of the use of institutions, rather than the institutions themselves, is a major hindrance to the life, mission, and unity of the Church." [6] The church is hopefully inner-directed in its institutional forms by way of its tradition, its theology, and its mission. It is outer-directed in its responses to the environment. At this point we are primarily concerned with the latter.

When the church becomes acculturated so that it is dependent upon its environment, it is victim of one of the chief sources of institutionalism. An illustration is the homogeneity of most congregational life as against the racial and ethnic pluralism of urbanized life. The exclusive character of the church in its institutional form is a reflection of the socio-cultural patterns and mores surrounding it. In many instances the local church resembles more a social club in its homogeneity than an inclusive fellowship.

A second illustration is the bureaucracy of the church. One primary form this takes is the separation of laity and clergy, with the latter regarded as the expert and the administrative authority, while the laity assumes the role of the "assistant Christian," or the "assistant to the pastor." Without parity in the life of the church its mission is primarily the mission of the chief executive. The laity tends to become auditors (not in the Biblical sense) but not participants in the revelatory drama of the Christian faith. As Muelder points out, bureaucracy breeds the organization man and overconformity.[7] Diversity of thought and action are discouraged for the sake of a pattern of conformity where things run smoothly.

When the church's response to the environment merges with the environment, the educational function has essentially lost its

---

[6] Walter G. Muelder, "Institutionalism in Relation to Unity and Disunity," in Paul S. Minear, ed., *The Nature of the Unity We Seek* (St. Louis, 1958), 94.
[7] *Ibid.*, 97.

cutting edge. Christian education is then safe, which is what Americans seem to want lest any real content in the church school upset the *status quo*. When the church is acculturated, it has so blended into the hues of life around it that its distinctiveness is lost. It has become domesticated. This makes it irrelevant for many and favors inertia for others. Domestication, irrelevance, inertia do not make for a viable context in which to carry on adult Christian education.

Lack of Meaning

We now move more precisely into an area adumbrated in the previous section of this paper which deals with the contemporary mind and has as its diagnosis essentially a lack of meaning. In the following description of our culture, generalization is our primary tool, with its dangers of oversimplification and abstraction; it presupposes analysis done by competent critics of Western culture.

In the contemporary United States the good life is attached to good things. Good things come out of department stores, discount houses, supermarkets. The good life is a *quid pro quo* merchandizing matter. Since the good life is marketable the means for the market are of first importance. Consequently there is a heavy emphasis on the means for achieving the good life. The means for the market are tangible means and become a focus of concentration of skills, motivation, and attention. The very meaning of a materialistic civilization, which is what ours has been called, is that of preoccupation with means-ends in terms of the market place. Where values are primarily sensate, non-sensate values are difficult to articulate, and their reality takes on a tenuous kind of existence. They are not necessarily denied. They are held to be of little consequence. Indeed, the meaning of secularism is not that God does not exist but that he is not relevant to daily living.

In the context of the good life measured by marketing criteria, amid the glut of good things, it is hard to be motivated to be a pilgrim, a servant, or even an understanding friend, key models in gospel language. The whole thrust of American life is opposed to the other-worldly and eschatalogical concerns which are integral to the Christian faith. Resistance to these concerns is subconscious but very earthy and real. Granted that Christian education is not always in touch with life as it is, yet to so many it seems to deal with a completely different time and different world.

Akin to what has been said above is a quite pragmatic approach to life, an approach which is concerned with results. Our problem-solving concerns itself primarily with the technical rather than the philosophical. It is already true in education and business. This is becoming increasingly true in both the physical and social sciences where there is some anxiety over the increased movement of scientists from pure science to its practical application. The accumulation of knowledge as classified data has a pragmatic insistence to it, and consequently knowledge is not noticeably utilized as the broad base for wisdom. Wisdom calls for reflection; reflection for the luxury of leisure; leisure is almost exclusively the enjoyment of the United States in comparison with the rest of the world. Yet leisure is not used reflectively for the end result of wisdom. Instead, it is surfeited with operational designs that are under duress to immediacy.

A friend of the writer's who is involved in research for the church is of the opinion that women respond in the life of the church both numerically and existentially better than men partly because women are more cosmopolitan. Men, although they travel more widely and have wider contacts, are perhaps more provincial because they are so narrowly focused vocationally. As specialists, their eyes are closed save to quite narrow limits. The woman, although she is more rooted in one place than the man, has a more viable relationship to the nuances and overtones, as well as to the movement itself, of life. One sees what he is looking for, and many a man is looking for the immediate result which can be turned into cash. He lives and moves and has his being within the idiom of his trade.

In keeping with its pragmatic outlook on life the contemporary mood sees no real need to educate the adult in anything quite so esoteric as faith, belief, or even ethics, and this especially when the religious understanding of many is compounded of superstition, straw men, illusion, error, and is pegged at about the junior department level. Believing as we do that our power will somehow be balanced by *our* goodness and that surely rational men will act rationally, we are neither disposed to question our belief nor to hear when prophetic religion questions it. So our concern with Biblical religion and its rituals is as spectators who doff their hats when the flag goes by.

The contemporary mind suffers also from fragmentation. Population mobility, which includes inner-city as well as regional movement, contributes to our increasing fragmentation. With approximately 25 per cent of Americans moving each year, the need for roots is apparent. The very movement itself suggests superficial coverage of ground. A piece of real estate comes to have psychological significance. It is difficult for one to know who he is unless he knows where he is, that is, where he stands. Identity is a socio-psychological category and its opposite is, as Erik Erikson has shown, role diffusion. The insecurity of our time is certainly due in part to geographical as well as social movement.

Fragmentation is also due to the stresses and strains of competing institutions and mores in a given community. In a recent study of family life within the United Presbyterian Church, U. S. A., one of the research techniques was group-interviews of parents. A major complaint of parents interviewed was the competing pulls in all directions felt by the family. One mother described her home more like a bus station with herself as the dispatcher. Each age is pulled or lured in several directions and by worthwhile organizations, too. The family also feels the strain of social and cultural pulls and pressures. In this sense we not only are, but are afraid not to be, organization men. This is the plight of "other-directed" society. As David Riesman says, "The other-directed person is, in a sense, at home everywhere

and nowhere, capable of a rapid if sometimes superficial intimacy with and response to everyone." [8] The malady of the
other-directed person, according to Riesman, is a "diffuse
anxiety." The anxiety is a feeling born of estrangement, not
estrangement due to sudden loss, but estrangement due to fragmentation and brokenness. The social whirl is aptly descriptive
of the centrifugal social force keeping us strangers from one another. With the kind of movement herein described, which is
both geographical and social, life seems to be only one dimen-
sional. Fragmented existence is tragically superficial but its very
movement creates motion enough to lull us into the false sense
that *something* is going on. This is a poor context for Christian
adult education, for people swirling in motion do not pause to
hear nor do they understand.

When one considers the contemporary mind, one is driven to
the conclusion that modern man, at least in our culture, thinks
of himself as rational man. This has more meaning than simply
using one's head. It means that by using his head man can solve
all of his problems. It means that man is autonomous within the
cosmological setting of means-ends. In its classical use reason
was regarded to be the structure of the mind by which it could
grasp reality. In this form, too, it ever threatened to become
autonomous, and did so, for example, in Hegel. Yet in the form
of ontological reason it had always the possibility of its own corrective: Ideal Forms (Plato), Logos (Stoics), Pure Being
(Plotinus), or Absolute Spirit (Hegel). However, in our time
reason has become technical reason concerned almost exclusively with means. Separated from ontological reason, technical
reason is impoverished; and impoverished it has become autonomous reason in our scientifically-oriented society. In its
instrumental function reason is implicitly, and often explicitly,
the governing law of our lives. John Dewey's *A Common Faith*
and Julian Huxley's *Religion Without Revelation* are illustrations of autonomous technical reason. What is most suspect in
both books from the church's point of view is the exclusive

---

[8] David Riesman, Nathan Glazer, and Reuel Denney, *The Lonely Crowd*,
abridged ed. (New York, 1953), 41.

emphasis upon human activity. What is real is what is observable, capable of experimentation, of recording, and of reflective thought.[9] It is the doings of man, his rational capability and activity, which are of decisive importance.

The church itself has contributed to this form of man's feeling of self-sufficiency. It has espoused a supernaturalism that is more Platonic than Biblical and a theological position which itself has been pleased to accept the support of technical reason in the arguments for the existence of God, in its equating orthodoxy and right doctrine, and in its moralistic approach to ethical living. Every time science has made a new breakthrough the church has felt threatened or it has dismissed that particular area as not really crucial for Christian faith.[10]

Actually much of what has passed for Christian education has been in the service of technical reason. The whole man has been forgotten, as though he had only a head and vocal cords, the head with which to learn doctrines and the vocal cords with which to parrot them back. Although Christian education theory has passed the stage of transmissive education, it has somehow not taken hold of the church schools which are still the primary locus for such education. What the profound drama of the Christian faith is, and how to get an adult to participate in this drama, are both difficult to teach within a cultural context that through an incomplete use of reason has lost the dimension of depth.

Paul Tillich has dealt with the meaning of depth. He says that it is that which is "ultimate, infinite, unconditional in man's spiritual life." [11] Reason becomes autonomous when it does not have regard for that concern which is ultimate, the final revelation of which is Jesus Christ. For Tillich reason really implies the whole question of revelation, for it is incomplete in itself apart from final revelation. Reason that is autonomous does not ask the question of revelation, for it is reason

---

[9] John Dewey, *A Common Faith* (New Haven, 1934) , 32.

[10] Cf. Tillich, *Systematic Theology* (Chicago, 1951) , I, 74 ff; Tillich, *Theology of Culture*, 129, where the author agrees with Einstein that theologians should not build their doctrines "in the dark spots of scientific research."

[11] Tillich, *Theology of Culture*, 7.

which has no ultimate concern. If the Christian faith is, as we have suggested earlier, primarily concerned with God's self-disclosure in Jesus Christ, and if what we have been saying about the role of reason in our culture, inclusive of the church, is true, then Christian education especially for adults has the very difficult problem of making itself heard, of bridging the gap, of becoming relevant, without prostituting its own gospel. It must challenge the rationalistic presupposition of our culture without itself being captured by that presupposition or without its becoming irrational or anti-rational.

From varying vantage points we have been dealing with the lack of meaning in our culture. We have, of course, begged the question all along of the meaning of "meaning." We have assumed the meaning implicit in the Christian faith, meaning which must always have the adjective *ultimate* in front of it, meaning which is caught up in the word, as Christians use it, God. When we say that our culture lacks meaning, God as he is revealed in Jesus Christ is our point of reference. We are saying then that our culture is primarily horizontal and not vertical, or that we have lost the tautness of the vertical intersecting with the horizontal.

The plight of Christian education is that the Christian message must be heard as an answer to ultimate questions which our culture is not asking. Perhaps it is that Christian teaching depends upon right Christian preaching; that is, upon Christian preaching that helps people to begin to ask the right questions. In that case part of the failure of Christian education is the failure of preaching in the American churches, preaching that is moralistic, culturally-informed, unbiblical, and superficial, preaching that supposedly is concerned with ultimate meaning, with depth, with God who is disclosed in Jesus Christ.

If much American preaching is a projection of infantile needs and cultural concerns, with questions and answers which essentially derive from the culture, Christian education is stymied, for the damage is done at the 11:00 A.M. hour where the masses are and it cannot be overcome in the 9:45 A.M. hour where the drowsy are. While I am much impressed with Tillich's method of correlation and the need to ask the existentially important questions, the Gospel itself must teach us to ask some questions which will not necessarily be asked out of the culture. This is part of the function of preaching in our time and without its fulfilling of this function the role of the Christian educator is made all the more difficult. The radical questions are not being asked; therefore, the radical answers seem irrelevant.

Impoverishment of the Self

It has become fashionable of late to speak of conformity in derogatory terms. Anyone, however, who has read with care Riesman, Erikson, Horney, Sullivan, Fromm, Mead, or Benedict, among many others, will know that conformity is both inevitable and necessary. Riesman in *The Lonely Crowd* has developed three categories: tradition-directed people, inner-directed people, and other-directed people. Each of these insures conformity in its own way: through following tradition, or through internalizing a set of goals, or through becoming sensitized to the expectations and preferences of others, respectively.[12]

Riesman's thesis is that the new American middle class—the salaried employee, the white collar worker, the worker involved in the service trades, etc.—is other-directed with heavy emphasis on attitudes and behavior which are "socialized" in terms of success patterns. The human agents to bring about conformity in these terms are parents, teachers, peer-groups, and the storytellers (primarily the mass media of communications in our time). The peer-group and the mass media give primary reinforced guidance in our other-directed society by keeping the attention of the people focused on signals from others.[13]

A culture which is other-directed, taking its signals from others, whether bureaucrats or managerial experts, whether television or the movies, whether Madison Avenue manipulators or suburban neighbors, is so diffused as to roles, so given to

---

[12] Riesman, *et al.*, *The Lonely Crowd*, 23.
[13] *Ibid.*, 36, 37, 54 ff.

playing to the balcony, so reactive that it is difficult for the nuclear self really to develop. The feeling of emptiness which counselees describe to their counselors is a result. These are the hollow people whose own ego identity is unclear, whose core of selfhood is seemingly missing, whose sense of values is precariously determined by how others might view them.

A vast creeping impersonalization has engulfed us. People make fewer and fewer decisions that matter although they go through the motions as though their decisions did matter. Job anonymity makes one little more than a cipher. The sense of impending fate in the international threat; sheer enormity of governmental operations; sprawling bureaucratic corporation life; mass housing tailored to a monotonous pattern; masses of people in urbanized centers; spending that is induced through the mass media; fashions that are imposed from without; these among other factors help to create the climate in which inertia sets in, wherein there is no passion, and in which a sense of helplessness takes over as though one is carried by a relentless tide. Private initiative is lost, and if there is commitment, it is commitment only to a degree.[14] Kierkegaard's fear of the crowd was precisely his fear of the individual's losing himself in the crowd. The impersonal structures of our day would be the crowd Kierkegaard inveighed against become more dangerous to the self than even he imagined.

A self that feels the encroachment of impersonalization is the self caught in Buber's category of the I-It where the self is not really a subjective center of personality but is an object talked at, manipulated, organized, treated as a thing. The I-Thou relationship is crushed by impersonal forces and its effects are most poignantly experienced in the home between husband and wife and between parent and child. T. S. Eliot has caught up the resulting sense of estrangement in the words of Celia to her psychiatrist in *The Cocktail Party:*

> . . . it isn't that I *want* to be alone,
> But that everyone's alone—or so it seems to me.

---

[14] Sören Kierkegaard, *Purity of Heart* (New York, 1958), Chapter 7.

They make noises, and think they are talking to each other;
They make faces, and think they understand each other.
And I'm sure that they don't . . .[15]

Other-direction and impersonal structures both contribute to
a society the competitive aspects of which run deep. This is true
of other-direction because the standards for success are the
signals that come from others and they insist on a matching
contribution. It is true of impersonal structures because when
personal structures are deficient the self develops neurotically
in the attempt to overcome its lack of love-acceptance. The
neurotic is notoriously competitive, whether aggressively or
compliantly so. Karen Horney makes the point that the "whole
pursuit of success is intrinsically unrealistic." [16] She argues that
compulsive drives for success are not natural but neurotic.

The self that is lost in a competitive culture seeks to extricate
itself by various compensatory stratagems, acting out patterns,
defense mechanisms. One way the neurotic tries to fulfill his
need is through imagination. He creates in his mind an idealized image of himself and through serving this image carries
forward his search for glory.[17] The tragedy is that the self is lost
and has to try desperately to find itself through all kinds of
maneuvering. It has to compete although its very competition
is doomed to frustration because even a victory is empty of satisfaction.

It has to search for itself although it is looking in the wrong
places because the very places in which it is looking have contributed to the desperate plight of the self from the beginning.
So the self has come full circle without ever becoming a self:
spawned by a culture that is not productive of selfhood; seeking
to know who it is by way of a culture that depends on others
for its own definition; circling on a gigantic merry-go-round of
ups and downs but never really growing into the full potenti-

---

15 T. S. Eliot, *The Complete Poems and Plays* (New York, 1934) , 360.
16 Karen Horney, "The Search for Glory," in Clark E. Moustakas, ed., *The Self*
(New York, 1956) , 230.
17 *Ibid.*, 225. For a fuller discussion of the Idealized Image see Karen Horney,
Our Inner Conflicts (New York, 1945) , Chapter 6.

ality of its own intrinsic nature; suffering continual frustration, the self is lost. Karen Horney could with some accuracy speak of the neurotic personality of our time: boredom, meaninglessness, depression, isolation are all hallmarks.

The Christian faith must make its appeal to this lost self to become a real self. Christian education has the advantage of speaking to the most desperate need of every individual but it has the disadvantage of saying what a desperate self, neurotically deafened by its culture and its reactions to that culture, cannot hear. This would seem to suggest that the Christian educator must become more involved in primary process-thinking; that is, thinking that is subconscious or at the feeling level. Through the Christian fellowship (*koinonia*), where love is experienced as a reality, where acceptance is genuine and lasting, a faith-response (transference) can possibly take place, first on the neighbor-to-neighbor level and then hopefully in depth as ultimate concern comes into focus. On the basis of this process can secondary process-thinking, which is intellection at the conscious ego level, begin to move. This would seem to be the proper sequential approach to doctrinal teaching. A barrier to the lost self is that it does not really believe it can be found and so it is basically afraid to try. However, the Christian faith has the church as the agent [18] of reconciliation. While ostensibly the church is a community of grace which is a totally accepting fellowship, its offer is more often like the fig tree whose blossom promised fruit but there was none; yet, when it is doing its proper work it offers that peculiar friendship which encourages a fearful self to try.

The concern of the church is to make each person inner-directed by way of the transforming Reality, Jesus Christ. Mere autonomy lacks depth. But selfhood grounded in God gives to man a rootedness, a stance, in life. While the culture itself is shy of resources for the self's renewal in terms of depth, a theonomous orientation in which the self is related to God can provide each self with an inner-direction which not only knows who it is

---

[18] The singular is used intentionally to signify the singleness of the ministry of the church: the church is ministry which ministry takes manifold forms.

and where it stands but allows it the courage to grow toward the fulfillment of its own life style. Then it is that a person is free to be a rebel in Camus' meaning of the word: when man becomes aware of himself and of his identity with humanity and is able to say "No" to any and all forms that deny either himself or that common humanity. The plight of the Christian educator is that he is confronted by the anomaly of trying to provide what every man inwardly wants and needs, a self, but what man in our other-directed culture is so afraid really to accept and work for.

In summary, Christian education must work through the church, which theologically and sociologically is not well, to provide a depth of meaning to a culture that is one-dimensional, and to enable each to become fully a self when the would-be self continues to curve in on itself in reacting to its milieu.

3. Recent Developments in Curriculum Theory and Some Implications for Christian Adult Education

RYLAND W. CRARY

Associate Professor, Foundations of Education
University of Pittsburgh

Any program of intended learning, which is curriculum, must be realized in a dual dimension. Learning is both intellectual and emotional, though these are, of course, interrelated. Although it is not my purpose to return to an antique psychology for sanctions, this double emphasis warrants clarification.

Man has an endowment of reason, held the ancient humanist. That reason and faith are not incompatible was the sum of the Thomistic synthesis of Aristotle and Augustine. Man, indeed, is a rational being, ran the exaggeration of the Enlightenment. In the general view of the American pragmatist, intelligence is the distinguishing characteristic of man. Infused with Rousseau's romantic optimism about the innate goodness of man's nature, a good deal of the Western intellectual heritage has conduced toward a large confidence in the human mind and the development of its capacity by education.

The view of man as predominantly rational has not been without challenge. Much theology has refused to believe that man's intelligence constitutes the primary or exclusive basis for human distinctiveness. Not all Christian thought has viewed man as a creature of what might be called spiritual determinism, but some of it has.

Newer fiats have challenged the view that man can be intelligent; that is, he can be self-determining, the master of choice, the maker of self. Adam Smith saw man subjected to the determinants of the market; in a more inclusive economic determinism, Marx found him to be the creature of deadly materialistic historical forces. Modern social science, not altogether by any means but to the degree to which it gave sanction to pure behaviorism or to theories of social and cultural forces, has tended toward a view of either environmental or societal determinism.

Beyond these, other intellectual forces have pressed toward a diminution of the stature of man. In turn, science destroyed man's confidence in the centrality of his mortal abode in the universal scheme of things, then his idea of special creation in a divine image, and in our time even the sure sense that what he could make he could control. The naturalistic view of man taught him well the ramifications of his animal nature, and the novelist has not, at least since Zola, ceased to explore this dimension. Modern man, instructed in the naturalistic view of self, can see amazing complexities and exciting sensory manifestations of his creaturehood. He cannot, however, so easily gain a sense of human dignity by the view of self as an ever-so-superior forager on a world-wide animal farm.

Least of all has the Freudian view of mind enhanced the self-esteem of modern man. It is not the seeking of help that is debilitating, for man in community has ever found dignity in seeking aid from his fellows; the basic premise of interdependence implies that a man may count on such help. But, however scientific it may be, the Freudian analysis brought degradation to the rational image of man. The man in trouble seeks help; through Freud he is invited to find the solution in the primitive and instinctual irrational, to regard the conscious and the willed dimension of intelligence as the lesser force in his life.

What is the gist of this analysis? It is this: a basic current in Western thought from antiquity has enhanced the self-esteem of man by building confidence that his reasonableness is great; and that, by force of reason, he could construct a satisfying life and community for himself. In the nineteenth century he had even begun to believe in a Law of Progress. History shattered the nineteenth-century illusion with the cataclysms of the twentieth. And other views of man, many founded on serious evidence, diminished his view of self, even to the point where the concept of human dignity seemed imperiled.

Curriculum appears to face a Hobson's choice here. None of the three alternatives appears too tenable.

1. Learning may be built exclusively on the intellectual pillar, on the historic precept that man is reasonable, that intelligence is his unique distinguishing characteristic. If a choice based on an illusion can be noble, this one is; for from the humanistic standpoint there is no nobler illusion. The difficulty lies with the evidence, and with experience. Auschwitz, Buchenwald, Budapest, Hiroshima, and Little Rock fail to support the precept.

2. Learning may be built upon a contrary assumption: it may follow a set of arbitrary and confident strictures regarding the nature of man and the world. In the event of such a priori conclusions dictating the educational pattern, the primary exercise of intelligence (in a Marxian setting, for instance) is to learn the rules and the rationalizations which sustain them and to follow them in all the ramifications of personal and social behavior. Choice remains, and the erectors of closed systems may call it free; but it is a freedom to choose between fixed truth and error, and to choose the latter becomes by definition an evidence of unregenerate character, a matter of heresy or treason.

3. Learning may even be built upon the structure of what Bertrand Russell calls "naked power." In the early stages of

totalitarian systems there may be some effort to cloak the coercive use of education with the garments of philosophy. Alfredo Rocco and Giovanni Gentile attempted this masquerade for Italian fascist education, and the Soviet is not without sophistication in camouflaging the ultimate persuasion behind its teaching. The brutal assumption of brutish man that man is irrational, coercible, venal, and animalistic never paraded itself so candidly as in the years of the Nazi beast. The lesson was simply take and rule; the teacher had the gun. This is the ultimate hazard when man loses confidence both in his reason and in systems of historically vindicated patterns of social control.

A harder concept undergirds my own philosophy of curriculum. It does not deny the noteworthy quality of human intelligence. It admits that free choice must consider alternatives where the principles and consequences are alike unknown. It elevates the conscious and the will above the instinct in the arena of the mind. It includes the knowledge that man can be a brute but denies that he must be or that he should be. And it faces honestly his complexity.

"Man," wrote Unamuno, "is said to be a reasonable animal. I do not know why he has not been defined as an affective or feeling animal. Perhaps that which differentiates him from other animals is feeling rather than reason. More often I have seen a cat reason than laugh or weep. . . ." [1] The mind is not all that must be schooled. Wisdom, indeed, elevates and sustains man. But circumstances impose choice where wisdom fails and courage or love must take over, or the man must flee. The Persian poet found the doors of philosophy interchangeably marked as *Exit* and *Entrance,* and his flight was into hedonism. St. Augustine explored well "the lust of the eye," the world of rational perception, the realm of humanistic scholarship. He did not find himself fully until he traveled far into the affective, into the spirit.

The curriculum of Christian education finds deep sanction for this complex rationale. Jesus taught with high regard for es-

---

[1] Miguel de Unamuno, *The Tragic Sense of Life* (London, 1931), 3.

sential human intelligence. He reached out to teach sensibly to all, even the children, as though they might be instructed by sense. His parables were not so obvious that they put no tax upon the wit of the hearers. He argued but little from the a priori; he made sense within the evident context of time and place circumstance. Yet he knew how to teach with tears and anger. He asked an extreme reasonableness of man, but the very extremity of the demand on reason—to turn the other cheek—is a demand for disciplined emotion. The Sermon on the Mount may be characterized, perhaps, as a disquisition on the rewards of affective achievement. Meekness, purity of heart, peacemaking—these are not unreasonable qualities to be sought, but there is much in rational man which argues hard and effectively against, as well as for, them. They are scarcely to be learned by the discipline of the mind alone.

"Perhaps," as Norman O. Brown puts it, "the time is now ripe when the mystic can break the glass through which he sees all things darkly, and the rationalist can break the glass through which he sees all things clearly, and both together can enter the kingdom of psychological reality." [2]

The first curriculum principle here asserted, then, is that *learning is both intellectual and emotional.* A hard study of its implications may resolve many of the problems of educational effect so often worried over in every realm of teaching.

The second principle to be developed is that *learning is related to conceptual awareness and in the adult area is particularly a process of conceptual criticism and a development of conceptual depth.* A concept may be defined as an intellectualized and behavioral codification of meaningful experience. In order to develop the concept, an articulate generalization must be devised to state it; a factor analysis must be made; its kinetic potential must be present and realized. Action is implicit in the concept. The experience must be internalized and personalized. The action resulting must be willed and understood.

Perhaps, stated extremely, this implies that the curriculum

---

[2] Norman O. Brown, *Life Against Death* (New York, 1959) , 34.

for human learning is basically the same at all stages, for the child and the adult alike. The curriculum for Christian adult education is a dimension of the desirable life learning of the human, not a supplement, nor a corrective, and certainly not set against it; that, at least, is the assumption in this essay.

How then do we clarify this matter of conceptual development?

An illustration may assist. If you visit a nursery school (public, private, or parochial, as the case may be) you will not be around long without discovering an emphasis on sharing. The children share, even with a certain self-consciousness of virtue. Even against the grain of natural or acquired selfishness, the five year old may share to gain either adult or social approval. In the intermediate grades and the junior high school, the term "community" occurs frequently, and courses in community study are not uncommon. Go to college and even in a graduate seminar you will hear the phrase, "the interdependence of man," or "of society," or "of human communities," or "of nations."

Literally, in the kindergarten and in the seminar, the students are learning about the very same thing. It is, throughout, a concept of formidable depth, with a tremendous potential for action. Internalized and codified, it directs the child to wait his turn on the slippery slide; likewise it directs the adult to philanthropy, to social legislation, to missions, and to institutions of world order. It is a concept rich in unexplored dimensions, both of understanding and of action. It is patently derived from a great religious insight or observation, the fundamental recognition of the brotherhood of man.

This illustration may be referred to in reinforcing our first curriculum principle. Clearly, the concept of brotherhood is unlikely to be developed or utilized fully without the involvement of both the intellectual and the affective attributes of the individual. But we should remember that complex though its origins may be, the action potential of any concept is great. A concept, indeed, travels around the world and through history. Furthermore, conceptual learning does not diminish nor wear out. The cliche that one "forgets 90 per cent of what is learned" may apply to formalistic categories of subject matter learned for their own sake or for purely academic purposes; it does not apply to the concept.

Jesus taught, for example, a genial tolerance for children and phrased an ultimate respect for them: "of such is the kingdom of heaven." Sooner or later, behavior in the Christian world had to begin to feel the force of this concept: the school had to cease being an institution where children were punished for being born; love and respect had to enter the curriculum. And in time this concept did richly infuse Western civilization. The Madonna and the Child lent it the affective weight of the genius of the Renaissance. In the nineteenth century, anger at the abuse of children was the inspiration for Charles Kingsley's *The Water Babies* and for much of the work of Charles Dickens. John Steinbeck's tender "parable of the penny candy" in *Grapes of Wrath* is a Jesus-inspired story. Albert Camus, deeply affected by the Christian tradition, is nowhere more moving than in *The Plague,* where his protagonist's deepest human feelings are reached by the meaningless suffering and death of a child.

No illustration serves better the dual purpose of illuminating our first two curriculum principles. For a concept can betray if it should be developed in the chaos of the child-centered school or the child-dictated home. The child, too, is human; his tyrannies, though less dangerous at the time, are no better than adult ones. The child may be betrayed by emotion; or call it zeal. The Children's Crusades were conceived in spirit devoid of sense. It is well to beware of the errands upon which we send children—or humanity.

For Christian adult education this concept illustrates the great and continuing task remaining before us. Children are still abused most grievously. They cry in hunger in most of the world today. In Europe they ran in packs amid the rubble their missing parents made their legacy. In New Orleans they went to school in the face of threatening mobs of hateful adults who in many instances did not blush to go to church. Our Christian nation must fear to calculate the number of infants incinerated in their cribs at Hiroshima and Nagasaki—I have never seen an estimate.

This is by no means the only concept relevant to Christian adult education. But until its substance is fully explored and its action-dictate realized by all who struggle for Christian understanding, there will be the continuing problem of adequate content for Christian adult education.

If the conceptual approach to education is tenable, and surely it can not be dismissed out of hand, it has peculiar relevance to certain common problems of Christian adult education. It implies, of course, that the curriculum is a continuum, that there is not much different about adult education except the age of the learners. This is at least partly true, but there is a more significant implication.

The greater implication is this: you cannot reverse concepts in midstream. This dictate is so often ignored in religious or moral and ethical instruction that the confusion in the common culture is scarcely to be marveled at. A concept is meant to grow with a person through a lifetime. Obviously, a child cannot be taught all there is to know about an automobile (which is a concept as well as an instrument) , or of love, or of sex, or of prayer. But the child had better be instructed in the essence of the concept, or he will be the worse for it.

If you would raise the child to handle his car on the road in respect for life and self, best not in childhood set him as rear-window sentinel to alert the driver to the presence of a traffic cop. If you teach him to regard the amount of indulgence as the measure of love, you cannot expect him in adulthood to establish relationships enriched by generous self-giving. If you nurture the child on evasion and mythology about sex, do not expect his adult sexual behavior to be open, healthy, and realistic. And if you encourage a child to pray for ponies, gifts, and favors, expect him as an adult to pray for the winning of games and wagers and for the consummation of successful business deals.

As a college teacher, I am well aware of the acute revulsion against religion which affects college youth. It is not to be written off as "sophomoric." It should give religious educators great pause that this phenomenon takes place among the intellectually select at a time when they are segregated for pursuit of truth more than at any other period in life, and when idealism and serious-mindedness are encountered in a dimension of pristine excitement.

It has always been assumed that the college youth revolts against the teachings of his elders because he is young and his youth requires it of him. It has often been assumed that he revolts because the college itself is inimical to religious faith. It is more probable that the student is in revolt because trauma from the exposure of the defectiveness of the conceptual structure in which he was first instructed has exceeded his capacity for tolerance and adjustment.

The principle of conceptual continuity is to be ignored at the risk of destroying faith, faith in learning at the very least. Adult sense is not derived from nonsense in childhood; neither is religiosity the parent of religion. This has everything to do with adult religious education. Many a congregation is afflicted by a lack of full communication between its ministry and its laity. Possibly too little educational and theological attention has been given to the identification of religious concepts which can be internalized and acted upon by children and yet more deeply internalized and more broadly acted upon by adults. The concepts taught the children in many churches where the ministry is full of religious sense are not prior to and part of mature religious understandings; rather they are apart from and even contradictory to the concepts upon which maturity is built. Thus the adult laity is often in a confusion of immature or shaky theological constructs.

Many children bridge the gap between the childish concept and the conflicting mature concept, through good teaching or because of the rare flexibility of the human mind. Many, however, suffer an incurable sense of betrayal; or worse yet, they may conclude that the mystery of faith lies in contradiction and that the supreme test of sacredness is incredibility.

Where the whole program of religious education is not based on conceptual continuity and consistency, adult religious education is stultified. It becomes largely a matter of intellectual and spiritual housecleaning, well worth the effort, no doubt, but probably not the noblest work for faith.

The third principle of effective curriculum is *recognition of the content-method nexus.* In brief, this means that subject matter, compiled and classified knowledge, does not comprise educational content. Content exists only when a method is present by which the subject matter may be learned. Not all subject matter is learnable in any useful or meaningful sense. Remember that in this context learning is seen as concept development; therefore the learning must be internalized and have behavioral consequence.

The intent here is not to assert that religious education, which in our terms would mean the behavioral impact of religious experience, has been historically unimpressive. Great teaching has characterized the spread of the great religions of man. The measure of the learning, however, is in behavioral terms: the blood of the martyrs, the works of the saints, the repeated phenomena of moral and spiritual heroism—these are the evidences of complete conceptualization and expression in action. It is apparent, however, that there is an educational need. Man in history, man in this century, has not learned well enough the great sustaining concepts; his troubles and his moral afflictions make that clear. Our problem is to search modern educational theory for insights that may bolster the work of religious education.

Although religious education is often less effective than the good intent behind it, its instructional errors do not make it unique. Its fault, like the fault of the schools, has been that it has remained too academic. Its teaching has often lacked consequences beyond a formalistic, verbal response or a polite and superficial acquiescense. Its motivations have often been extrinsic, honorific; the rewards have been in social recognition, pins and awards, and self-satisfaction. Often the methods have been authoritarian. These are the classic errors of pedantry to which our schools may again be succumbing in a frenzy of academic competition and from which it would be gratifying to save some area of educational endeavor.

Religious education has a tremendous asset in its content. Indeed, the conceptual force of Christian teaching is perhaps the largest reason for its great survival. Historically, it has endured through institutionalizations, creeds, theologies, and teaching which have had little to do with the faith and intent of Jesus. But a great obstacle to Christian adult education lies in the too common belief that religious education must be authoritarian. Dogmas and creeds, church organizations, the Scriptures, and sometimes sacred history may be held to be authority. The minister may say, the Bible may say, the Church may say. The saying may be true and the source authoritative, but—as preachers and teachers know only too well—saying does not establish an effective learning situation.

Authoritarian positions of denominations or congregations are perfectly acceptable in our community of free conscience, in our society of cultural pluralism. But the degree of authoritarianism certainly affects the method and philosophy of learning, and its effect on conceptual learning can be adverse. The transmission of authoritative codes is not educational. It may be worth doing, in the view of the cultural group, but the word for it is indoctrination. Education implies inquiry, and unrestricted inquiry at that.

If religious instruction functions in a context of minimal authoritarianism, it has its largest chance of being educational. However, this does not suggest that education may not become authoritative. It becomes decisive in individual choice, which is for the free man his authoritative gift. He utilizes his willed intelligence to give a meaningful act, whereby he participates actively in the continuing creation of self, society, and the meaning of life.

Participation is a key to method. But lately participation has been ritualized in education. Participation does not necessarily mean getting the talk well distributed or naming everyone to a committee. Group process may be an instrument for democratic decision-making; it may also be a tool for psychological coercion. Participation means intellectual and emotional involvement, in this case, in learning. It is well to remember that, although an adult religious education program may fail in methodology, it may also fail in other dimensions. It may not be religious; it may not be serious; it may not be adult.

The curriculum of education, perhaps particularly of religious education, has a quarrel with the common culture. The common culture, for these purposes, is simply what most people think about most things most of the time. If adult religious education has no quarrel with striving after money, status, and power; if it takes no issue with social class pretensions; if it does not take sides when humanity is exploited, maligned, and tortured—then, it may well leave its job to the mass media; for these, corrupted as they have been, are doing this job, and are occasionally doing it well.

The philosophical bias in this article is no doubt quite apparent. It regards education as serious business, directed toward the development of endurable value structures and responsible human behavior. If this be true, it is difficult to distinguish Christian adult education from education in general. It will be necessary for the denominations to provide their own distinctions; historically, they have proved themselves quite capable of doing so. Whatever the distinctions, however, a concurrence is assumed in the goal of an austere individual moral responsibility.

Summation

The curriculum occurs within. Effective learning reaches and develops the human quality of the whole man. Intelligence is a significant attribute of human distinctiveness, but it is not the whole of man. The affective quality is real and also the province of education. It is not apart from intelligence; there is but one man. Intelligence is a quality to be developed and integrated in the person, however. It is not the binder; the binder is human-ness. This quality of the human expresses itself in being and becoming, in acts of wisdom, love, and courage. It communicates. When the human acts, he behaves responsibly; he defines his meaning by what he does. The director and integrator of his actions is the willed intelligence.

Learning is the conceptualization of meaningful experience. Man is capable of learning. Not all men learn; not all groups encourage learning. The creature whose potential is to be human has also a potential of the brute; he is also prone to capture through conditioning and coercion; he is disposed toward ease and may become a zombie, the automaton in society living merely by the conditioned and witless reflexes of the common culture. Education in any dimension must awake man to his potential and his responsibility. It translates mugs into men.

The content of learning is composed of the skills, knowledges, experiences, and values which assist in realizing this goal. The method is intrinsic within the content. It consists of involving the man in meaningful, humane action. It imperils the goals when it is perceived as extrinsic either to the aims of education or to the nature of man. A content-method nexus conceived soundly does not diminish man's esteem, it does not purchase his precious time with the spurious awards of tinsel and sham, it does not set man away from man or against himself.

Education may be served through many institutions, but—allowing generously for individual, racial, and cultural differences, and for mortal caprice—it must serve a certain conceptual consistency. Christian adult education, to be sure, includes a unique dimension of the concept of human responsibility. It offers the Cross. The acceptance of the burden of man in the ultimate sense affords to this educational institution its reason for being and its opportunity to make a unique contribution to the educational enterprise. Is there a justification for Christian adult education if it avoids the Cross or too often lays it down?

Education must respect, above all, the infinite potential of the human. Its prescriptions must not be bound by its institutional limitations or its professional literal-mindedness. In life there is the dimension of the unknown and the unknowable. In religious experience there are mysteries, spiritual and psychic phenomena, mysticisms, symbols, visions, miracles, and prophecies. The discipline of conceptual consistency is not intended to deny this. The incredible exists, but there may be error in attempting to make it credible.

Education does not necessarily proceed from myth to stodgy literalism. To do so robs both the child and the adult. The concept, too, of mystery is a continuing one; it belongs on a continuum of its own. The sense of wonder at the amazing potential in the world of mind and spirit belongs not to the child nor yet to the adult; it is an endowment of the human. Education must not use it as a tool to manipulate or to corrupt the person. In fine, it is reverence, and reverence is not to be demanded of one for another nor to be held as an institutional discipline. The wonder, the awe, the reverence in man is his own feeling of the marvel of the human potential. Among men reverence is the climate in which they meet in full and share their apprehensions of the best.

4. Communication Theory and Its Implications for Christian Adult Education

ROBERT S. CLEMMONS

Director, Department of Christian Education of Adults
Board of Education of The Methodist Church

A RECENT MOTION PICTURE portrayed a father who was taking a course in public speaking. As he prepared his speech, he tried out sections of it on members of his family. His daughter, who was primping for a dance that evening, was too preoccupied to listen. His son, who was getting ready for a sports event, went about his activities without paying heed to anyone. And even the mother, who was preparing the evening meal for her busy family, had no time for her husband's oratory. After these valiant but disappointing attempts, the earnest communicator scrawled across the bottom of his notes, "I have a message for no one."

How frequently God, whose message would deliver us from evil, save us from ourselves, and lead us into a realm of right relationships, must feel like that father whose family was so preoccupied with its own little plans that it had no time to listen to a message of importance. How much like that father do we feel as Christian communicators? We may have a message that is crucial for our time, yet the status seekers in suburbia respond with selective attention, and the only ideas that get through to them are those which will give them a boost up the ladder toward a higher class position.

One of the great anomalies of our time is the fact that we have the greatest mass media for communication and simultaneously the greatest amount of confusion among the peoples of the world. Moreover, in a culture where an explosion of ideas is taking place, the Christian teacher finds himself caught in a trap each Sunday with an adult learning group whose pace becomes ever slower and slower. It seems to me that the time has come to review our theory of communication in the light of the Christian purposes that impel us, the new perceptions concerning adult learning that enlighten us, and some new factors in interpersonal relations discovered by the social sciences that may aid us.

In this study we are interested in the communication process as it relates persons to God and to one another in a Christian manner. This process includes feeling and relating, speaking and listening, thinking and understanding, reading and discussing, viewing and identifying, mediating and acting, and worshiping and witnessing. It includes the field of influences that impinge upon adults in the church, affecting their development as Christian persons. Likewise it includes a host of perceivable responses by adults that enable them to move toward the purposes of the church or cause them to become arrested in their development. This is a dynamic view of communication theory which assumes that both God and man are in action. It assumes further that they have the kind of relationships that can facilitate changes in the attitudes, understandings, and actions on the part of man toward God, who is ever seeking man with an unbounded love. Also it assumes that any change in any part of the relationship will have a dynamic effect on all other parts and thus affect the field of relationships to God.

As an ordered structure within which we may explore more

fully this field of dynamic relationships, I propose that we look at the process of communication on three levels: (1) feeling, (2) idea, and (3) image.

Feeling

All change involves risk and risk heightens feeling. When adults are asked to move from what is known to what is unknown, their anxiety is aroused and their resistance goes up. Past experience plus one's style of learning will be involved in any learning venture. This is no new phenomenon. Remember Jahweh's call to Isaiah, "Go and say to this people: 'Hear and hear, but do not understand; see and see, but do not perceive.' Make the heart of this people fat, and their ears heavy, and shut their eyes; lest they see with their eyes, and hear with their ears, and understand with their hearts, and turn and be healed." [1] Could the resistance of any people be higher? Yet it was to these people that Isaiah was sent to communicate the message of God.

One of the basic conditions of communication in religion is faith. However, faith is more than trust in the word of an authority. It is readiness to participate in the adventure of a search. As Paul Tillich asserts, "It is participation in the subject of one's ultimate concern with one's whole being." [2] This kind of faith calls for removing the roadblocks of resistance and letting the traffic of ideas and feelings between man and God start moving. It enables response in the presence of hearing, search amid the profusion of printed media, and perception when confronted by images. It is a basic condition of communication in Christian education. When the disciples gathered in the Upper Room at Jerusalem, they waited until they were empowered by the Holy Spirit. When they felt their faith in God had been renewed in the depth of their being, they began to change in their attitudes and to respond with a new wholeness to the purpose of God. They were able to alter their own feelings, to overcome despair with hope, and to adventure in com-

---

[1] Isaiah 6:9-10.
[2] Paul Tillich. *Dynamics of Faith* (New York, 1957), 32.

municating to their fellow men the meaning of their renewed relationship to God.

The horrors perpetrated upon the Jews by Adolf Eichmann teach us that feelings of hatred fan the flames of passion. They bring a holocaust of destruction upon the heads of men. As communicators of the Christian spirit, we need to follow the lead of William Lee in reassessing the place of feeling in the process of communication: "If it is true that destruction follows in the wake of misdirected passion, it is even more true that nothing of any consequence whatsoever follows from the objective, passionless, uncommitted speculations that characterize the ideal of modern knowledge. The language of the minister must speak to the depth of man, it must evoke the atmosphere of reverence, of awe, and of the presence of mystery." [3] To communicate the gospel to people in our time, we must break through the veneer of rationality with a spirit of contagious love that enables us to accept people who differ, express a deep concern for their worth as persons for whom Christ died, and seek to help them clarify their own personal relationship to God.

During the past few decades we have been so enamored of the tasks of Christian education that we have neglected the vital relationships involved in the learning situation. Yet reminders come from the strangest sources. Now the social scientists remind us that Mary, who established a listening and learning relationship to the Master, had just as vital a function as Martha, who was doing all the busy work in the household of the Lord. As these social scientists point out, the climate for learning is created and maintained as persons learn how to listen with a view to hearing the difference between anxiety and faith, hostility and love, confusion and clarity, so that they may be able to speak the word that is needful to the spirit of the persons with whom they are communicating.

Moreover, persons in the group need to give an authentic expression to the moods and feelings of themselves and other

---

[3] William Lee, "Language, Witness and Communication," *Oberlin Graduate School of Theology Bulletin,* (Spring 1957) , 5, 6.

members. Always someone needs to give an authentic witness to the faith that lies within him. Others need to be warm, friendly, accepting, and encouraging so that their neighbors will know that the ideas which they express will fall on fertile ground. Some members of the group need to set the pace, for people must not acquiesce in mediocrity. Someone needs to bring the shining light of the Christian ethic upon our relationships to the end that consciences may be quickened and our ensnarement in the throes of sin confessed. Moreover, there is an abiding need for members of the group to be reconciling, redemptive channels for the communication of God's grace, giving support to the fact that his love is still at work in the world. The maintenance of these relationships on the feeling level is quite essential to the Christian education of adults if we expect our words to become flesh and to dwell among men.

If our education is to produce the kind of maturity that has something of the wholesomeness of Christ our Lord, then persons acting under their own self-discipline need to venture in faith and seek to express the Spirit of Christ as a controlling factor in their attitudes and feelings toward their fellow men. In this manner the church becomes the living embodiment of His Spirit. In this kind of community the Word takes on a new ring of reality because people see and feel the kind of support that gives authenticity to the gospel which they read and hear. In a world where people are clamoring for an authority to exercise control over them, we need to communicate the gospel on a feeling level; individuals must discern clearly the Spirit of Christ as an operating, dynamic, and guiding force in the lives of those who declare they are followers of Jesus Christ.

Idea

The second dimension of our theory of communication views the ways we handle ideas. It assumes that effective communication of biblical truth involves an essential mastery of the message in the context within which it was stated, personal identification with its meaning, and the ability to translate it into the thought form of the culture so that its power may do its work in the minds of the hearers. This approach to communication was made abundantly clear in the Second Letter to the Corinthians: "God was in Christ reconciling the world to himself, not counting their trespasses against them, and entrusting to us the ministry of reconciliation. So we are ambassadors for Christ, God making his appeal through us." [4] God's revelation of himself which had been made to the people in Galilee had now become a very empowering force in the mind of Paul. He identified himself with it. This new and inclusive relationship between man and God he sought to communicate to the people of Corinth in a manner they could understand.

This is the fact which Jules M. Moreau states so accurately: "As God in Christ entered concretely into a specific culture at a given time and place, so the message of his revelatory-redemptive act must become incarnate in and for each generation by entering the culture of that generation and redeeming it. This is the task of the church as it seeks to share this unique and unrepeatable act of God with the world which he created and which he redeemed by his new act of creation in Christ whereby he also finally revealed himself." [5]

In the current debate over lecture or discussion as the best medium for communicating the gospel to people in a democratic society, it seems to me that one very important ingredient is often obscured, namely, the exercise of the mind. In *The House of Intellect,* Jacques Barzun tells the story of a school teacher who came to him complaining because he had given her a "C" on an important paper. She had quoted well from many encyclopedias, her footnotes were all in order, but said the eminent educator, "You have failed to exercise your own intellect."

The mind of the listener must be actively at work. It must

---

[4] See II Corinthians 5:19-20.

[5] Jules L. Moreau, *Language and Religious Language* (Philadelphia, 1961), 194.

make a distinction between what is essential biblical truth and what is purely descriptive data, presupposition, or myth. It must be alert to fallacies of reasoning and seek to discover the validity or errors of interpretation. Continuously it must seek to relate biblical truth to similar situations in our daily life. A person needs to listen with a view to discovering the true message of the Bible for him. He is not to be taken in by such slogans as "The Bible says," or "Paul says," or "Isaiah says," but he must search behind these words to discover what God is saying to him through Paul and Isaiah that will have meaning and relevance for his life at the present time.

Only as people feel themselves in common union with the Holy—the God who makes us whole—can they sense the impact of the truth which he seeks to communicate to them. There is much more to the lecturing process than telling a few jokes to get attention, stating a major premise, a minor premise, and drawing a conclusion, while filling in all the rest of the skeleton outline with one's opinionated judgment about what happened last week.

In his preparation the instructor must study the Bible and theology long enough for the purposes of God to become the purpose with which he is identified. Only as the instructor is cognizant of the fact that "the love of God controls us" and is willing to take leadership in helping his people become an inclusive church, not merely members of a middle-class status cult, can he ever say, "I am an ambassador for Christ, God making his appeal through me." [6]

Bible study requires depth of listening and thinking. The adult participant needs to discover the meaning of the words spoken at a particular time and place. Today there is an abundance of information discovered by biblical scholars. From this material the adult student can begin to discern the meaning of the message for the persons for whom it was originally intended. But this is only the beginning of the process. The student must go deeper. What was the meaning of the message that

---

[6] II Corinthians 5:14, 20.

the writer wanted to convey? What had God revealed to him? What does this passage mean for people in our day?

Since the Protestant Reformation adults have been brought into direct contact with the Bible, reading it in their own language. If it is to be a living book, it needs to speak to their own experiences. This means that adults need to engage personally in a dialogue with the Bible. What does this passage mean for my relationship to God? To other persons? Do I intend to take it seriously? Do I need greater spiritual maturity before I can accept it for my life? What changes in my motives and actions would I need to make if I tried to live by this biblical truth for my life? Trusting in the guidance of the Holy Spirit, the adult student now searches the scriptures as well as his own experiences at a deeper level of thought to discover the living reality of the message of the Bible for his life.

Testing in the classroom or in one's own mind is necessary at the next level of thought. How would people respond if I acted according to these changes? Am I ready to take the consequences? Do I know who I am? What do I want to become? Can I live with myself if I respond in this way? The Bible is a living book as the meaning of its message becomes alive in its students.

When adults discuss current ethical concerns, they need to do more than identify the problem, analyze the alternatives, set up hypotheses, state proposals for action, and test them. They need to accept responsibility for the quality of the learning that is taking place within themselves and among the members of the group. This means testing ideas for their validity, coherence, historical accuracy, and relevance. It means recognizing and identifying with the goal which the church seeks to attain. It means being resourceful in bringing one's experiences, Christian insights, and disciplined attitudes to bear upon the question being explored. It means listening to others and seeking to understand what they have to say, picking up and building on their ideas, exercising restraint when others are confused. It means speaking to the point of the discussion in such a way that you support the group in its movement toward the chosen

Christian goal. This kind of mature behavior calls for the exercise of the mind and disciplined participation in discussion that is timely and relevant.

In Abbott Kaplan's *Study-Discussion in the Liberal Arts,* the Fund for Adult Education reported that participants in contemporary discussion groups (1) enroll because of interest in the subject matter and the desire for intellectual stimulus; (2) are divided about subject matter; (3) become more open-minded and tolerant of opposing views; (4) are not stimulated by discussion experience to engage in community activity; and (5) are stimulated to continue educational and cultural activities. The book concluded that discussion leaders (1) need a higher level of educational background and cultural interests than the participants; (2) need more adequate substantive backgrounds in the subject matter under discussion; (3) need to be able to raise alternative points of view and ask pertinent questions.[7]

If the data gathered by this independent research organization has a bearing upon effective communication among adults today, it would seem to me that it points toward the recognition by participants that there is an active search for meaning and understanding implicit in any kind of discussion group. This search has caused people to move beyond simply repeating what someone else has said to the point where tested experience is shared with others in a relevant, clear and timely way. In an active search, as Margaret Mead has pointed out, we need to move from *"vertical* transmission of the tried and true by the old, mature, and experienced" to *"lateral* transmission, to every sentient member of society, of what has just been discovered, invented, created, manufactured or marketed."[8]

In a world where most of the knowledge did not exist in the textbooks when adults were in school, we need to cultivate a climate wherein we can learn from each other, younger and older adults together. This means that the dialogue must begin

---

[7] Abbott Kaplan, *Study-Discussion in the Liberal Arts* (White Plains, N. Y., 1960) , 128-37.

[8] Quoted in A. C. de Porry, "Virginia Vista," *Adult Leadership,* 9 (1961) , 301.

between doctors, merchants, engineers of the space age, housewives, religious leaders, and others, so that we may begin to develop a Christian perspective that provides an adequate theistic understanding of life in our time.

Image

The third dimension of our theory of communication involves the way persons look at the situation and the forces that impinge upon them. It assumes that people tend to behave according to the way in which they view these factors. This places the controlling element for behavior within the person. If a person's response in a situation, therefore, is a matter of his total personality, not simply the response to a stimulus or the conditioning effect of his environment, we must learn to relate to persons in such a way that we may help them perceive life from a Christian perspective.

Perception psychologists place strong emphasis upon an individual's self-image; as the social roles and work roles of the individual change, the attempt to identify one's self is a prominent personality characteristic. The individual's view of himself is affected by his needs, goals, values, security, and integrity. In recent years it has been assumed that as persons grow older they experience difficulty in restructuring their perceptions, but, as Harry Kay points out, the difficulty is not in the capacity of adults to learn but in the situation, the materials, and the speed with which the learning tasks must be completed.[9] Each individual selects only a small part of the total number of stimuli that confront him each day, depending on his experiences and needs. Hence, one of the great problems in adult education is the ability to understand and utilize the past experience and wisdom of people who are in the learning situation.

In his life-span psychology, Howard McClusky develops an

---

[9] Harry Kay, "Theories of Learning and Aging," in James Birren, ed., *Handbook of Aging and the Individual: Psychological and Biological Aspects* (Chicago, 1959) , 614-49.

interesting formula between the load of living and the power to carry the load. The load is the bundle of external requirements for living on the job, in the family, in the community, and in relation to the church, etc. Power consists of an individual's view of himself, his expectancies concerning life, his beliefs, his scheme of values, and his own assessment of his internal strength and abilities. As adults face the responsibilities of life, they are making a continuous reassessment between their own inner power and demands that are being made upon them. In the opinion of McCluskey, the ratio of power over load gives the person the strength with which to choose from among the many alternative opportunities that life places upon him. Facing a decrease in the ratio during the middle and later years, people need to be related to Christ in such a way that sources of spiritual renewal and strength in the Christian religion enable them to keep developing.

From the Christian perspective life is never completely encased in the circumstances that surround it. Unlike in Greek tragedy, man is not caught in the web of fate from which he cannot extricate himself. Within us is a hope born of our perception of what Christ has done for us that renews our relationship to God. Although we recognize the limitations of our creaturehood, we need to help adults get a truer perspective of man in a space-time context. Whereas our images of man and the world are bound by a sense of gravity and by Euclidian forms and objects, we need to perceive that there is a whole field of energetic forces which transcend these restrictions. By placing man in a world with depth and shape and object, we tend to obscure the whole field of forces in space to which he belongs. If any significant breakthrough is to take place in communicating the gospel to men and women of the space age, we must begin to change the images we use so that these will not be a naturalistic block to the perceptions of man in a world of magnetic fields, energy in motion, and an eternal space-time continuum.

Of the three dimensions of communication—feeling, idea, image—in my opinion the greatest is the image. Through the powerful media at our disposal—television, motion pictures, symbols, projected pictures, painted pictures, or diagrams—we may bring a number of impressions to the individual with such an impact that they will outlast the feelings and the ideas associated with them. Protestant educational forces need desperately to move ahead in the creation of visual media which will give a much more accurate reflection of the embodiment of the Spirit of Christ in our age. They need to reflect the reality of Christianity at work throughout human relations and intergroup relations. Though our problems are manifold, we need to strive toward the goal of the individual experiencing the reality of Christ.

Shunning a repulsive literalism on the one hand and avoiding the creation of Jesus in our own image on the other, we need to confront adults with Christ the living Lord who is regnant in the hearts and lives of people today. This perspective needs to support our personal relation to Christ and our clearly delineated interpretations of an image that evokes wonder at the reality of what God has done and is doing for mankind.

Basic Principles

Here, then, are some basic principles which a more adequate theory of communication must encompass if it is going to be effective in our time:

1. God and man are in an active relationship.
2. This relationship can be interpreted to persons in ways that can help them change attitudes, understandings, and behavior.
3. We communicate on at least three levels: feeling and relationship; idea and understanding; image and perception.
4. A change in any part of the relationship affects all other parts.
5. Adults are participants in the communication process and need to accept responsibility for the quality of the life and learning in the group.
6. Communication involves listening with a dimension of depth, delineating, weighing, understanding, and witnessing with integrity.

7. Persons who enter into the communication process accept a relationship that implies change. As they listen and are influenced by others and as they seek to influence others, they are a part of a change process.

Significant Breakthroughs

For current Protestant curriculum resources, this theory has one very definite implication. If we are going to reach adults with the Christian message in a more significant way, we need to make a multiple approach that utilizes all three dimensions of communication.

In recent years there have been some significant breakthroughs in the production of printed resources for adult classes and groups in some major Protestant denominations. *The Seabury Series,* developed by the Protestant Episcopal Church, summons its adults to *be* the church. It seeks to develop those understandings of the church that will enable adults to give support to the Spirit of Christ. By developing a program of in-service training, parish-life conferences, and spiritual life conferences, they are giving new credence to responsible participation in the Christian community. This new image of what it means to be a responsible participant in the church is given further support by training sessions for leaders which involve the rector in the local parish.

Other significant breakthroughs have been established by the Presbyterians in their *Laymen's Theological Library* and by the Methodists in the *Adult Bible Course* and the *Basic Christian Book* series. These publications exemplify the ingredients and the rules for selection of material as compiled by curriculum makers in the secular field who produce the *Great Books* series: basic and background information on the issues or problems to be discussed; cogent statements representing opposing positions or different points of view; assignments for each discussion that are fairly discrete and do not cover too broad a range of material or ideas; basic material, rather than information that becomes dated too readily; and material that is well written and not too technical.

Printed resources, however, are not enough. We need to correlate visual resources with the printed page. Moreover, in the content material itself we need to include guidance for participation by members of the group, so that they will see clearly the meaning of responsible participation in obtaining the goals which the materials seek to reach. These resources are not the private domain of the so-called "teacher." Rather they are the common property of all members of the Christian community who seek to be responsible participants in a learning enterprise.

But even this is not enough!

In recent years the Foreign Policy Association has made a bold new venture in its "Great Decisions" program. It has dared to supplement its printed resources, which include visual materials, with radio and television programs. Thus there is a two-way flow of opinions and ideas between the small viewing groups and the leaders who initiate the programs. Moreover, at the end of the discussion of each of these great issues of our time, a poll is usually taken and the varied opinions of the members of the group are sent to the State Department. Churches as well as communities that have engaged in this consensus-gathering process have felt a new sense of responsibility as they seek to understand the nature of the problems. They have thus come to a deeper recognition of the forces that play upon us and of the way in which we should relate to them. By making decisions in a purposeful way, one adds stature to his maturity and integrity to his living. In such a process cherished values become living realities.

In like manner, the twenty-six *Talk Back* programs produced by the Television, Radio and Film Commission of The Methodist Church, and scheduled for television broadcasting in 162 cities by the Broadcasting and Film Commission of the National Council of Churches, have sought to involve their audience in discussions of some of the major religious problems of our time. Churches involved in viewing and discussing these issues have found a readiness on the part of adults to identify with people in their contemporary predicaments. Through probing thought, the sharing of experiences, the delineation of ideas and values, and clarification of beliefs, they have been able to take a new look at their own self-images and discern more clearly the ways in which they need to change.

If we are to move forward in adult education, it seems to me we need to strive toward a much greater correlation between the procedures we are suggesting for leaders and participants, the content which is disseminated on the printed page, and the images that are produced to give vitality to the gospel we communicate. It seems to me that curriculum planners need to take into account these three dimensions of the communication process so that teachers and members of the groups will have all of these resources in the same package. If we are to take seriously Margaret Mead's idea of distributive education, then the adult participant needs to have a clear interpretation of the educational process, a mature statement of the basic ideas with which he will be working, and immediate access to the images that give credence and embodiment to the Christian spirit. By providing these resources as the common property of all, we may set free the minds of adults, and continuing education within the Christian community may become an adventure in discipleship for the entire Body of Christ.

5. A Theory of Christian Adult Education Methodology

MALCOLM S. KNOWLES

Associate Professor of Education and General Consultant
in Adult Education
Boston University

THE PURPOSE of this paper is both modest and limited. The intention of the author is to engage with the reader in an inquiry into the relevance of secular adult education to those aspects of the work of the Christian church that are concerned with adult learning.

This purpose is modest in that the reader is put into the role of exploring open-mindedly, not of accepting a dogmatic set of beliefs. The purpose is limited in that the exploration is restricted to phenomena of human learning, the assumption being made that other phenomena of personal change, such as those attributed to grace, are not within the scope of educational investigation.

It has become almost a cliché in the social sciences that nothing is so practical as a good theory, for practice without theory is blind (just as, conversely, theory without the test of practice is likely to be sterile) . A good theory provides a conceptual structure for understanding a given body of phenomena and for predicting how these phenomena will respond to various influences. A theory can be said to be adequate, therefore, when it explains all the phenomena with which it is concerned and when its predictions come true. But few theories are wholly adequate or final in this sense, especially in the social sciences, in which phenomena are so complex and variable. So the best theories about human phenomena have built-in provision for constant revision in the light of new discoveries about the realities with which they deal; they are growing theories which resist becoming fixed doctrines.

The practical effect of a good theory is to provide a set of guiding principles for the selection of means that will most effectively accomplish given ends. An adequate theory of Christian adult education methodology would, therefore, help Christian adult educators in several ways: (1) by enabling them to define educational objectives more precisely and realistically; (2) by guiding them in planning sequences of learning experiences that would move consistently toward ultimate goals; (3) by providing a basis for selecting (or inventing) methods that would most effectively accomplish each objective; and (4) by providing criteria against which the results of their efforts can be tested.

Because a theory of Christian adult education methodology is dealing with phenomena of human learning, certain requirements would seem to be imposed on it by the very nature of these phenomena. At least some of the more obvious conditions that an adequate theory of Christian adult education methodology would have to meet are the following:

1. It is based on a coherent conception of the purpose of education.
2. Its methodological principles are consistent with existing knowledge about the nature of the learning process.
3. Its methodological principles take into account the unique characteristics of adult learners.

4. It provides criteria for selecting methods appropriate to different objectives.
5. It provides a basis for measuring outcomes.

The propositions stated below represent a beginning attempt to bring insights from the findings of the social sciences to bear on the construction of a theory of Christian adult education methodology which meets these requirements.

A Conception of Education

The prevailing concept of education in the history of civilization has been that it is the process of transmitting knowledge or culture. According to this concept, the principal aim of education is to gain acceptance by the learner of the facts, skills, attitudes, and beliefs which the existing culture deems it important for him to have. The role of the teacher is to transmit a body of content and the role of the student is to absorb it. The test of the efficacy of education is the student's ability to recall the information transmitted and the conformity of his behavior to the attitudes and beliefs transmitted.

A counter concept reached its first flower during the Golden Age of Greece in the teachings of Socrates and Aristotle, only to wither and lie dormant until revived (with mutations) in modern times in the contributions of Bacon, Comenius, Pestalozzi, Herbart, Spencer, and Dewey. This concept defines education as a process of guided growth of the learner toward his full potential as a whole person. According to this concept, the principal aim of education is to help an individual develop his full capacities and to use them not only to exist in a culture but to change a culture. The role of the teacher shifts from that of being primarily a transmitter to being a guide to self-discovery. The test of the efficacy of education in this frame of reference is less in terms of what he knows and how well he conforms than in terms of how well he is able to think, inquire, create, and perform.

In actual practice, of course, these concepts are seldom applied in pure form. Even the most person-centered education requires some transmission of information, and even the most content-centered education would fail without some concern for personal growth. But these concepts describe two basically different orientations to the nature and purpose of education which lead to different ways of organizing and conducting learning experiences.

Placing these concepts in the context of religious education, the "transmission concept" would result in programs keyed to indoctrinating adults with those facts and beliefs about the Bible and the Christian faith which are approved by established authority. The methods most appropriate to this purpose are reading, sermonizing, and recitation. On the other hand, the "personal growth concept" would result in programs in which the adults are provided with guidance and resources in discovering the facts and beliefs about the Bible and the Christian faith which have meaning to them. The methods most appropriate to this purpose are, not surprisingly, the methods of scientific inquiry.

To state the choice facing Christian adult educators even more sharply, it is between producing dependent believers, adults whose intellectual understanding of religion is derived from others; and producing mature believers, adults whose intellectual understanding of religion is the result of guided self-inquiry. The choice is a free one, for there is no authority vested with the power to say that one alternative is right and the other is wrong. The choice depends upon which consequences are desired: a religious community that is more dependent or more self-directing, more conforming or more inquiring, more imitative or more creative. In addition, one of the consequences of choosing the former alternative would be that religious education could look to secular education less and less for reinforcement and mutual development of techniques, for the moving edge of secular education is in the direction of teaching how to learn and think rather than what to learn and think.

The first requirement of an adequate theory of Christian adult education methodology, therefore, is a coherent conception of the purpose of education. Methods are only means, never ends in themselves. Until the ends of education are clearly defined in terms of the kinds of people education should produce, it is not possible to think relevantly about methods.

The Nature of Learning

Few aspects of education have received as much attention in the last quarter century from psychological researchers as has the learning process, for understanding what happens when a person learns is prerequisite to solving almost all other educational problems. As a result of this research, no concept in education has undergone such drastic change as has that of the nature of learning. Briefly, the direction of this change has been away from a focus on the product of learning (the acquisition of subject matter) toward a focus on the process of learning (what takes place inside the person).

Certain generalizations can be extracted from the existing body of research findings about the nature of learning that seem to have special implications for a theory of methodology. Perhaps the central insight is that learning is, indeed, a wholly internal process. The learner governs what is learned. In this sense, a teacher cannot really teach; he can only help a learner to learn.

The learning process is therefore described psychologically as a process of need-meeting and goal-striving by the learner. This is to say that an individual is motivated to engage in learning to the extent that he feels a need to learn and perceives a personal goal that learning will help to achieve; and he will invest his energy in making use of available resources for learning (including teachers and readings) to the extent that he perceives them as being relevant to his goals and needs.

The central dynamic of the learning process can now be seen to be the experience of the learner, experience being defined as the interaction between an individual and his environment. The quality and amount of learning are thus clearly influenced by the quality and amount of interaction between the learner and his environment and by the educative potency of the environment. The art of teaching is essentially the art of managing these two key variables in the learning process, environment and interaction, which together define the substance of the basic unit of learning, a "learning experience."

The ultimate product of the learning process thus has come to be defined by modern educational psychologists as *a change in behavior effected by the experience of the learner.* The mission of the teacher consequently becomes defined as engaging with learners in constructing situations in which individuals experience the satisfaction of their needs and goals for more effective behavior. The notion of education as behavioral change is one of the most pervasive in modern educational thought. The assumption is that new acquisitions of information that are not translated into new behavior are not truly learned. A "learning" is something that can be transferred from the situation in which it is learned to other situations, thus demonstrating an internalized change in behavior.

This new emphasis on the behavioral character of learning has produced a growing interest on the part of educational thinkers in what they call "change theory." Several fruitful lines of inquiry that are now being pursued by social scientists regarding the dynamics of individual and social change are already greatly affecting educational methodology. For example, research into the phenomenon of resistance to change has produced some useful ideas about how to create conditions that make it more possible for people to change in learning situations (such as by establishing an atmosphere of mutual acceptance, non-competitiveness, objectivity in observation of behavior, and support in experimenting with new behavior). Other research is yielding insights into the unique effects of different kinds of content acquisitions, such as knowledge, understanding, skills, attitudes, interests, and values on different kinds of behavior. An example is the insight that changes in relationships with other people are less affected by acquisitions of knowledge than by acquisitions of understanding, human relations skills, and attitudes.

Perhaps the research along these lines that has most direct application to religious education methods is that having to do with environmental forces affecting individual change. For example, a large number of studies of the dynamics of small groups indicate that a group is likely to be an effective instrument for change and growth in individuals to the extent that:

1. Those people who are to be changed and those who are to exert influence for change have a strong sense of belonging to the same group.
2. The attractiveness of the group to its members is greater than the discomfort of the change.
3. The types of changes attempted are relevant to the basis of attraction to the group.
4. Those who attempt to influence for change have prestige in the eyes of other members.
5. The members of the group share the perception that change is needed, thus making the source of pressure for change lie within the group.
6. The direction of changes attempted is in keeping with the norms of the group.
7. Information relating to the need for change, plans for change, and consequences of change are shared by all relevant people in the group.
8. Changes by one individual are supported by relevant changes in other members of the group.
9. It is a group norm that change in behavior is possible and desirable for all members.

Similar research regarding the dynamics of institutions and communities suggests that they, also, vary in their quality as educative environments; that, for instance, the attitude toward membership responsibility which an individual learns in a given church will be influenced by the climate (e.g., authoritarian or democratic) established by the actions of the minister and board of trustees.

A second requirement of an adequate theory of Christian adult education methodology, this line of reasoning would seem to suggest, is that the principles it proposes for the selection of methods be in keeping with what is known about how people actually learn.

The Characteristics of Adult Learners

While adult learners possess some of the same characteristics that youthful learners manifest, there are some crucial differences. The unique characteristics of adult learners might be summarized as follows:

1. Adults enter into learning situations with other than learners' roles. The normal role of a youth is to be a learner, while the normal role of an adult is to be a producer or doer—parent, worker, citizen. The adult acquires an image and status in his own eyes, as well as in the eyes of others, from these "outside" activities which he brings with him into a learning situation. Accordingly, if he finds himself being treated like a child in a learning situation (e.g., being talked down to or told what to do), he finds his image of himself as a responsible adult threatened. And adults tend to reject or withdraw from situations which threaten their self-images.

2. Adults enter into learning situations with more experience than youths have been able to accumulate. Simply by virtue of having lived more years, most adults have accumulated a greater quantity and wider variety of experiences than most youths. This fact has two consequences for learning: (1) adults have more to contribute to a learning activity out of their experience; and (2) adults have a richer foundation of experience to which to relate new experiences.

3. Adults enter into learning situations with a different quality of experience from that of youths. Few youths, for example, have had the kind of experience that comes from being a breadwinner, a spouse, a parent, a voter, or an employer. One of the consequences of this difference in quality of experience is a difference in learning readiness. For example, when an individual becomes a parent he tends to become ready to learn about child development in a different way from which he learned as the result of an academic interest in this subject in his youth.

4. Adults enter into learning situations with intentions of more immediate applications of learnings than is usually the case with youths. Most learning is regarded by youths as being an end in itself (e.g., disciplining the mind) or as a means to some postponed end

or use (e.g., a degree, a job, a happy adulthood). But an adult typically enters into learning in order to be able to deal better with immediate problems or to get answers to questions that arise out of his present experience. Youths tend to be more subject-centered in their orientation to learning; adults tend to be more problem-centered. One of the consequences of this difference is that adults tend to find a curriculum organized around life problems more congenial than one organized on the principle of logical subject development.

A third requirement of an adequate theory of Christian adult education methodology, consequently, is that the principles it proposes for the selection of methods take into account the unique self-images, experiences, and purposes of adults as learners.

Educational Objectives and Methods

Since, as has already been stated, methods are only means to ends, a prerequisite to the choice of the best methods for a given learning experience is the clear formulation of the objectives it is designed to accomplish. And, since the methodology we are concerned with in this paper is that of Christian adult education, the principles we develop should distinguish between the uniquely Christian religious education objectives and the objectives achieved through other institutions providing for the education of adults.

What are the uniquely Christian objectives for the education of adults? There are probably two chief sources from which these objectives can be derived: the needs of individuals and the needs of the church as an institution. How the needs of individuals are defined depends largely upon which conception is adopted. If the transmission of culture conception is adopted, then the needs of individuals will be defined in terms of the mastery of the approved doctrines, values, attitudes, and bodies of information. The educational objectives would then be formulated in terms of the development of the ability to recall this information and to conform to prescribed behavior.

On the other hand, if the personal growth conception is adopted, then the needs will be defined in terms of some model of a mature Christian person. And educational objectives would be formulated in terms of the development of these competencies. Since maturity is a compass bearing (like East) rather than an absolute condition, these objectives can probably be most usefully stated in terms of direction of growth rather than target points.

Without presuming actually to propose what these objectives should be (a task which only those engaged in the Christian education enterprise can legitimately undertake), Figure I illustrates the types of objectives that might be included in such a formulation.

FIGURE I

POSSIBLE DIRECTIONS OF CHRISTIAN MATURATION

Movement	
From	Toward
Dependence on others for religious ideas	Ability to identify and think about religious issues for one's self
Ignorance of the traditions and literature of the Christian church	Informed understanding of the traditions and literature of the Christian church
Passive conformity to prevailing patterns of behavior of church members	Creative questing for continuously more effective ways to translate Christian ideals into behavior
Narrow interest in religious matters	Constantly expanding interest in religion
Selfish concern for personal problems	Altruistic concern for welfare of others
Vague definition of personal value system	Clear and integrated perception of personal value system
Self-righteousness about the state of personal religious development	Humility about the state of personal religious development
Fragmentary application of Christian ideals to life	Total application of Christian ideals to life

The needs of the church as an institution can perhaps be derived most simply from an analysis of the roles required for the effective operation of the institution and the competencies required to perform these roles adequately. For example, the most universal role in the institution is that of the "good member." What competencies does the church need its members to have in order to be good members? Some examples of the kinds of needs that might emerge from this type of analysis are the following: a feeling of identification with the loyalty to the local church, the denomination, the Christian church, and the cause of world brotherhood; a sense of responsibility for financial support of, and service to, the activities of the church; ability to participate confidently and constructively in the religious, educational, governmental, and social activities of the church; and a tolerance for differences among people, especially other church members.

The church also needs a corps of leaders for its various activities and committees, with such competencies as the following: the ability to see the total program of the church in perspective; the desire to contribute extra time and energy to the welfare of the church; an understanding of principles and techniques of democratic leadership; sensitivity to the needs, feelings, goals, and problems of individuals and groups; the ability to diagnose what is wrong when groups are not operating effectively; the ability to perform a variety of leadership functions; the ability to share leadership responsibilities with others, to involve others, to delegate tasks; the ability to evaluate one's own performance objectively; concern for the growth of other persons.

Once the individual and institutional needs have been identified, it is possible to extract from each one some notions about the changes in behavior (which become the educational objectives) required to satisfy the need. For example, the following changes in behavior are probably required to help an individual achieve progress toward "ability to identify and think about religious issues for one's self" (Figure I) : increased knowledge of the historical development of the Christian and other religions, their central ideas, and the sources of information about them; increased understanding of the thinking of great religious figures about religious issues; increased skill in identifying religious issues and thinking critically about them; a growing attitude of tolerance toward differences of opinion; broadening interest in the role of religion in human affairs; deepening appreciation of the value of the spiritual dimension of life.

As each educational objective is identified, it can be grouped with similar objectives derived from other needs and assigned to a particular learning experience or to a sequence of learning experiences. Once a cluster of educational objectives has been defined for a particular learning experience, the problem then becomes one of selecting the most effective methods for achieving these specific objectives. Figure II presents the present writer's notions about which methods tend to be most effective for each basic type of learning.

FIGURE II

MOST EFFECTIVE METHODS FOR BASIC TYPES OF LEARNING

Type of Educational Objective	Most Effective Methods
The development of knowledge	Purposeful reading. Lectures. Audio-visual aids. Field trips. Exhibits. Socratic discussion. Recitation. Research projects.
The development of understanding	Problem-solving discussion. Case study. Team-inquiry projects. Writing assignments. Laboratory group analysis.
The development of skills	Demonstration. Role playing practice. Discussion practice. Drill. Participant observation. Practice teaching. Laboratory experimentation.
The development of attitudes	Role-reversal role playing. Permissive discussion. Feedback laboratory groups. Counseling. Field trips. Intercultural collaborative projects.
The development of interests	Satisfying exposure to new interests: field trips, exhibits, demonstrations, assignments, group projects, visits, etc.
The development of values	Biographical reading. Sermons. Visits with great personalities. Value-clarifying discussions.

The designing of learning experiences involves the artistic combination of those methods that will most effectively accomplish a given set of objectives. While this task is in the final analysis an artistic one, some guiding principles can be suggested for certain kinds of choices:

1. Participants are likely to feel more involved and more motivated to invest energy in activities they have helped to plan than in those planned for them. This principle suggests the desirability of involving the students in assessing their own needs and interests, formulating educational objectives, choosing and helping to execute methods, and evaluating outcomes.

2. New knowledge is likely to be more meaningful and more readily internalized when it is provided in response to a learner's recognition of the need for it than when it is introduced from the teacher's need to transmit it. More bluntly put, an individual tends to be more interested in listening to the answers to questions he has raised than to answers to the questions for which the teacher thinks he *ought* to have answers. This principle suggests the desirability of providing experiences that will demonstrate the need for knowledge before transmitting it. According to this principle, a better case can be made for having the rhythm of an instructional course be questions-lecture than lecture-questions.

3. In general, the more actively an individual participates in an activity the more he will learn from it. This principle suggests that if there is a choice between two methods for accomplishing a given objective, the one that involves the greater participation by the learners is preferable. It also suggests the desirability of inventing ways to use participative devices in conjunction with non-participative methods (e.g., using listening teams, reaction panels, buzz groups, and the like, in connection with lectures).

4. Learning experiences with an aesthetic quality are likely to produce greater learning than those that are dull and routine. This principle suggests that the same qualities that make for good art, drama, music, and literature also make for good learning experiences: warmth (a feeling of friendliness, informality, concern for persons); color (lightness, brilliance); rhythm (experience-questions-lecture); balance in masses (large meetings, subgroup meetings, large meetings); unity (a central theme or problem); etc.

A fourth requirement for an adequate theory of Christian adult education methodology, this line of reasoning suggests, is that it provide criteria for selecting methods appropriate to different objectives and for arranging them into learning experiences of esthetic quality.

Evaluation of Outcomes

Evaluation is necessary if the learners are to be able to measure their progress toward their goals and if they are to learn from their experiences. Evaluation is also an essential ingredient in program improvement. The first requirement of effective evaluation is already provided for in the theoretical framework proposed above: the clear statement of objectives in measurable terms. This requirement grows out of the very definition of educational evaluation: the measurement of the amount of learning achieved in the direction of a defined goal. Since it is also proposed that learning be defined in terms of behavioral change, the implication is that evaluation should be based on units of change in behavior.

A second requirement of effective evaluation is that there be an assessment of the status of a learner in regard to the objectives before the learning experience (or at least at the time of entry), as well as during and at the end—and, ideally, at intervals after the learning experience. This requirement suggests the need for ways to get data about behavior that are comparable over a sequence of collections. Most standardized tests meet this criterion, but few of them are concerned with actual behavior (as distinguished from aptitudes, abilities, interests, and factual recall) of the sort with which religious education is concerned. Perhaps the value tests are the devices of this type that are likely to be most directly applicable. Religious educators, indeed, are confronted with an almost unlimited frontier for creative development in the whole area of behavioral data collection in their field of work. Devices now available for getting information about behavior include diaries, the solution of hypothetical case problems, situational projective tests, observation schedules, internship experiences, and the like. But much remains to be done before these devices provide reliable data in comparable units of measurement.

A final requirement of evaluation is that the data be made available to all relevant parties. It is this feedback process which makes experience educative both for individual learners, teachers, and program planners.

Conclusion

No doubt other elements of an adequate theory of Christian adult education methodology can be identified. Perhaps those examined above are sufficient, however, to determine whether or not it will be fruitful to look further to the social sciences— and particularly to secular adult education—as appropriate resources for this undertaking. If this essay serves no other purpose than to stimulate further inquiry in this direction it will have served a useful purpose.

Perhaps it would be cowardly for me to withhold my personal conviction that Christian adult education faces a value choice on which its future vitality depends. If it chooses to define its mission as that of inculcating prescribed doctrines, I believe it must accept the consequence of being attractive primarily to dependent personalities. If it chooses to define its mission as being that of helping adults become increasingly able to inquire into matters of faith and morals—to grapple actively with deep theological issues—I believe the consequence will be a good deal of somewhat uncomfortable ferment, but a sense of vitality that would bring into active involvement many presently passive members and many more of the unchurched. In this latter case the social sciences would have much to contribute, especially in the enormous task of training lay and professional leaders required for such an undertaking.

6. Insights for Christian Education from Research in Adult Motivation

WILLIAM A. KOPPE

Research Psychologist, Character Research Project
Union College

I

THE TERM "MOTIVATION" used in the context of education almost always gives me a feeling of a mysterious something
to which we must adjust if we are to bend someone's will to
think what we want him to think, to believe what we want him
to believe, to learn what we want him to learn. When we suc-
ceed, we may say that we have educated someone or, more
properly, that we have motivated him to learn. Motivation,
used in this context, has some impolite names, such as "brainwashing" or "hidden persuasion." For convenience here, let us
call it the "hard sell." Brainwashing and propaganda are highly
effective forms of education for specific purposes; they are designed to capitalize fully on human motivation.

My objection to the hard sell has grown from observations of
an overemphasis on the argumentative approach in printed
Christian education literature. Regardless of the methods curriculum editors and writers intend to use in their materials to

motivate learners, the most predominant is to convince them. Implicitly, instructions directed to teachers and learners alike tend to be predictated on the hypothesis, "If I can only convince them to understand, then learning will take place." [1] I have three basic objections to using the hard sell in Christian education.

I object, first, on very practical grounds. Propagandists and advertising personnel deal with fairly specific concepts leading usually to a single, well-defined response. Motivational research in advertising, for example, is "an attempt to discover motives, especially hidden motives, that may be appealed to in order to induce people to buy, or motives that must be circumvented lest they refuse to buy. There is no attempt to relate goods to real needs but only to relate sales appeal to favorable attitudes and motives." [2] Religious education cannot be simplified to make this definition of motivation appropriate.

My second objection is that the hard sell concept of motivation de-emphasizes individuality. This, too, is a practical matter. Even after the denotation of a concept has been precisely understood, and even after it has been learned to the point of becoming a belief, its connotations, reflecting the personality of the learner, may become incongruous with the meaning intended by the educator. Edmund deS. Brunner and his associates suggest: "Substantively, the prime concern is with the meaning for himself of each individual's acts of goal-directed behavior—how does he evaluate his own behavior; how does he assign primary or secondary importance to his own actions and to his own reasons or motives for these actions; how does he compare his own motivations with those of other people." [3]

In the Character Research Project investigations the individual's perception of learning was found to be a more profound force than any principles he learns. Ernest Ligon writes:

---

[1] William A. Koppe, "Toward a Developmental Theory of Character Education," *Religious Education,* 56 (1961), 441-45.

[2] Horace B. English and Ava Chapman English, *A Comprehensive Dictionary of Psychological and Psychoanalytic Terms* (New York, 1958), 330.

[3] Edmund deS. Brunner, *et al., An Overview of Adult Education Research* (Chicago, 1959), 41.

"Effective curricular material must take into consideration the full range of individual differences. Effective teaching of curricular material presupposes their adaptation to the individual expected to do the learning." [4] Learners are not receptacles into which knowledge can be poured nor plastic clay which can be modeled to conform to the educator's preconceived attitudes or beliefs. The learner determines how he shall learn and much of what he shall learn. Reuel Howe states the problem in terms of cracking the meaning barrier between the teacher and the learner, the lesson arising from the dialogue between the two.

Finally, I object to hard sell motivation because it implies a conflict of will between the educator and the learner, a conflict in which the learner does not necessarily realize his will is being assaulted. Howe's illustration of the young men who were persuaded to enter the ministry without having the opportunity to consider alternatives is a case in point. According to CRP research, all learning must be expressed purposefully as a *personal learning goal*.[5] When the learner knows what he is learning and why he is learning it, his learning experiences are regularly more revelant to his concerns and, hence, intrinsically of greater importance to him.

If Christian adult education is to make an impact on society, commitments made in a religious setting must grow from personal conviction that goes beyond acquiescence to the teacher's demand. A personal learning goal is an immediate decision to invest energy in testing what has been learned. In turn, this may contribute to firm conviction. In allowing freedom of response, the educator must inevitably risk that the learning which takes place will differ somewhat from his preconceived notions.

II

There is no intention in this paper to produce a comprehensive review of motivation in adult education; this task has been

---

[4] Ernest M. Ligon, *Dimensions of Character* (New York, 1956) , 97.

[5] The Union College Character Research Project, *Powerful Learning Tools In Religion* (Schenectady, 1958) . See Chapter II.

dealt with admirably by Edmund deS. Brunner.[6] For example,
I have purposely avoided motivations that are really adult-level
responses to the pushes and pulls of society, the culture, and
personality variables such as anxiety and guilt. Although the
educator must be aware of these presses, he must also attend to
felt needs of the learner. Herbert F. Wright makes a clear
distinction between (1) "normative needs" such as the need for
optimum health, for recreation, and for a useful education and
(2) "psychological needs" such as the need for rewarding social
contact. "The point in calling these needs psychological is not
that they are always known to the individual who has them.
The point is simply that, as states of the person, they belong to
the network of psychological determinants. When they get
linked with goals in the environmental part of this network,
directed actions occur. Then, psychological needs become
charged, as normative needs never do, with motive power." [7] If
adult education is to be vibrant, it must be based on achievement as well as fear of failure, pride as well as shame, purpose
as well as passive response.

It should be made clear that the terms "motive," "motivation," and "to motivate" are simply convenient conceptual constructs. We cannot observe a motive. We can only observe behavioral manifestations which can be described more meaningfully if we infer something like a motive. In fact, when
Cofer reviewed the literature on motivation in 1959, he wrote:
"The major conclusion I would reach from the material reviewed here is that, if the present trends continue, motivation as
a distinctive concept, coordinate with other psychological concepts, may well disappear. It apparently has no automatic response indicators, if it is true that activity, consummatory responses and reaction to pain are or may be heavily influenced
by learning and experience." [8]

Cofer could not find a single, unique concept that character-

---

[6] Brunner, et al., An Overview of Adult Education Research, Chapter III.

[7] Herbert F. Wright, "How the Psychology of Motivation Is Related to Curriculum Development," The Journal of Educational Psychology, 49 (1948), 149.

[8] Charles N. Cofer, "Motivation," Annual Reviews of Psychology, 10 (1959),
194.

ized motivation, and a standard psychological dictionary lists several meanings for the term "motive." [9] However, it remains a useful word that answers the question, "Why?" We cannot jettison the term just because it has diverse meanings in different settings. We still want to know why people learn and how to take advantage of this learning.

III

In any educational experience, we must take into consideration the motivation of the educator as well as that of the learner. Obviously, educators have needs and aspirations, many of which are subconscious. Consider the probable differences in teaching between a teacher who looks to authority for security and a teacher who thinks largely in terms of inquiry into new ideas. The first will probably be concerned with motivating learners to discover and to accept authoritative principles and sources. The second may disregard resource materials, attempting to motivate learners to explore, to experiment, and to generalize from experience.

Beyond needs and aspirations, educators differ widely in their philosophies of life. For example, it is generally recognized in research that women are more idealistic than men. The sex of a program director, curriculum writer, or class teacher is profoundly influential. We have found that when fathers participate in religious instruction, they tend to introduce systematic evaluations of learning. When mothers lead the teaching, they tend to emphasize adaptation of the lesson goals to individuals. Fathers stress what can be done within the realistic limits of the world; mothers stress what ought to be done. Fathers organize resources; mothers often are concerned with details. As religious educators, women tend to motivate learners to seek higher ideals than do men. Men tend to motivate learners to do the best they can with the resources on hand, without expecting to achieve higher ideals.

---

[9] English and English, *A Comprehensive Dictionary of Psychological and Psychoanalytic Terms*, 330.

Finally, educators vary in their theories of learning. Whether or not they can explicitly state the reasons they believe learning takes place, educators predicate their procedures on these reasons. An educator who believes that we learn best by experience will use quite different incentives than one who believes that we learn best if we understand principles.

IV

Through CRP research, we have developed a general model for religious and character education that can serve as a useful framework in which to consider diverse motivations.[10] Briefly, the model for character education is composed of three interrelated concepts. The first is basically convictions, including faith, beliefs, loyalties, and philosophy of life. The second concept is realism, including ethics, morals, and the nature of the world in which we live. These two concepts can reinforce one another in the form of mutual evaluation: evaluation of ideals in terms of the real world, and evaluation of the world in terms of ideals. The third concept refers to decision-making, the ability to organize resources in terms of value systems and to plan both short- and long-range purposive behavior in terms of them. When convictions are basically Christian, then assessment of the real world in terms of these convictions constitutes a basis for Christian decision-making and action.

Motivation to learn has different meanings for each of the three components of this model. The first area, our convictions involves much that is subconscious. This area is well shielded from reason and logic. Motivation to further develop one's ideals, convictions, and philosophy of life is not likely to be stimulated by reason alone. An adult is more likely to be stimulated to learn if he grows aware that he is capable of learning and if ill-defined religious principles are clarified in such a way that he feels he can do something about them.

The second area, our real situation, is rarely of our own choosing. We are rich or poor. We live in a free or a totalitarian

---

[10] Koppe, "Toward a Developmental Theory of Character Education."

society. We are Protestants or Jews. Still, in a very real sense, we make our own environment. Paul Bergevin points out as one of his four principles that "we behave the way we see things and not necessarily the way things are." Character Research certainly can document this statement extensively. We may interpret our resources in terms of their potentials for Christian living or in terms of their inadequacies for the same purpose. Admonitions to think positively are of little assistance. Realistic and optimistic organization of resources and use of these resources for worthwhile purposes are more adequate stimuli for learning.

Finally, the third area of the general model for religious and character education, decision-making, involves skills of leadership, action planning, and progress evaluation. The major incentives for learning the concepts in this area center around levels of aspiration. Adults first must be convinced that planning purposive Christian action is not sinful; then the experience of committing themselves to specific Christian actions and evaluating their successes and failures in order to correct their course for further action can raise aspirations to learn more. Nothing succeeds like success.

Let us consider each of the three areas of the model in further detail.

V

A body of religious convictions is important to religious decision-making. Research indicates that it is generally basic to Christian character. As religious educators, we must find ways to stimulate adults to clarify their convictions and their faith. It is clear that we cannot depend on adult interests alone. A wag has commented that adults want to *know;* they do not want to *learn.*

The Character Research Project held a conference for youth recently in which eighty-eight teen-agers analyzed over five thousand descriptions of youth's attempts to exert social influence. The most striking conclusion was that"teen-agers who wield the most effective social influence are those who have a firm, explicit set of convictions." [11] The delegates themselves found that they had great difficulty in making their own convictions explicit, as did the workshop leaders. Yet the fact that they tried and had some success is encouraging, especially in view of extensive research findings that adolescents tend to reconcile religious doubts by the late teens, but not necessarily in favor of strong faith. One gets the feeling from Ayad, Farnsworth, and Allport and his associates that reconciling beliefs may mean simply selecting those that fit present felt needs and rejecting all others, a process that in some cases results in atheism or agnosticism. [12]

Krech and Crutchfield have stated a series of rules of propaganda, one of which is relevant here: "A suggestion concerning an ambiguous situation will more readily be accepted than one concerning a clearly structured situation." [13] This rule can be considered from two points of view. On the one hand, once an educator has pointed out to an adult the ambiguity of his convictions, the adult is likely to be strongly motivated to seek a resolution of the ambiguity; he has a readiness for education that can clarify doubts and bring order from chaos. On the other hand, once an educator has helped an adult to establish his convictions, the adult is unlikely to change to concepts that are inconsistent with his organization of convictions. [14]

Allport, Gillespie, and Young have called the early twenties the least religious period of life. At the same time, McCann has indicated that lack of religious faith often leads to guilt feelings. Perhaps, as has been pointed out, this reinforces the convictions

---

[11] Union College Character Research Project, *Adventures in Character Education,* 17 (1958), No. 3.

[12] Gordon W. Allport, J. W. Gillespie, and J. Young, "The Religion of the Post-War College Student," *Journal of Psychology,* 25 (1948), 3-33; J. M. Ayad and P. R. Farnsworth, "Shifts in the Values of Opinion Items: Further Data," *Journal of Psychology,* 36 (1953), 295-98.

[13] David Krech and R. S. Crutchfield, *Theory and Problems of Social Psychology* (New York, 1948), 357.

[14] I have attempted to translate all of these rules of propaganda into terms of educational communication in William A. Koppe, *Helping Children Learn* (Schenectady, N. Y., 1956).

of parents who feel that it is their duty to teach their young children the fundamentals of their own faith and to see that they receive religious instruction.[15]

Most psychological and sociological writers imply that little or no change in values takes place after adulthood is achieved. This position is defended by the concept that mental rigidity increases as the individual grows older, as illustrated by Kuhlen, who indicated that likes and dislikes become stronger and interests tend to become more stable with age. Strong has pointed out that at twenty-five years the adult is largely what he is going to be and has acquired largely the interests he will have throughout life.[16] This indicates that under ordinary circumstances adults are not likely to be motivated to learn Christian values which do not essentially reinforce or build upon those learned during childhood.

Hurlock, citing a study by Havighurst and Albrecht, points out, "There is no evidence of a large scale turning to religion of people as they grow older." Busse, studying the process of aging, and Chandler, studying attitudes of superior groups toward retiring, independently indicate a shift to a less strict adherence to religious dogmas and a more tolerant attitude toward the church and the clergy.[17]

In spite of the general indication that adults cease to change attitudes, some potential change is indicated. An interesting graph developed by J. W. Still shows potential peaks in arts, science, and administration between the age range of thirty to sixty years and an abstraction peak involving philosophy be-

---

[15] Allport, Gillespie, and Young, "The Religion of the Post-War College Student," 4; R. V. McCann, "Developmental Factors in the Growth of a Mature Faith," *Religious Education*, 50 (1955), 147-55; J. H. S. Bossard and E. S. Boll, *Ritual in Family Living* (Philadelphia, 1950), 121.

[16] Raymond G. Kuhlen, "Age Differences in Personality during Adult Years," *Psychological Bulletin*, 42 (1945), 333-58; E. K. Strong, "Interests of Negroes and Whites," *Journal of Social Psychology*, 35 (1952), 139-50.

[17] Robert J. Havighurst and R. Albrecht, *Older People* (New York, 1953); E. B. Hurlock, *Developmental Psychology* (New York, 1959), 573; E. W. Busse, "Studies in the Process of Aging: The Strengths and Weaknesses of Psychic Functioning in the Aged," *American Journal of Psychiatry*, 116 (1955), 896-901; A. R. Chandler, "Attitudes of Superior Groups Toward Retirement and Old Age," *Journal of Gerontology*, 6 (1950), 254-61.

tween the age range of fifty-nine to ninety. Bayley's studies of intelligence indicate intellectual growth at least through the age of fifty years.[18]

In Character Research Project longitudinal investigations of the same children over a ten-year period, it was found that the children who learned the most from lesson materials were those who had teachers and parents with growing philosophies of life. These parents and teachers looked upon the Christian education of their children as a cooperative venture. Although we can only conjecture at this time, we suspect that the basic motive is expectation that learning can and should take place.

Although religious values usually are resolved by adulthood, the probability is that at least two important motivating factors can contribute to growing Christian philosophies of life. The first of these is expectancy that religious growth is possible. Adults tend to develop expectancies about the limits of their learning which they rarely test. Perhaps, in the course of teaching their children religious concepts, some parents discovered that they themselves could learn more than they had previously assumed was possible. It is perfectly within reason that this discovery can come about in other ways. The most powerful incentives to learn Christian principles (or any other type of principles) cannot be effective motivational forces if the adult has little reason to expect growth. Research is needed to discover ways to raise an adult's anticipation that his philosophy of life can grow.

The second motivating factor is organization and clarification of religious principles. The deepest convictions of adults tend to go unfulfilled because they have not been effectively evaluated in terms of resources necessary to carry them out. An adult may be surprised to discover that he can find ways to implement his highest ideals at some level if he evaluates them in terms of the resources available. Now let us turn to the realistic situation in which adults find themselves.

---

[18] Still's graph was prepared for a *New York Times* article and is reproduced in E. B. Hurlock, *Developmental Psychology*, 467; N. Bayley, "On the Growth of Intelligence," *American Psychologist*, 10 (1955) , 805-18.

VI

Lest I mislead you, I should make a clear distinction between "real-life situations" and "a reality." Ideals, beliefs, convictions, and faith are as much realities as jobs, mental ability, and grocery bills. However, the former refers basically to our value systems, the framework of emotional states on which we predicate our behavior.

When I speak of realistic life situations, I refer to the resources of the world in which we live: our own assets and liabilities; the legal, moral, and ethical system of our society; and the possibilities and limitations for our behavior determined by such factors as time pressures, wealth, and technology. In short, what do we have to work with? A major block prevents most people from answering this question effectively, for among all human phenomena the tendency of the individual to fret about what he can not do is the strongest and the strangest.

It is not difficult to analyze the motivations for accentuating the negative and at the same time wistfully aspiring to think positively. Everyone projects plans in his life that involve wishful thinking about resources; and unfortunately the ideal resources are rarely available. Since the discrepancy between the dream and the actuality is always more dramatic than the relatively mundane successes of life, it is far simpler to view existence through the frame of reference of failure. I have a strong belief that as long as we motivate people to dwell on their imperfections and the inadequacies of their situations, particularly in religious education, we shall simply give them increased experience in recognizing problems they did not know they had. Ligon writes: "Our own point of view in this regard is that eliminating the weaknesses in personalities brings us up only to the zero point, and that the most important elements in character education are over and above this point, sometimes actually in spite of these weaknesses." [19] Our experience is that it is very difficult to shift thought patterns from the negative to

---

[19] Ligon, *Dimensions of Character*, 52.

the positive. The CRP Positive Potential Study indicates that some children and adults alike who did emphasize the positive, experienced new dimensions of religious character that went beyond curricular materials. Of course, human inadequacies must be dealt with when they hinder progress, but it remains a truism that most adults have never learned the skills of assessing their actual resources in terms of their aspirations.

In Christian adult education this problem is sharpened. As has been indicated from the psychological literature, adults tend to *resolve* their religious convictions during the early twenties. I emphasize *resolve* since we have found that the solutions are not necessarily realistic or healthy. But let us assume for the moment that they are healthy. In a world that is changing as rapidly as ours, implementation of religious beliefs can never be as anticipated. This is due not only to changing technologies, but also to changes in life patterns. Travel, for example, has revolutionized human interaction.

Havighurst makes clear distinctions among developmental tasks during adulthood.[20] Early adulthood is dedicated to selecting a mate and starting a family, establishing an occupation, and finding one's self in social groups and in society. Religious education must help young adults establish themselves and discover in their potentials and limitations the ways to implement a Christian vision.

The emphasis in middle age is divided between achievement and the maintenance of one's economic and social standards of living. Havighurst cites acceptance of responsibility as focal, and other researchers have indicated that middle age is a period of high achievement in terms of productivity.[21] We can anticipate that the religious interpretation of the resources of life will tend to be conservative.

Havighurst's developmental tasks of later maturity involve

---

[20] Robert J. Havighurst, *Human Development and Education* (New York, 1953).

[21] H. C. Lehman, "Jobs for Those Over Sixty-Five," *Journal of Gerontology*, 10 (1955), 345-57. For an opposing view see Wayne Dennis, "Age and Productivity Among Scientists," *Science*, 123 (1956), 724-25.

adjustment to declining strength, social group, and living arrangements. I personally believe Havighurst is somewhat pessimistic. Work in gerontology has repeatedly supported the position that, with longer life spans and better health, older people have potentials not yet explored. It has been noted that the aged do not return to religion as was formerly thought. Yet it is possible that one of the major motivating forces religious education can have among senior citizens is to help them reinterpret their situation in order to find religious purposes for their useful role in life.

In summary, adults can be motivated within the framework of religious education if, as they pass through their maturity, religion helps them reinterpret their resources optimistically. They can then make the most of these resources, meet the tasks of their age level, and develop within the framework of their Christian ideals.

VII

From the point of view of motivation in education, the concept of "levels of aspiration" is probably Kurt Lewin's highest achievement. Briefly stated in terms of motivation, this theory holds that individuals will strive to achieve tasks that appear to them to be difficult but not impossible. It applies to concept formation as well as social, emotional, and physical skills.

The key to levels of aspiration lies in the interplay between actual ability and perceived ability, or even perceived ability to judge one's own actual ability. Much of the research focused on this concept seeks to discover the conditions which contribute to raising or lowering aspirations. For example, it is pretty well established that referent social group, past experience of success or failure, and increasingly realistic evaluation of actual performance profoundly influence a subject's optimistic or pessimistic anticipations regarding future performance. Levels of aspiration research place high value on the motivating force of the need for achievement.

Psychologists have variously explained the level of aspiration in terms of motivation as an attempt of the individual to find a balance between a desire for achievement and a fear of failure; a response to the habit of expanding abilities during childhood growth and social pressure (especially in Western culture) to continually improve one's self. Let us consider some of the implications of levels of aspiration for adult religious education. Aspirations imply goals toward which the individual can orient himself, skills of assessing and organizing resources to make progress toward these goals, and objective evaluations of progress. Transcending all three of these, and possibly almost synonymous with levels of aspiration, are skills of decision-making. Brunner and his associates make a summary statement that during mid-life "goals must be modified and made more specific." [22] The implication for adult education seems clear— for personal adjustment, as well as for learning, it is important that goals be well-defined and clearly related to action.

In the Character Research Project, we have found distinct developmental sequences bearing on levels of aspiration in Christian decision-making. Pre-school children can learn that it is possible to decide on certain aspects of their behavior; elementary children can develop meaningful plans to carry out various principles they have been learning; adolescents can learn to organize their resources and to capitalize on their assets, to implement their growing philosophies of life.[23]

Motivating an adult to make Christian decisions and to implement them by realistic plans and action must be based on these three steps. First, he must feel that it is legitimate to plan his own actions. Second, he must be helped to learn skills that he will use in planning meaningful action; this involves an evaluation of his actions. Finally, in one way or another, adult education must help him organize his resources so that he can relate clearly his activities to his Christian philosophy of life.

---

[22] Brunner, *An Overview of Adult Education Research*, 38.
[23] Koppe, *Toward a Developmental Theory of Character Education.*

VIII

Motivational research in education has been caught on the horns of a dilemma. On the one hand, permissive educators concern themselves only with satisfying the interests and the needs of the adults who choose to be educated. On the other hand, educators who desire to improve the level of our society seek incentives to influence learners into action.[24] I am reasonably sure that neither position is substantial. Both assume that the educator has the facts and that the learner will be better off for them if he wishes or can be motivated to accept them.

A background of Character Research Project data leads me to believe that at least one attitude and two skills are prerequisites to motivation in adult (as well as children's) religious education. An adult must expect that he can evaluate his environment and his values to formulate an idealistically realistic philosophy of life. He must learn simple skills of evaluating beliefs, life activities, and the effectiveness of his plans. Finally, he must be helped and encouraged to plan action based on his own philosophy of life. When he can recognize his own religious growth and achievement, we suspect that he may rise to levels of Christian growth not known today.

Character Research Project evidence among children and youth has established at least five principles for motivating students to learn meaningfully. As Knowles has pointed out, although adults bring more to the learning situation and feel a stronger need for a clear purpose for learning than children, these principles are relevant to both groups.

1. The learner who *expects* to learn something significant will be motivated to gain most from the learning experience. At times, the hard sell may be necessary to raise this expectancy.

2. The educator who concerns himself primarily with the learner as a person and tries to appreciate his normative and felt needs stimulates more enthusiasm for learning than one who is primarily concerned with content.

---

[24] Brunner, *An Overview of Adult Education Research,* 28.

3. When teacher and learner explore material to be learned together, each seeking for deeper insights, the learner tends to be more enthusiastic.

4. When teacher and learner have satisfied themselves that each has a clear purpose for learning, learning itself becomes a goal-directed activity.

5. Finally, learning experiences become significantly relevant to a learner when the study periods are conceived as an introduction to new ideas that lead directly into life. This means that learners commit themselves to act on learning in at least a limited way within the immediate future, preferably within the next few days.

7. Some Contemporary Lay Movements and Their Implications for Adult Education in the Churches

---

LLOYD M. BERTHOLF
President
Illinois Wesleyan University

WHEN ONE SPEAKS of adult education in the churches it is assumed, of course, that he speaks of the education of adult laymen. And the first questions that come to mind are "how" and "why" and "what" questions: How important are the laymen of our churches? Why have an educated laity? What kind of education are they getting? How does this compare with the apparent need?

I

Hendrik Kraemer assigns a tremendous role to the influence which the laymen of the Free or Dissenter churches exerted in seventeenth-century England. He regards this "dissenting independist" movement, which was mainly the work of the laity, as the forerunner of the modern period of Western history. It

was here, he claims, that the seeds were sown which have resulted in modern political democracy, in the principle of tolerance, and in the modern art of discussion which enables persons
of widely differing points of view to sit around a conference
table and arrive at mutually acceptable procedures for solving
common problems.[1]

Another evidence of the importance of laymen in world affairs is the part which the Christian conscience, stirring in the
hearts of many laymen in the eighteenth and nineteenth centuries, seems to have had in the abolition of slavery. Both
Catholic and Protestant groups were involved in this. Among
Protestants, the Quakers and the Methodists probably deserve
special mention, though the Methodists divided over the issue.
Alfred North Whitehead pays this tribute to the early Methodists:

In an age of aristocracy in England, the Methodists appealed to the
direct intuition of working men and of retail traders concerned with
working men. In America they appealed to the toiling, isolated
groups of pioneers. They brought hope, fear, emotional release,
spiritual insight. They stemmed the inroads of revolutionary ideas.
Also, allowing for many qualifications, they must be credited with
one supreme achievement. They made the conception of the brotherhood of man and of the importance of men, a vivid reality. They
had produced the final effective force which hereafter made slavery
impossible among progressive races.[2]

In considering the importance of Christian laymen in influencing the events of history, we must not overlook the great
wave of evangelistic and missionary activity that took place
among laymen in the nineteenth and early twentieth centuries.
This was the time of the rise of the Y.M.C.A., the Y.W.C.A.,
World Student Christian Federation, John R. Mott's Laymen's
Missionary Movement, the Student Volunteer Movement, the
Oxford Group Movement, and others. The members of these
organizations were primarily churchmen, although the organi-

---

[1] Hendrik Kraemer, *A Theology of the Laity* (Philadelphia, 1958) , 26.
[2] Alfred North Whitehead, *Adventures of Ideas* (New York, 1933) , 28.

zations themselves were outside the church proper. As Kraemer sums up these activities:

The work as it has been carried through has always been mainly in lay hands. This is also true in regard to the aggressive 19th century evangelistic campaigns. Moody and his companions were, all things considered, charismatic laymen. It cannot be too strongly stressed that these great expressions of Christian lay-vision and sense of responsibility have performed *vicariously* a task, which in principle lies within the calling of the Church, but for which the church as a whole was in the 19th century too clumsy, too defensive and empty of real vision.[3]

There is not much evidence that in the first half of the twentieth century the church had become any less "clumsy" or any less "defensive" or less "empty of real vision" than it was in the nineteenth century. That is not to say, of course, that Christian ideas had ceased to be of influence. One has only to note what tremendous force has been exerted, for example, by the idea of non-violent resistance, which was so prominent a part of the example and teaching of Jesus. In the hands of the untouchables of India and the Negroes in our own Southland and in South Africa, this has done more to eliminate segregation and racial discrimination than all other methods ever used. But it has not been used primarily by churches—by many church laymen, yes, but not much by the ecclesiastical leadership of the churches.

This estrangement of the laity from the church as an institution seems to have gone much further in Europe than in America. Whatever its causes, we seem to be seeing in recent years a real effort by the churches to recognize the importance of their laymen not merely as an untapped reservoir of power and of financial support, but as the essential expression of the church and of its calling and function in the world. Margaret Frakes has asserted that on both sides of the Atlantic a new concern has arisen for a renewal of the life of the churches. It expresses itself, this time, not as attempts to form new denomi-

---

[3] Kraemer, *A Theology of the Laity*, 30.

nations but rather in the opposite direction, toward unity. And it is characterized, she says, by a revived recognition that it is primarily through laymen that the church witnesses in the world.[4]

There seems, therefore, to be no question about the importance of church laymen, no matter whether we mean importance to the life of the church as an organization or importance to the social advancement of mankind. It seems unnecessary, also, to argue that this importance will surely be related basically to the amount and kind of inspiration and education to which these laymen have been subjected. We turn, therefore, to a discussion of some of the significant things that are being done to bring this about.

II

The efforts which the churches are making to challenge and educate their laymen and involve them in the expression of the church in the world are partly denominational and partly ecumenical. I shall deal first with the efforts the denominations are making—not denomination by denomination, for that would take too long, but only those efforts which are common to many denominations.

The first and most obvious is the preaching service. If there is anything that is more universal in Protestant churches than preaching, it is hard to think what it would be except, perhaps, the singing of hymns. Certainly preaching is designed to challenge and inspire, as well as to educate, and no one can be unaware of the tremendous influence the "preached Word" has had through these nineteen centuries of Christian church history.

The popularity of preaching lies partly in the fact, presumably, that it requires almost no effort on the part of anyone except the preacher. But its ineffectiveness as a method of education lies precisely in the fact that there is no reaction called for on the part of the congregation. In fact, it is becoming less

---

[4] Margaret Frakes, *Bridges to Understanding* (Philadelphia, 1960), 8.

and less fashionable to show any reaction whatsoever to a sermon—no handclapping, no amens, no tears, not much, if any, change in facial expression. And one suspects that along with this there is very little change in attitudes or purposes or conduct throughout the week. And if the experience of the European churches gives us any premonition of things to come, there is likely to be a falling off of attendance at American preaching services unless more effort is made to supplement preaching. But more of this later.

Another very old and very common activity of Protestant churches in the field of adult education is that of the adult Bible class. This has, without doubt, had a most important influence down through the years. Its success has been spotty, but where handled by a good teacher, the educational value of the adult Bible class is hard to overestimate. The trouble is that it often degenerates into another sermon; and although this has fine educational value for the teacher of the class, it is usually far less valuable to the rest of the members than the minister's sermon, because the teacher ordinarily lacks the theological background of the minister. As a consequence, I think we must conclude that the adult Bible classes that are doing a significant job in influencing the lives of laymen today are few and far between.

What is much more successful in the average church is the Women's Society. It is usually in their weekday activities that these groups find their greatest expression, and the serious educational work now being done by many of these societies is impressive. The extent of the organization is also impressive, extending as it often does into larger and larger areas, and supporting national and even worldwide projects. It is only when, as sometimes happens, the predominant concern is the raising of money through bazaars, sales, and dinners that educational effectiveness is minimized.

The organization of men's groups (men's clubs) in the churches is a more recent development but one that has reached considerable proportions. The movement started just after World War I, and soon almost every denomination had an organization, frequently bearing its own name, such as Baptist Men, Presbyterian Men, Methodist Men. Typically, these are closely related to local churches, but they also have district and state and even national conventions. A fairly extensive set of publications has been developed for most of these groups— handbooks giving the history and background of the movement, its constitution, and suggestions on how to organize a local club; instruction books for each officer and committee chairman; record books; program books; project suggestions; report blanks, etc.

The effectiveness of such clubs in increasing the level of churchmanship among laymen is often considerable. They give a new outlet to lay activity, with responsibility falling on many men—as officers, committee members, leaders of projects, and participants in monthly programs. The emphasis on projects, the attempt to relate religion to the work-a-day world, training in church polity, and the fellowship of common tasks all help to transform men into churchmen. On the other hand, there is often a conspicuous failure to deal with vital issues or to involve the men in any significant educational processes.

The Roman Catholic church, also, is giving new attention to its laity. In an article in the *Chicago Sun-Times* of April 28, 1961, George W. Cornell, on the eve of the Pittsburgh meeting of the National Council of Catholic Men, called this new rise of the laity in the Catholic church a "manpower reform." He considers it noteworthy that a church which for centuries has functioned chiefly through its clergy, with laymen left in a comparatively passive role, should now be attempting to bring clergy and laity together as a team, as evidenced not only by the activity of Catholic Men but by a host of other twentieth-century organizations: social action groups, interracial councils, lay retreats, lay theological studies, sodalities, and family-life movements.

These and other new developments involving Catholic laymen are described by Leo R. Ward. He points out that in the first half of the twentieth century the altar rail served as a sort of daily reminder of the barrier that exists between laymen and priest. But the movements now underway are destined, he thinks, to remove much of this barrier and to give laymen a new sense of belonging to their church. They are not there merely to multiply the hands of the priest. The layman has his own work to do in the church, a proper work in which he substitutes for no one, and in which he is simply doing his own work as a Christian.

Ward describes, for example, the Christian Family Movement. This started about 1947 when three young couples came together to consider how they could help to bring "Christian life in modern society." The groups read books, have reports and discussions, engage in group devotions, study problems of the home and family, promote church attendance, and seek to Christianize community life. By 1957 there were almost twenty thousand families enrolled in these groups, and the movement was only just started.[5]

The Pre-Cana and Cana Movement is another "couples" organization, devoted to the problems of getting ready for marriage and of marriage. From October 1947 to June 1957, 401 Cana conferences were held, attended by nearly twenty-two thousand couples; and during the same period, 218 Pre-Cana conferences attended by approximately six thousand couples.

There is the Grail Movement for girls and women, the National Council of Catholic Men, the National Council of Catholic Women, the Confraternity of Christian Doctrine, and several others.

It seems evident that the churches, both Protestant and Catholic, in the United States at least, are becoming very much aware of their laymen and are seeking to meet their needs as persons and to involve them constructively in a greatly enlarged total church program.

III

The other new spurt of lay activity in recent years, primarily since World War II, has been the ecumenical movement. This

---

[5] Leo R. Ward, *Catholic Life, USA* (St. Louis, 1959), Chapter III.

has had its origin and its greatest activity in Europe. For in Europe the interest of the laity, especially of the laymen, in the organized church and its activities has been waning sadly over a period of two generations and more. Whereas in America church membership and attendance is still socially acceptable, in Western Europe the churches stand largely empty. In countries having state churches, the membership is high, naturally, much higher often than in the United States; but attendance, except on special holy days, is small.

Concern over this lack of interest in the conventional program of the church has existed for a long time, and as early as 1915 Manfred Björkquist in Sweden began to organize a movement to challenge intellectual doubters with a concept of the Gospel big enough to permeate every phase of daily life. This resulted in the Sigtura Foundation, with headquarters on the shore of Lake Maler near Stockholm. A similar concern led George MacLeod to found in 1938 the Iona Community on the Island of Iona off the western coast of Scotland.

But the main interest in such movements came in Germany after World War II. Much has been written about the "German miracle," that remarkable recovery in military, political, and economic strength made by Germany just after the war. But Franklin H. Littell maintains that the true German miracle was the way in which in a ruined society, demoralized and starving, roots were put down for the "most significant laymen's movement in the world today."

According to Littell, the opposition to Hitler was far more general than the American public was ever allowed to know, and a large part of the resistance was centered in the churches.[6] The first real evidence of church resistance to Hitler was that of the conferences at Bormen in the Ruhr Valley in 1934. Here 140 delegates from nineteen territorial churches—Lutheran, Reformed, and United—adopted a six-point platform which became the fundamental Confession of Faith for such men as Martin Niemöller, Dietrich Bonhoeffer, Karl Barth, and Hendrik Kraemer, and thousands of their followers.

---

[6] Franklin H. Littell, *The German Phoenix* (Garden City, N. Y., 1960), 4.

It was this same general group of resisters that formed the Evangelical church in Germany and prepared the Stuttgart Declaration of Guilt in 1945. They confessed their solidarity with the guilt of the German nation, identifying themselves with the sin of their own people—and this at precisely the same time that the Nazi war criminals were pleading not-guilty in the docket at Nürnberg!

And it was from this group that came the leaders of the Evangelical Academies of Germany. The people they called together were not necessarily Christians; communists, socialists, agnostics, orthodox, and liberals were all welcome so long as they agreed to follow the rules of full and free discussion. Most were engaged in vocations that had been debased and demoralized by the Nazis: law, medicine, civil service, journalism, industry. Many were repelled by the church. They were not interested in the sacraments or in the observance of a historic church calendar of celebrations or in the liturgies or the catechisms. They wanted to ask questions of their own choosing and to be able to disagree and to challenge—which is not at all the atmosphere of the typical church worship service. Even the environment of the church building repelled them. And so the conversations began to be held on "neutral ground," in resort areas, abandoned castles, and other isolated locations. According to Margaret Frakes, the first of these to be established as a regular meeting place in Germany was in 1945 at Bad Boll, a large resort hotel fifty miles southeast of Stuttgart.[7] But others sprang up almost at once: Bad Nauheim (later Arnoldshain), near Frankfort-am-Main, in 1946; Loccum in Hermannsburg, near Hannover, also in 1946; Tutzing on Starnberger Lake in Bavaria; Haus der Begegnung, near Mulheim in the Ruhr area; Friedewald, near Betzdorf in Westphalia; in addition to one in Berlin and at least four in the East Zone, and many smaller and temporary locations throughout Germany.

In Holland, also, a number of these Academies have sprung up since the war, Kerk en Wereld, near Utrecht, being the largest. Part of the program at Kerk en Wereld is somewhat in

---

[7] Frakes, *Bridges to Understanding*, 8.

the nature of a lay theological seminary—a four-year course in preparation for service as Wikas, a new kind of church worker who serves in parishes and social centers, in villages where industries are changing the old patterns of life, in human relations programs in factories, and in civic centers. But Kerk en Wereld also conducts shorter workshops and conferences for a great variety of groups of business and professional men, trade unionists, and technicians. Eight other lay centers are active in Holland today.

In France there are at least six retreat centers. In Italy there is the important center called Agape, an ecumenical village in the heart of the northern mountains. In Finland there are two or three of these institute centers. In Switzerland there is the well-known Boldern institute near Zurich, founded by Emil Brunner, and the even better known Ecumenical Institution at Bossey on Lake Geneva, as well as the YMCA-sponsored program at Castle Mainan on an island in Lake Constance.

This does not give a complete picture of these centers in Europe where institutes, retreats, workshops, and conferences of various kinds are held, for new ones are being established continually; but it does show something of the size of a movement which has grown into immense proportions since World War II.

Who attend these academy conferences, and what do they talk about? Frequently the main thing the members of a group have in common is their occupation. Those attending may be teachers, engineers, physicians, nurses, midwives, architects, economists, farmers, contractors, artists, journalists, business men, industrialists or industrial workers. Sometimes it is a common interest in a subject such as theology, the church, peace, automation, politics, the family, aging, personal religious living. Much stress is placed on good fellowship, relaxation, meditation, and (for those who wish it) worship.

The subjects discussed arise out of the felt needs of the participants. A favorite topic in the early days of the Institutes had to do with the problem of being Christian in the work-a-day world—"Serving Christ at my job." But there is also much questioning about the basic theological issues: the nature of God, how man can properly relate himself to God, and whether or not this is a moral universe. International relations, atomic warfare, and disarmament have also been much discussed, and, of course, the influence of communism, fascism, and intense nationalism. Race relations have come in for much consideration, and other themes are urban expansion, aged people, the dangers of prosperity, modern poetry, and the Bible and freedom. Women factory workers have discussed the rival claims of family and job; mayors, the temptations of bureaucracy; artists, the significance of modern design; soldiers, the ethics of the soldier; older workers, preparation for retirement; teachers, the literary work of Albert Camus; jurists, capital punishment; pharmacists, the use and misuse of drugs; secretaries, the problems of the career woman; and war widows, the rearing of a family without a father and adequate income. One conference at Tutzing in Bavaria brought jazz musicians and pastors together to explore the significance of rhythm in life. Another brought together models and designers to talk about the motivations behind clothes fashions and their implications for the good life.

From the foregoing it can be seen that there is a tremendous ferment in Europe, an attempt to probe deeply for answers to fundamental questions. The religious leaders are to be congratulated on their flexibility in cutting across denominational lines and setting up the facilities outside the church where a frank and honest search for these answers can be carried on. (In many cases, of course, this search is also being carried on within the churches.)

IV

Before leaving the European scene, we should mention another dramatic movement that has taken place among Protestants in recent years: a new type of lay assembly, best represented by the German Kirchentag. The term was first used in the nineteenth century for the church congresses called by Johann Hinrich Wichern, who founded the Inner Mission Movement in Germany in 1849. The newly revived Kirchentag

Congresses have caught fire in a remarkable way. The first was held in Hannover in 1949. Under the dynamic leadership of Dr. Reinold von Thadden-Trieglaff, it sought to bring together the laity of all churches "in order to develop and express a new sense of Christian responsibility for and in all the life-sectors of the world, and to educate the laity for a courageous and spiritually intelligent witness in the world." [8]

That Hannover meeting was such a local success that it was followed in 1950 by the first national Kirchentag at Essen where 25,000 came for an entire week and 200,000 assembled for the closing session. Annual assemblies were held for the next four years, and the numbers grew until at Leipzig in the Eastern Zone in 1954 some 60,000 came for the week and 600,000 for the closing service. Thereafter the assemblies have been on a two-year schedule, with comparable attendance.

Dr. von Thadden has built up a full-time staff that concerns itself not only with the mechanics of getting ready for the next Kirchentag but with the spiritual preparation of those planning to attend, and with a follow-up program for those who have already attended. He summarizes the purposes of the entire movement as follows:

It has set itself the task to call Protestant lay Christians to their responsibilities in all sectors of public life and to make them active, particularly in the economic, social, and political fields where Christian principles are on trial and where Christian obedience has to stand the test. The layman is anything but some sort of a marginal figure on the outskirts of the church. He is *the essential interpreter of the Christian message in the battlefield of the world.* Therefore he must be spiritually prepared for open confession of his faith, and for active service in *everyday life as well as in the congregation.* . . . The Kirchentag is not a meeting of elected representatives of the church: it is aimed at bringing together the voluntary lay forces in Germany. It has no membership—and no records from which to register what it has achieved. The Kirchentag is not, and does not want to be, a church itself. Its nature cannot be understood in isolation from the church, but only in relation to it. It is, and wishes to

---

[8] Kraemer, *A Theology of the Laity,* 40.

remain, a voluntary and spontaneous contribution to the building up of the church. It has no party program on national or international problems, or on political or ideological difference. But within the limits of our specifically Christian obedience, it seeks to make clear to all people the responsibility of the church in the spheres of present world and national issues.[9]

At other places in Germany "junior Kirchentag" meetings are held from time to time with essentially the same purpose. In Holland the movement takes the form of regional Church Days, when whole families are encouraged to attend. In Scotland seven Protestant denominations have united to put on a Kirk Week, held in Aberdeen in 1957 and in Dundee in 1959. France, also, has been holding what are called *Rassemblements Protestant;* they are based on the Kirchentag plan.

When we add the activities of these lay assemblies to that of the Academies and Institutes discussed in the previous section, the total is most impressive and encouraging for the churches of Europe. But how is it in the U. S. A.?

V

In the United States and Canada we have not been entirely unaware of these European developments. There has been a real desire on the part of the National Council of Churches, the Canadian Council of Churches, the Y.M.C.A. and Y.W.C.A., and a large number of other inter-denominational or non-denominational groups, as well as most of the denominations themselves, to give adults on this side of the Atlantic the same opportunities for serious and frank discussion of the basic issues of our times that are being enjoyed by Europeans.[10]

One of the most successful of these new efforts is the Evanston Ecumenical Institute, inaugurated at Evanston, Illinois, in October 1958. This arose, to some extent, as an outgrowth of interest aroused by the second World Council of Churches As-

---

[9] Quoted in Frakes, *Bridges to Understanding,* 91-92.
[10] Further details on most of the developments mentioned in the following paragraphs may be found in Frakes, *Bridges to Understanding.*

sembly, meeting in 1954 in Evanston, and represents a creative effort to relate the Christian faith to modern problems. It is sponsored by thirteen theological seminaries in the Chicago area, and is directed by Dr. Walter Liebrecht, who is intimately acquainted with the German academy movement. Its program of lectures, discussions, retreats, study courses, and workshops is similar to those conducted in Europe.

A similar movement, emphasizing perhaps more of the personal aspect of religion is the Yokefellow Movement, with headquarters near Earlham College, Indiana. The Laymen's Movement for a Christian World has since 1941 conducted seminars and retreats for business men at Wainwright House near Rye, New York. It now has over fifty "cells" in American cities and has branches in approximately forty-five foreign countries.

The Camp Farthest Out holds a series of week-long retreats in camps throughout the United States every summer. Stanley Jones conducts his Ashrams in a similar way. A "movement for power among the churches" was initiated in 1942 at Kirkridge, a rural mountainside center near Bangor, in eastern Pennsylvania. Packard Manse at Stroughton, Massachusetts, operated by the Christian Fellowship Foundation, is used by groups in that area who are interested in conducting a dialogue between church and world. Parishfield, near Brighton, Michigan, is an ecumenical center devoted to problems of industrial life.

Many denominations are also operating institutes, seminars, and retreats modeled somewhat after the European Academies. The United Lutheran Church in America has for several years conducted a series of Faith and Life Institutes throughout the United States and Canada. The Protestant Episcopal Church has been putting on an extensive series of Parish Life Program conferences. The Presbyterian Church in Canada has a lay center at Clarendon Hills, north of Toronto. The United Church of Canada operates four lay centers, the Five Oaks Christian Workers Center near Paris, Ontario, being the oldest. The Quakers for many years have conducted programs of lectures, study, discussion, and worship at Pendle Hill, near Philadelphia.

To this list must be added practically all other denominations in America, most of which have many retreat centers where laymen can go for serious consideration of problems of every-day living. Furthermore, many of the regular theological seminaries are putting on lay schools of theology which are proving popular.

One would suppose, judging by all the church activity of American laymen, that there is little need for additional programs of adult education in our churches. Over 60 per cent of Americans belong to some church, and, according to a 1958 Gallup Poll, on an average week nearly 50 per cent of the adult population attend a church service. Having attended church, these laymen, one would suppose, carry the Christian principles expounded there back into their homes and offices and factories, back into the social and political and business life of everyday America. This was the assumption of the 1954 Assembly of the World Council of Churches as it closed its Evanston session: "The real battles of faith today are being fought in factories, shops, offices, and farms, in political parties and government agencies, in countless homes, in the press, radio, and television, in relationships of nations. Very often it is said that the church should 'go into' these spheres, but the fact is that the church already *is* in these spheres in the person of its laity."

All this may be true, but if the church is really in these various spheres we shall have to confess that it is a largely impotent church. Church members are there, to be sure, but crime rates continue to rise; materialism and secularism and expediency seem to have gained as the bases of action; racial tensions are greater than at any time in recent history; delinquency, divorce, greed, and mental breakdown are increasing. From this we must conclude, I think, that much of the so-called lay "activity" is merely that, without anything significant happening to transform lives or change basic concepts, attitudes and practices.

What some of the basic concepts are, for Methodists at least, was brought out in a survey conducted in 1959 by the Board of Social and Economic Relations of the Methodist Church. Replies to a questionnaire were received from 5,020 respondents, most of whom were laymen, and were reported in a recent volume by S. Paul Schilling.[11] It is interesting to note, first of all, what these Methodists conceived to be the nature of the Christian church. Only 23.7 per cent agreed with the classical Reformation position that the church is "the faithful congregation in which the pure Word of God is preached and the sacraments rightly administered." The largest number, 34.6 per cent, took the historic Methodist position that the Church is "the community of those who have been renewed through Jesus Christ and empowered by the Holy Spirit." But most surprising was the 6.3 per cent, at the one extreme, who took the essentially Catholic position that the church is "the custodian of the authority and grace committed by God to the apostles and their successors," and the 30.4 per cent at the other extreme who adopted a basically humanist view that the church is a "society of those who have joined together in their quest for the religious life." In commenting on this result, Schilling writes: "If this is an accurate and serious expression, there is sound warrant for the judgment of some concerned students, that for many Protestants the church is little more than a social fellowship or merely one of the many human organizations." [12]

Perhaps even more pertinent to the present paper is the response to a question on the nature of the laity. More than one-tenth of the respondents assign laymen to a marginal role, either as "those who are ministered to by the clergy who are the true church" or as "people in part-time Christian service." The largest response, 59.9 per cent, was to the statement that laymen are "non-ordained Christians whose function is to help the clergy do the work of the church." Only a disappointing 24.8 per cent regarded laymen as "members of the people of God called to a total ministry of witness and service in the world," which is essentially the position taken by the World Council of Churches and by most of the leaders referred to in this paper. As Schilling points out: "The replies to this question make

---

[11] S. Paul Schilling, *Methodism and Society in Theological Perspective* (New York, 1960) , Chapter V.
[12] *Ibid.*, 161.

plain that the currently stressed idea of the ministry of the laity as the church at work in society has made relatively little headway among Methodists, possibly because it is not well known or understood." [13]

VI

Comparing the activities for the Christian education of adults to the need, what may we conclude? So far as measurable results regarding the Christian education of adults in this country are concerned, the answer will have to be rather pessimistic. We seem not to have developed a very effective lay apostolate. The carry-over from Sunday sermon to Monday job is not very great. The concept of the church, of the Kingdom of God, of the social gospel is not at all clear in the minds of laymen. Ignorance of the Bible is probably greater than at any time in the past century. Evidences of lack of personal integrity on our campuses, in the entertainment field, in the great corporations, and in public office are shocking. Crimes of violence increase, racial tensions build up, and international crisis follows international crisis with sickening rapidity.

But on the other hand, never have there been such opportunities to perform the educational task we are discussing here. Church conferences are well attended. Summer camps are overflowing. People travel across the country to attend almost any kind of meeting—even one called by a church, with no expenses paid! In the Methodist church alone, the one with which I am most familiar, it is probable that within a single year the total attendance at all the conferences, assemblies, retreats, and conventions of the church amounts to more than five hundred thousand! Furthermore, it is not difficult to get people to buy literature. The yearly sale of Bibles continues to break all records. Other books and magazines, particularly paperbacks, have never been so widely bought and read. Enrollment in adult education classes is increasing.

It would seem that if ever the church had an opportunity to

---

[13] *Ibid.*

educate people, it is now—but not merely by more preaching. This is not to imply that good preaching should be decreased; it is to suggest that sermons need to be supplemented with many other educational devices and methods. At the same time, a continual search needs to be made for meaningful language in which to express spiritual realities and explain what the church is and does. To say, for example, that the church is the "mediating society of God's grace" leaves most laymen cold. More understandable equivalents for many traditional words and phrases need to be discovered.

The success of the small, intimate, face-to-face discussion group in dealing with problems of real importance and concern has been amply demonstrated in countless situations, particularly when discussion is followed by action and this in turn is reported back to the group. The experience of our European brothers seems to indicate that much more significant use can be made of this method than we have done thus far.

And let's not neglect the college students in our churchmanship education. These are young adults, too, and will have a lot to say about the church and much to do in creating a climate favorable to spiritual values in the future. If they are not educated in college years or before, the job will be doubly hard at a later date.

But whatever the procedures, we as Christian educators can hardly expect to hear a "well done, thou good and faithful servant" if we fail to use the opportunities that are now before us. In the words of the Stuttgart Declaration of Guilt in 1945: "Our hope is in the God of grace and mercy that He will use our church as His tool and give it authority, to proclaim His Word and to create obedience to His Will among ourselves and in our whole nation."

8. Insights for Adult Religious Education from Other Sources

PAUL BERGEVIN

Professor of Adult Education
Indiana University

Introduction

A COMPREHENSIVE TREATMENT of the insights into adult Christian education that could be gained from the many current patterns of adult education would result in a work of encyclopedic proportions. Adult education makes use of many disciplines and relates them to the problems of adult maturation. This discussion presents a few examples which serve to illustrate what we might look for in our quest to improve and extend a specific field of adult education.

Most individuals recognize that their behavior varies from situation to situation but that they are essentially the same persons. Yet our needs and expectations differ to some extent in each one of the institutions that compose our social life. And each institution is, to a degree, unique in its expectations and needs. As the nature of an institution is studied, its peculiar characteristics are revealed; its needs and expectations are exposed. A problem of the adult educator is to determine the unique relationship of the person and the institution in question and to develop a program of learning which, so far as possible, relates and fulfills the needs and expectations of those concerned, both the individual and the institution. If we become specific and speak of the Christian church, then we are obliged to examine our problem in terms of the nature, scope, expectations, and purpose of this body.

Basic principles of learning and educational insights can be applied in the education of adults in any grouping or institutional environment. But the relative success of the educational venture will depend to a surprising degree on the diagnostic skill of the adult educator and also on his ability to translate educational insights and learning principles to meet the specific problem at hand. This implies a considerable amount of training of the adult educator. Because a philosophy of procedure proved productive in some factory or community program of adult education is not sufficient evidence to indicate that it would be successful in a church-centered program of adult education.

Unique Characteristics

Although Christian adult education is characterized by a number of unique features, this does not enjoin us to stand aloof from ideas developed and used by sources outside the church; we must examine the secular ideas carefully and adapt the effective ones. Many of us in the field of education have seen programs from one source lifted *in toto* and used with little or no modification in another situation. Use of procedures without study or adaptation is sometimes done because we have not examined carefully the nature and the need of our particular work. We feel that adult education is adult education wherever it is carried on, and that if we substitute religious study materials for whatever materials might have been used, the outcome will be a person better informed about religion.

The fallacy is that the learning experience involves more than study materials. The reading of the Bible will not, of itself, make us better Christians. Something has to happen in the learning process in order to bring about the kind of learning which causes change. The use of quality resource materials is of very great value, but resource materials of themselves cannot guarantee a complete learning job even if they are carefully read and assimilated.

True Christianity is an active state presupposing kinds of adult learning which cause dynamic change. A knowledge of resource material is needed, and concomitantly training experiences are required to put this resource information to work. Either one without the other puts adult Christian education in the same category as the countless number of study groups and courses which hope that by some magical process real learning will come in direct proportion to the number of courses taken, books read, or the length of time one has attended study groups.

We also must be aware of the differences which exist between the non-religious idea of the development and growth of human kind and the religious idea. These differences are vital and must be considered in the planning, conducting, and evaluating of a program of Christian education. Some people believe that education in the usual channels plus consideration of moral standards is essentially what is needed to bring about a mature person, the goal of secular society. Christian education, it seems to me, views maturity as a means rather than an end, the end being to know God and to serve him.

If this distinction is within reason, then circumspection should be exercised in the way we select and use educational concepts employed elsewhere than in the church. Clearly, some of these can be used without much translation or selective adaptation. But others seem to require the skilled and discreet hand of the professional educator who knows the objectives of Christian education and who is capable of attacking problems of Christian adult education. This person can act as the translator, carefully adapting many valuable educational concepts to the need of the Christian community.

It is true that some of the basic areas of concern are the same whether the educational problems of adults are approached from the view of the church-related program or from the secular position. The church, for example, is concerned about the whole person and his total life. Its interest is not limited, as is erroneously thought by some people, to a person's regular attendance at a particular building on Sabbath days. Some secular programs also are interested in the development of the total person. At first glance it might appear, then, that the two programs are related closely, if not identical. If this were true, the problem of careful selection of resources and methods from non-religious programs would be minimized or non-existent. Some religious educators have embraced this view. Their programs use educational ideas, which in themselves are valuable, without much change except perhaps the substitution of religious resource materials for the secular ones.

Here the adult religious educator becomes ensnared in the same fallacy that besets adult education generally: books and other learning resources become the end. When religious learning neglects a purpose, we tend to become Bible worshippers rather than God worshippers. We, as learners, become befuddled with words.

Before we go too far in our search for new ideas and insights from other sources, we should inquire whether these new views could be used or skillfully adapted to help us to: (1) increase continually our understanding of God's meaning for us by knowing God better; (2) practice more effectively the percepts in Christian living, such as love, forgiveness, and humility in order to extend our understanding of God and His purpose for us; (3) establish conditions which will make possible willingness on the part of the learner to allow an infusion of the Holy Spirit to take place. If such criteria are used when we borrow from others, we will have established nuclei around which new educational insights can be assessed and productive programs built. Evaluation is possible only if we begin by setting some standard for achievement. In a sense we should know at the outset what we would like to do and now and then examine the program in its various stages to see if we are accomplishing our objective.

Another problem that should not be overlooked as we observe, select, and translate adult education concepts from other sources is the environment which spawned the concept. Today's world is a vocational and commercial one. We are trained to be "go-getters," to conform, to press forward our material standards of living. From fawning over the power of man to the worship and use of the creative, releasing power of God is a long step which adult Christian education must help one make.

Two other factors worth considering when selecting the proper educational methods are that adult Christian education should involve some understanding of the reality of the supernatural as it affects the maturing adult, and that the participants are to learn to be in this world, yet not of it. So far as the supernatural is concerned, I must approach it from the viewpoint of a layman. I know little of the theological interpretation of this power. I do know as a Christian that there is a power transcending the ordinary course of nature. I am not thinking of magic or mystery or an invention by which many sincere and religious people have been enslaved in religious ignorance, not always without the help of the clergy. I am thinking of a reality, a power which defies full explanation and identity by means of the knowledge we have at hand. While the supernatural may not be realized by reason or by a direct encounter with an intellectual activity, education may have something to do with developing the will to believe through which the supernatural can be known. Inclusion of the concept of the supernatural as a factor in Christian adult learning is essential. It forms, in a sense, part of the antithesis of materialism which characterizes much of present-day adult education.

Pointing out how to participate in our world, yet be not of it, is surely another major item in the repertoire of the qualified adult Christian educator. This concept clearly identifies the spiritual quality of adult religious education. There may be better examples than these, but the point I am trying to make is that although adult Christian education affects the whole life of the adult, it concerns life in a permanent sense, not as a temporary vocational, materialistic, or sensuous concern. It certainly does not ignore these latter points, but rather tempers them and relates them to a dominant spiritual motivation.

These points, I think, are unique characteristics of adult religious education, concepts which uniquely identify it: (1) it teaches that the maturation process is a means rather than an end; (2) it lends direction to our need for worship; (3) it helps one appreciate the supernatural; and (4) it encourages our learning to live in our world yet not be of it. When we become aware of our particular task and its nature, our programs can prosper. When we fail to identify our task as a specific and peculiar one and borrow indiscriminately from less specialized forms of adult education without careful adaptation, we are not performing the teaching mission of the church. We may be contributing to general cultural advancement, but it is doubtful if the program could stand up well under careful evaluation in the field of adult Christian education.

Some Insights Which May Have Significance for Adult Christian Education

In recent years more emphasis has been placed on the continuing education of adults, and concomitantly more persons have been concerned about improving its quality. In some instances, experimentation conducted by adult educators has revealed new insights of value to the student of adult education. Lay adult leaders, teachers, and institutions have made valuable contributions by trying different approaches which, in many cases, resulted in productive ideas. Also, social scientists have provided the adult educator with a reservoir of insights, many of which are being applied successfully toward the advancement of the area of continuing learning for adults.

Because of the extent of the information available, it is impossible to present a comprehensive view of this area. It is hoped, however, that a few selected examples may serve as an introduction to a vast number of possibilities which might be examined and adapted to serve our specific needs. The several concepts which are treated briefly here have been selected arbitrarily because they are current, fairly representative, and have value as stimulators to those who would pursue this inquiry further. The first four can be interpreted as examples of principles which could be applied to programs; the others represent programs or plans which others have found useful. No attempt has been made to explain the how-to-do-it phases.

Four Principles Which Could Improve Our Programs

1. *We behave the way we see things and not necessarily the way things are.* This concept may explain why some of our programs are not productive of good results. Since our behavior is a result of our perceptions rather than of the direct forces which are exerted upon us, we must be concerned with process in the learning situation. The emphasis in this concept should be on helping the learner to see things differently by growing from within. The teacher should provide conditions which will help the learner help himself to become an active ingredient in the learning process; he should help to establish the best learning conditions possible, while offering a minimum of assistance, and then let learning take place. This idea is predicated on a kind of discipline which comes from within and helps give the learner an opportunity to learn.[1]

2. *How we behave toward others depends on how we look at people.* This concept combines philosophical, theological, and psychological approaches. It is basic and vital to any program of adult education worth conducting. As I understand the concept and its implications for those of us charged with the responsibility of developing and maintaining meaningful programs of adult education, it is this: if we think of a person as largely a living result of influencing forces, then we in adult education who set out to cause change must do so by manipulating the forces which are exerted on the learner. This stimulus-response approach represents a view of the nature of humankind upon which a program of adult education can be constructed.

---

[1] A brief description of this idea can be found in *Learning More About Learning,* a pamphlet published by the National Education Association in 1959.

We may think of a person as a child of God, subject to forces revealed by Christ, or we may think of him as a mechanistic creature, subject to external forces of a rather vague nature. In any case, we ought to come to a decision and make our attack accordingly. Some of our Christian adult education programs have little or no foundation in the Christian idea of the nature of humanity. Others are so thoroughly structured and theologically oriented that the participants drift into a kind of exclusive intellectual society for the propagation of the knowledge of God.

3. *Creative Christian adult education demands programs which promote desirable change.* A mechanical learning procedure usually does not cause much to happen to the basic views of the learner. It is true that when we read about the plight of the poor people of the world we may be moved to send a pittance to CARE. Or we may hear a sermon which arouses a feeling of guilt in us. But we soon find some way to rationalize our past behavior and carry on pretty much as before.

Productive programs of Christian learning cause change in the participants. The maturing person in an effective program of learning is not satisfied with the temporary feeling of well-being realized each time he leaves a class or a sermon where he was told in different ways that we must fight against sin. Conquering his tendency to traffic in hate and pride and slander is not simply a matter of learning how awful somebody else thinks these vices are, and then hoping he can absorb this aversion and be freed of them. In order that meaningful change may result, adult educators need to provide the opportunity for the creative release of the learner and to help him secure the freedom and discipline necessary to come to grips with himself, his fellow men, and his relationship with God.

A specific program of learning can be designed to accommodate this kind of desirable change. It is not based on tricks or gimmicks, nor do the participants need to learn a new language or be psychoanalyzed. It is based on the idea that careful training is necessary to bring about change. One important factor for causing desirable change in a learner is that the teacher needs to change, too. Little success can be realized unless those in a position of leadership understand something about change by being involved in the process themselves. And some of us in positions of leadership, very much like the student, find it extremely difficult to allow learning to help us.

Change does not always take place; indeed, it is a slow and sometimes painful process for most of us. The adult educator must provide the opportunity for change by understanding and using the procedures that usually cause change. This kind of experience begins with all the learners helping each other to plan the change, and making certain they recognize and understand the need for change.

4. *Diagnostics.* An important insight into adult education which barely has come to general notice is the diagnostic skill. Seldom have we in adult education made sufficient progress in developing a means of determining accurately the learning problems and needs of a particular group or institution. A large number of programs in the church and elsewhere have been started by guesswork. Often there has been no real evidence that the work offered the participants would satisfy their actual need.

To attempt to develop a program based on need, one uniquely suited to a particular group, requires the skill, partly scientific and partly artistic, which is diagnostic. To identify real needs from symptoms is a procedure which must precede any program planning.

Using diagnostic skills to determine need in adult religious education involves a careful analysis of the problems and needs of the individual, of the group, and of the church locally, nationally, and universally. Symptoms are discovered and studied by persons trained to recognize them as manifestations of need. The results reveal what the people actually need rather than what we thought they needed. Obviously, then, productive programing toward meeting this need can be established and effective evaluation conducted. Diagnostics is accomplished by persons trained to do this work, but to successfully complete the diagnostic process the clergy, the laymen, and the adult educator must work together.

Studies of the Aging Process and Their Contribution to Adult Education

During the past decade educators have shown an increased concern about the aging process. Adult learning becomes productive when it is based on an awareness and knowledge of the physiological and psychological changes which take place in the normal adult from the time he reaches physical maturity until death. Changes in vision, hearing, interest, and attitudes have significant implications for both professional and lay educators of adults in the church. Although there is not as much material available about adult learning in its several stages as about children, enough is obtainable to make spectacular changes in our programs if the insights gained were used.

Roman Catholic Christian Adult Education

In this particular area of adult Christian education, Sister Jerome Keeler has gathered a large number of viewpoints and summarized them in the following statement: "The general opinion seems to be that, if a program stresses only facts, skills, and techniques, and neglects fundamental truths about God and man, it is rather superficial, fruitless, and a waste of time." [2]
Roman Catholic adult education is broad and diverse. Exclusive of the many institutions of higher learning which conduct credit night-school programs, there are Institutes of Industrial Relations, Inter-Racial Centers, Cana Conferences (marriage preparation) , and scores of colleges conducting noncredit short courses in a vast academic area.
Two interesting and valuable programs for the education of the Christian adult are being carried on by the Roman Catholic

---

[2] Sister Jerome Keeler, "Where Are We in Adult Religious Education?" *Adult Leadership,* 7 (1959) , 235.

Archdiocese of Chicago. One is the work done by eleven Adult Education Centers, and the other is called the Christian Family Movement. In the Adult Education Centers the usual program consists of courses offered in neighborhoods where the centers are located. Last year a special Lenten program entitled "The Christian Man and the Modern World" was conducted. Six courses were given: St. Paul: Apostle for the Layman; The Matter of the Communist Challenge; Great Decisions, 1961; Five Important Questions for American Catholics; God and Man in the Modern World; and An Investigation of Great Music. A total of about eighteen hundred people attended the eight sessions given in each of these six courses. The work, of a rather formal nature, was conducted by persons distinguished in each field. In addition to the regular courses, there are a number of individual lectures offered in these centers. These cover such topics as Our American Culture: Prejudice Between Catholic and Protestant; and The American Consensus: What Can Unite a Religiously Divided Nation? Approximately twelve hundred people participated in the lecture program.

About two-thirds of the expenses of the operation of these Adult Education Centers is borne by the Archdiocese of Chicago. Physical facilities for this adult education work are donated by the Catholic high schools and local neighborhood parishes.

The Christian Family Movement, coming out of the Archdiocese of Chicago, is of international scope. It is an informal adult education program and clearly a lay movement. Small groups meet in the members' homes and use group discussion techniques to inquire into a variety of topics which are categorized as social inquiries. Economics, international relations, foreign trade, demography, and the United Nations are examples of the areas covered. In each session there is also a short scriptural and liturgical study. It is generally an accepted practice that a priest sits with the group, without participating as a regular member. If this is not possible, a married couple usually acts as leader.

Leadership training programs are available, but many of the present leaders have not been involved in any specific group leadership training activity. At the present time, there are no full-time headquarters personnel in charge of this enterprise.

Some Insights from Adult Jewish Education

Differences of opinion exist among adult Jewish educators, as among those in other areas. One of the sharp cleavages seems to appear between an approach that might be called humanistic Judaism and the more traditional view. The more traditional view, while not denying the importance of the liberal position, would probably feel that training for adults should not be exclusively worldly; that emphasis should be placed strongly on Torah; that an understanding of the heritage and the spiritual content of Judaism should take precedence over other areas of learning.

In the liberal area of Judaism the adult Jewish educator is not so much concerned about helping to make "good or better Jews . . . [as to] create mature, thinking human beings so thoroughly rooted in their religious heritage that they can draw on it for the benefit of themselves, their families, and their fellow men." [3] The traditional program would include a strong emphasis that might be called orientation in Judaism.

The attempt to clarify a point by such a brief comparison runs the risk of oversimplification. Generally, however, the differences exist in means rather than in ends and could serve to illustrate similar divisions within the Christian community.

The average Jew has the striking advantage of having been brought up in a religious and family environment which places a high value on learning. "An ignorant person cannot be pious," an expression of Hillel, exemplifies the kind of influence to which he is exposed. With this sort of candidate for further learning the adult educator has a fertile field which probably does not exist proportionately in other groups or institutions.

But there are also problems in this area of adult religious education. A basic problem lies in the average synagogue's fail-

---

[3] Lily Edelman, "Where Are We in Adult Religious Education?" *Adult Leadership,* 7 (1959) , 240.

ure to elevate adult education to a first-class status. Usually more funds and attention are given to other areas within the synagogue than to adult education. This problem is, of course, no stranger to the adult Christian educator. An acquaintance of mine inquired of the head of a prominent seminary about developing adult religious education. He was informed that the idea was a good one, but that they had committed themselves and their funds for the next four or five years and, unfortunately, adult education was not included.

Many of the ideas, devices, and methods in adult Jewish education are the unique product of Jewish creative thinkers. We can find much stimulation by considering such of their productive ideas as Living Room Learning. In a pamphlet prepared by Lily Edelman of the Department of Adult Jewish Education of the B'nai B'rith a study-discussion type of adult learning is described. The idea of Living Room Learning is to stimulate a concern for "the opening up of new mental vistas" and to provide "an adventure in friendship." While the basic idea of this sort of study-discussion group is not unique, there is a creative approach here that bears investigation.

Another program worth consideration is the Congregational Institutes of Jewish Studies. These studies provide sustained programs ranging from six to thirty weeks of study one evening each week. They provide a congregation with the opportunity to participate in group study and lectures in such areas as Hebrew, the Bible, and Jewish history.

Finally, the Institutes of Judaism should be explored. Internationally known Jewish scholars provide the background material for this type of Jewish adult education. The Institutes are designed to provide "group exploration into the world of Jewish tradition." It is one of their hopes that the participants will become inspired enough to continue their studies in year-round adult religious education programs.

Conclusion

Actually the surface scarcely has been scratched in the few examples given from academic disciplines and from on-going programs. I have tried, however, to make it clear that a study of the methods and techniques of general adult education and of several special forms can be most helpful, but that these ideas, methods, and techniques must be especially adapted in order to meet the needs of church-oriented adult education most effectively.

9. Challenges and Responsibilities for Christian Adults in Contemporary Public and International Issues

DONALD C. STONE

Dean, Graduate School of Public and International Affairs
University of Pittsburgh

CURRENT REVOLUTIONARY changes in community life, national affairs, and the world scene present a special challenge to Christian education. Today as never before the primary need is to develop spiritual resources and to stimulate in the individual awareness and understanding of his personal faith. A second need is to apply Christian imperatives in all realms of life.

The Spiritual Basis of Human Progress

Man's opportunity to improve his world is greatest when social systems are fluid—when he lives in a period of change. This is also a time of greatest danger, for he may find himself adrift and confused as old values give way before the onrush of new ideas and institutions.

All human progress has been attained through revolution, that is, abandoning the inadequate or irrelevant and adopting the more pertinent or appropriate institutions that will promote social progress. Change is essential to both individual growth and societal advancement. A function of Christian education, therefore, is to equip people to bring about essential, constructive, and effective change based on Christian ethics and morality.

Christ initiated the greatest revolution of all times. As a Christian, I consider the new life and the new society he launched to be the supreme form of revolution. His revolution enables men and women to free themselves from that which enslaves: greed, hatred, lust, selfishness, envy, and resentment. His revolution of human society based on brotherhood, compassion, integrity—love of one's neighbor as oneself—provides a universal answer to the problems of our times as well as the days in which Christ lived.

A task of Christian education is to assist mankind in applying these principles to an ever changing environment, and in coping with baffling and often overwhelming problems.

It was the application of these principles in the American colonies which produced the social and political revolution called the U. S. A. The same principles are appropriate and adequate for today's social, economic, and political revolutions; but it will take a tremendous amount of Christian education to develop the attitudes, knowledge, insights, and discipline to apply them. Christians must understand the real world in which they live and develop sufficient spiritual resources to cope with the complicated problems which mankind faces today and can expect in the future.

We live in a world totally different from that of our grandfathers, and the changes that we experience today are incalculably small compared with the conditions which our grandchildren will face. Yet we conduct our lives, educate our children, view civic responsibilities, and engage in religious practices as though we lived in the world of our grandparents; and most of them had little awareness of the real world in which they lived.

Applicability of Moral Imperatives to Government

Government and other social organizations, as well as individuals, must conform to the moral law of God. The initiative of the Protestant and Catholic churches in recent years in elaborating the implications of moral law on public issues is most encouraging. Much of our progress in developing morally defensible features in foreign policy has been due to this effort.

On the other hand, the number of church members who understand the moral and ethical issues in the role of government and public policy seems frighteningly small. I have found almost no literature or study guides in this field except as they relate to international responsibility.

A vast arena for Christian education is opened up, for example, by any sustained study of Biblical teachings about the state, and the function of public officials and magistrates. Throughout the Old and New Testaments, we learn that the state should be founded on justice, that it is instituted by God to enact just and equitable laws, that in the fulfillment of its mission it should be the organized expression of God's character and purpose.

The state—our country or any country—is judged by divine standards of righteousness and justice. Lawmakers, judges, and administrators are God's servants charged with bringing to all people the blessings of just, efficient, and humane government. Nations and individuals are accountable for their acts and are judged by God under the same moral and ethical standards. The people of a nation, as children of God, are charged with the responsibility to promote justice, freedom, equality, opportunity, respect, integrity, and mercy in all relationships. So, too, government, as the means by which the people carry out their collective public concerns and responsibilities, must fulfill these same obligations. This conception of the moral and religious foundation of government is reflected in the covenants of our country and in the official statements of our leaders.

These moral and religious foundations for government and public policy apply to the total community of mankind. They are the requisites for individual and group fulfillment at the level of the family, local government, state, nation, and international community. When individuals seek special privilege based on selfish interest, when they lack concern for the well-being of their fellow men and isolate themselves from responsibility for service to the general welfare of the community, then justice, freedom, economic and social progress, and public morality corrode and wither.

Likewise, when a nation, on the basis of narrow self-interest, endeavors to provide for its protection in isolation and seeks the economic prosperity of its citizens with little tangible regard to the misery, poverty, and ignorance which may exist outside its boundaries, or lends assistance to the economic development of other countries primarily for its own national interest and security and as a means of obstructing the machinations of an opponent, it, too, lacks adequate moral and religious foundations, and its policies will be frustrated and its actions resented.

Lack of Moral Foundations

As though turning our backs on the application of moral and spiritual imperatives, we deal with public issues mainly on an abstract or opportunistic basis. Political and administrative leaders today devote little attention to the fundamental moral aspects of the policies that are pursued, and they approach such questions with reticence, if at all, in discussions with representatives of other nations. Public expressions are largely materialistic, stemming from the divisive and egocentric principle of self-interest. In political and governmental circles, as well as in other areas of our national life, we too often consider truth and honesty as having only relative value.

Increasingly, social and economic measures become ends in themselves. The result is to place greater and greater reliance upon political and economic systems as the answers to our problems. We forget that it is people who make up the world and who serve and are served, and that their spirit, their quality, their convictions, their standards are what determine social progress or regression.

While a democracy operates on the principle of government by law, government, of course, is conducted by men. Men elect the representatives who pass the laws, and men elect or appoint administrators who carry out the laws. The character of the individuals who comprise these groups determines whether the desired corporate way of life can be achieved. The self-seeking, dishonest, dissipated citizen, politician, or administrator will breed a species of government of the same quality. By the same token, the community or nation which is torn by groups seeking to gain the greatest advantage for their particular following regardless of the public interest will falter in times of stress. Democracy cannot long endure when its moral foundation has been corrupted.

Democratic and effective government requires, as part of this moral foundation, honesty in the actions of those who institute governments—the citizens—as well as their public officials. Indeed, honesty in one group cannot exist long if it is absent in the other. Honesty prospers under two conditions: (1) when the material necessities of life are reasonably available; and (2) when people are conditioned to honesty as a principle of life and feel that penalties will inevitably occur from any other course.

Illustrations of Domestic Stress

Technological changes are occurring so fast that we constantly marvel over the tremendous developments of the past few years: television, nuclear energy, jet planes, penicillin, nylon, vaccines, to name a few. Many scientists report that we are merely on the threshold of a breath-taking technological age. Whatever the brain of man imagines, the genius of modern science brings into reality. Scientists predict that knowledge will double in the next decade.

The social and individual maladjustments which may accompany future changes give cause for sober contemplation. The relatively minor changes of the past few years have already produced a degree of instability and schizophrenia which has skyrocketed the population of our mental institutions, added many ciphers to the statistics of alcoholism, brought expanding rates of delinquency into our privileged suburban communities, and split marital ties to an extent that threatens this historic social institution.

During the past twenty-five years, the United States has changed from primarily an agricultural to an urban society. Two-thirds of our citizens are urban dwellers; 90 per cent of population growth is taking place in cities. In ten to fifteen years, three-fourths of our citizens will live in 190 metropolitan areas. With the passing of the farm and small-town family, our places of shelter, shopping, work, recreation, and cultural pursuits will be increasingly scattered. We will become fragmented as persons and as groups. This new environment is building a frontier as hazardous to the soul as the frontier of the forest and plains was to former generations.

Our cities are already blighted and inadequate for present populations. Citizens with sufficient resources are moving to the suburbs. Negroes are denied access to decent residential areas. The Federal Government, in its meagre appropriations for urban renewal and housing, has viewed this as a private, or at best, a state and local problem. With a hundred or more separate governmental units in a major metropolitan area, each going its separate way, our cities are largely paralyzed in trying to cope with urban sprawl, cheap developments along new highways, inadequate parks, smog, transportation crises, water pollution, and a thousand other difficulties.

Educators have projected requirements to provide for doubling and tripling the number of persons to be educated in the next twenty to twenty-five years. Instructional and physical facilities to meet this burden are not now on the horizon.

The Task of Christian Education

A major task of Christian education is to provide the principles, ideals, and analytical tools—the religious building blocks and individual skills—so that citizens may understand these forces and guide social change into moral and ethical channels.

The inadequacy of Christians in dealing with these issues has been due in part to their preoccupation with the tasks of earning a living, raising a family, and enjoying the opportunities for recreation and entertainment which increasingly absorb all of man's leisure time. Without leisure, Christian education would of necessity be highly restricted no matter how much the individual wished to engage in it.

Paradoxically, despite the great amount of leisure afforded by our national productivity, the acquisitive and material values inculcated in our culture have produced a degree of self-indulgence and hedonism which leave little time either for Christian education or Christian service. Most Americans appear disinclined to subject themselves to the discipline and work required in the development of a philosophy of life which they can articulate, and in mastering skill in the application of the principles of their faith in public and international affairs. Thus, part of the aim of Christian education must be to foster personal resistance to the corrupting values of an acquisitive society. Leaders need to be challenged as never before to become Christian revolutionaries in a world of change.

Christ's mission was to change men—to create capabilities and capacities, to generate qualities of leadership, and to develop group sharing, mutual support, and spiritual power capable of transforming the world. He did not produce a social security policy, formulate a housing program, or propose a plan of collective security. For Him, better society required better persons. With changed men, the social evils which he denounced would be corrected. In fulfilling this requirement, Christian education must accept as its primary task the development of persons with conviction, insight, and ability to reflect and articulate the Christian faith.

In business and public life today, it is not easy to tell who is or is not a Christian. The glow of Christian faith and the distinctive characteristics of Christian living disappear by absorption of nominal Christians into the value fog and by the practices of a secular and, in many respects, evil environment. For many church members Christianity appears to have little relevance to secular life. Christianity has become mainly a matter for discussion at special times in special places.

This tendency is especially evident when one travels abroad. Although there are a million and a half Americans and their dependents living abroad on overseas assignments and an equal number who are traveling as tourists, the proportion who give evidence of interest in spiritual and religious affairs is almost negligible. Thousands of Americans may be in Florence, Cairo, New Delhi, or Lagos on a Sunday, but I can testify from first-hand observation that very few attend church, even though row upon row of pews will be awaiting occupants. The staffs in the U. S. embassies are disturbingly ignorant on how to guide one to a Christian church service.

For most Americans overseas, religion presents a barrier rather than a bridge to international understanding and fellowship. It is a barrier because most Americans lack the personal commitment, the knowledge and understanding of religion to appreciate the common bond that exists among those who have sincere interests in spiritual and moral affairs. The individual who has a rational personal faith and concern for the spiritual interests of other people quickly finds a strong link with like-minded persons of other faiths with whom he can communicate and develop a community of understanding. Christian education can train persons to build spiritual bridges.

Obstacles to Christian Education

With the use of mass media, advertising, appeals to conformity, and the fostering of acquisitive tastes, the value system underlying American culture has been undergoing radical change. The environment in which parents today endeavor to raise children presents such obstacles to the development of Christian attitudes and standards that it is surprising that any youngster can become a responsible member of society. Just when training and development are most needed, Christian education in the home has been crowded out by other preoccupations. And the amount of time available for Christian education in the church is so small that its effect is often negligible.

Partly because people do not know how to deal with such matters in a non-doctrinal manner and partly because we have been intimidated by anti-religious people, appreciation of the relevance of moral and ethical insights to public education is being rapidly destroyed. At a time when penetrating scholars emphasize the need for greater understanding of the spiritual and religious aspects of life, education systems from kindergarten to universities are eliminating this vital element of general education. A related obstacle is widespread disinterest on most college campuses in becoming involved in matters of this type. Little evidence has been found that college studies, even of public and social problems, foster a sense of social and public responsibility or interest in working with civic, voluntary, religious, and private organizations. The culture of the campuses—the attitudes and values reflected in the dormitories, fraternities, and on the playing fields—are the primary determinants of the social and ethical values of most students. Indeed, the personality and attitude of a professor have far more impact than the course material he teaches.

Thus, the task of Christian education is not only to equip the young man or woman to apply the imperatives of Christianity in society but to bring about an awareness that Christianity has something significant to contribute to the quality of family life, to one's daily work, to the processes of public and private education, to the function of government, and to the conduct of international affairs.

Young men and women today are not confronted with these challenges, or they are unwilling to equip themselves to serve as partners in revolution, or the content and methods of Christian education are not adequate to the job. In any event, the youth of the world appear to be challenged more by the total commitment and alleged idealism of Communism and other totalitarian approaches to social change than by Christian democracy.

Older people tend to become conservative and disinclined to serve as combatants in Christian revolution. Many business-men assert that the church should not mix into their affairs, take a stand on a public issue, or even define the moral prin-ciples underlying economic and business practices. Enlight-ened welfare measures are often branded as socialistic and thus presumably evil. Churches which rigidly adhere to the *status quo* become identified with predatory and exploitive interests. Trade unionists and political reformers have not found an en-couraging or helpful religious haven in most churches. This has been true in other regions as well as in Western Europe and suburbia U. S. A.

Christianity and Vocation

Christian education should offer assistance to young men and women with regard to choice of vocation and to the conduct of work itself. I find little indication that many young people today select their fields of study and embark on careers with any real evaluation of how their work may contribute to society. On the contrary, one of the most disturbing aspects of contempo-rary life is the extent to which scientists, artists, lawyers, public relations counselors—persons in all professions—work for ob-jectives or enterprises which are socially injurious or otherwise impair the life and behavior of individuals. Evil practices be-come highly organized when they are commercially profitable, and they attract talented personnel. The assumption seems to be that the executive, engineer, advertising expert, or sales-man in such enterprises should be respected and professionally recognized on grounds of technical ability and financial success no matter how degrading or corrupting his job.

In selecting his field of work a man or woman should consider two important elements: first, he should make an assessment of his knowledge, skills, and competences; and second, he should consider whether a field of work contributes to the fulfillment of human needs. If the choice is made in prayerful search for God's purpose in his life, his selection and performance will enhance life and contribute to society in a manner harmonious with the teachings of Christ. Having gone through this process honestly, a young person should not be concerned if he is managing a grocery store rather than a multimillion dollar industry, assisting in road construction rather than serving as a judge, or perfecting methods of personnel testing rather than backstopping the United States delegation to the United Nations. In all of these occupations he can be a witness to his Christian faith and serve human needs.

There are many fields that permit conscientious persons to serve their fellow men. Some of the most essential fields, such as youth leadership, teaching, the Christian ministry, and public service, may not provide substantial financial return or status at the country club. But they pay large dividends in interesting work, creative helpfulness, personal satisfaction, and opportunities for "immortality."

The Public Service and Christian Vocation

In any appraisal of significant fields of service from the standpoint of Christian responsibility, public service should obviously be very much in the center. City, state, and national governments render most vital services to society: urban renewal, welfare, crime prevention, recreation, conservation, public health, sanitation, education, technical assistance, and countless other services. They require virtually every kind of occupational or professional skill. Top executives in government deal with more important and more interesting problems than those of private corporations. Yet few talented persons are guided into public service fields, particularly in community service. Instead they are encouraged by parents and counselors to enter fields which have high market place prestige, financial remuneration, or which are made popular by professional or trade organizations. Most choices are made in ignorance or by sheer accident.

Young people are deflected from public service by three principal factors. First, government is generally discredited by groups who do not want effective service, especially if it means higher taxes, impartial regulation, or the constructive influence on policy which derives from competent public administrators. Second, the patronage and privilege dispensed by some governments tend to discredit all government. Third, government is unable to engage in as effective promotional and recruitment practices and to offer as high salaries as many private organizations. The business associates of my father often expressed skepticism that I could be an honest man because I was working for government. Paradoxically, the government agencies which I was helping reflected higher standards of honesty than the businesses these men served.

Applying Christian Values on the Job

Regardless of the field of work, every individual has the opportunity to fulfill his Christian faith in his work, no matter what position he occupies. To be effective, he must have a genuine interest in helping people and in reflecting the service values of his faith in his working relationships.

Christian education surely should provide skills as well as motivations to carry on work in a spirit of helpfulness and to develop constructive work relationships. A person's attitude toward his job has a profound effect on fellow workers. The impact is incalculable when a cheerful worker gives his associates a lift at a time they need help and performs a full and honest day's work. By joining together with one or two others, any worker who is a truly effective Christian can build a new sense of service and team play into his unit.

By giving a courteous answer to a complaint, by defending a fellow worker and helping her to face up to her difficulties, by incorporating a needed apology in a letter she prepares for her employer, or by encouraging the boss to commend an employee who shows real courage in refusing an unwarranted permit, a secretary or any other worker can be an effective Christian.

Christian lawyers, salesmen, engineers, executives, foreign service officers, and representatives of other professional groups need to meet together in Christian education programs to consider ethical problems in their fields and learn from each other how to apply Christian values. This is the essence of the International Christian Leadership movement which has had such profound effect in the Congress, in the executive branch, in business, and in the professions, where members have disciplined themselves to this type of Christian education.

In an era of the organization man, the Christian administrator has many opportunities to apply the imperatives of his faith. An age-old problem in any organized effort is how to get the persons in the organization to work together harmoniously. A public administrator is always confronted with the need to offset the perversity of human nature and the disintegrating effect of individual desires as he tries to establish cooperative effort. Teamwork entails the wholehearted participation of the members of the team. Unreconciled differences, jealousies, incompetence, disloyalty, all contribute to the difficulty of the administrator's job. Every administrator has the challenge of providing an environment that will produce spontaneous and cooperative effort. This cannot be gained on a command basis but only by the upward pull of a leader as he seeks to secure the voluntary participation and cooperation of his associates in pursuance of a common goal.

Public officials and administrators must possess ideals and purposes adequate to cope with forces which create friction within their organizations and which seek to corrupt them from without. If employees are to respond positively in carrying out democratic principles, the scale of values which governs the life of the administrator must reflect the moral qualities of the Christian life. If an administrator tries to live by any other scale of values, he inevitably becomes defeated, full of inner conflicts, fears, and frustrations, and he bungles his relationships, official as well as personal. That this is the inevitable result can be amply demonstrated by psychological and psychiatrical analysis as well as by Christian teaching. To what extent does Christian education today serve the ever increasing number of administrators, supervisors, and foremen with insights and values?

Applying Christian Principles on the International Front

The conduct of international relations presents a special challenge to Christian education. Today the world is marked by stress and recurrent crises. Imperialistic and militant communism, bipolarization of power, conflicting ideologies, dislocations of uprooted people, and a woeful lack of the elementary necessities of life for vast numbers of the world's population create serious obstacles to harmony and integrity in public affairs. The combination of economic distress and social disintegration in many countries seems to be more than their spiritual and moral fibre can withstand. The changes taking place in pre-industrial countries are cataclysmic. Traditional societies which formerly experienced relatively little change from century to century are now leaping from a tribal culture into a nationalistic industrial age in a matter of months.

Three major forms of revolution are at work. One is the revolution of rising expectations. People everywhere are becoming familiar with the relative abundance and luxury in the United States and other industrialized countries. Determined to participate in this abundance, they respond to political leaders who demand more tolerable conditions of life—food, shelter, medical services, and education—frequently unmindful of the means, desirous only of achieving long-term goals within the shortest time possible and at minimum cost.

The second is the revolution of freedom and independence. Colonial peoples are determined to achieve political independence and to chart their own destinies. The omnipresence of this spirit of independence and freedom will close within a decade the final chapter of a centuries-old practice of political colonialism by Western nations. Subversion and infiltration may reduce new countries to communist colonialism, especially where the capacity for self-government is not deeply rooted nor the idea of an informed, articulate electorate widely understood. Most political leaders of the new and emerging countries, with encouragement from the U.S.S.R., appear to prefer precipitous independence with a loss of individual freedom to the orderly development of responsible government.

The third revolution is the determination of people to be respected and accepted. This revolution is, perhaps, the most significant for us as Christians who proclaim the sacredness of the human personality and the importance of human values. Aware of the non-white sensitivity to the widespread image of white arrogance and exploitation, we must approach these people with humility and apology, asking for a reciprocal Christian forgiveness.

We in the West cannot afford to withdraw from the responsibilities and obligations which we share with the pre-industrial countries as these revolutions take place. In less than half a century, the communist "revolution" has captured control of one-third of the world and has neutralized another third. Communist demonstration of rapid capital formation and economic development, as well as its dramatic space and military achievements, have brought the leaders of the non-industrial countries to consider seriously that the panacea to their Pandora's box of human ills may be founded in the totalitarian control of society as practiced in the Soviet Union or even Red China. Thus far the West has failed to foster a widely appealing counter strategy of life or to design effective alternative approaches to economic development and methods of assistance.

The forecast is not entirely gloomy, for a gratifying change has occurred in United States policy from the pre-World War II era when Americans chose to isolate themselves from the rest of humanity. Many of the policies and approaches of the 1920's and 30's were thoroughly immoral. But even with time and hindsight, our approaches and operations are not adequate if we are to keep step with world realities.

For example, we still cling to the traditional concept of sovereignty. In our definition of sovereignty, we include the right of a nation to decide whether it will or will not wage war.

Not only is the historic concept of sovereignty largely inoperative in today's world, but it is immoral and unchristian. Countries with a highly developed sense of responsibility have forfeited thereby the license to act counter to world opinion and universal moral standards. Irresponsible societies flout moral accountability and exercise their sovereignty to operate capriciously. This is not to suggest that we should disarm or renounce unilaterally the use of force, but rather to point out that we should recognize the moral issue and devote all our energy to bringing about collective security and the rule of law.

Likewise, Christian insight is sorely needed if we are to devise an adequate rationale for our overseas assistance programs. In 1951, official arguments began to justify economic as well as military assistance on the basis of narrow self-interests, to emphasize their value in counteracting Soviet imperialism, and to imply that we could buy with our material surplus the support and friendship of countries whose help we needed. The more aid that was justified on these grounds, the greater the volume of protest against aid programs, protest which was all too often based on the naive expectancy that people of other countries should be grateful for the programs which we ourselves declared to be carried out in our own self-interest.

How can right feelings of genuine mutuality be created among nations unless moral and psychological conditions essential to understanding, respect, and cooperation are fostered? Must we not give assistance because we are concerned for people as people, and because misery, ignorance, despotism, and selfserving exploitation must be relieved wherever they exist, so far as our abilities and resources permit? Christian education is already helping greatly in the development of acceptable approaches to questions of this type and to an appreciation that military force has only one justifiable purpose, namely, the maintenance of peace while all available energies are applied in the development of a system of collective security.

We are now engaged in a world struggle to decide which strategy of life will survive. Whole nations are in convulsion, and in a process of such rapid change the task of maintaining stability, order, individual freedom, and responsibility is staggering. Our present ineffectiveness in this struggle is due in large measure to our ignorance of how to develop a positive strategy which will be more appealing, as well as more potent, in meeting human needs and in offsetting the programs of communist and other totalitarian countries.

Moreover, Americans on the whole are not proving very effective in carrying out overseas assistance, informational, and other programs. The reasons are far less a matter of technical competence than lack of Christian motivation and genuine concern for people. With egocentric preoccupation and ignorance about other societies, religions, and cultures, Americans try to remake people in their own mold. They tend to do things to people rather than to work with them. With an underlying vein of arrogance and assumed superiority, they generally lack the warmth of spirit and selfless service which is found in persons who endeavor to function in a Christ-like manner. Christian education thus is challenged to provide the spiritual underpinning and the psychological and moral conditioning essential for effective service abroad.

Concluding Note

Our very survival depends on our becoming committed, knowledgeable, and effective in dealing with issues such as I have outlined. In the development of programs, approaches, and methodology to this end, Christian education has a tremendous challenge. The best minds and most experienced persons in these spheres of Christian practice are needed in the development of programs and materials.

Whatever the level of education and station in life, all persons must be aware that actions and attitudes on the lowest day-to-day scale reflect and determine the broadest realities. We must guard against discouragement. This is an imperfect world, but the smallest element of high purpose—even in carrying out a distasteful job—can have infinite ramifications for good.

10. Dialogic Foundations of Christian Adult Education

REUEL L. HOWE

Director
Institute for Advanced Pastoral Studies

A sub-title might be, "Christian Perspectives Underlying Christian Adult Education." Putting these two titles together suggests that the dialogical principle is the underlying assumption in education that would be Christian. In the pursuit of this theme I wish to develop four points: (1) The Dialogical Nature and Process of Education; (2) Incarnation: The Ground of Dialogue; (3) Relationship: The Source of the Curriculum; and (4) The Purpose of Christian Adult Education as Dialogically Conceived.

The Nature and Process of Education are Dialogical

One of the common misconceptions of Christian education is that it is accomplished by the monological method of communication. Many ministers and teachers come to their work with the mistaken idea that if they can only tell people what they ought to know, the message will be heard and accepted. Experience, however, disillusions them. They discover that people are not able to hear and understand. Undialogical instruction provides a veneer of content that bulges, cracks, and is destroyed under the heavings and tensions of people's living.

The teacher, on the other hand, because of his monological illusion about communication, suffers from what I call "agenda anxiety" in which he is so anxious about covering all the points of his curriculum that he does not get the people he is teaching into any kind of educational focus. The teacher, of course, is responsible for the content of education, but he should not let his anxiety about it be a barrier to communication with his students and to the meeting of meaning between himself and them. The bankruptcy of the monological approach to communication and education does not need to be elaborated. The results of the church's use of it are obvious, and all research in the area of communication indicates that it is the least efficient approach to the task.

The true concept or principle of communication is that of dialogue in which meeting occurs between the meanings students bring to the educational encounter and the meanings responsibly presented by the teacher. The attempt to tell people about the love of God in the abstract, apart from the meaning of their experience of love, will produce little or no result. On the other hand, if the teacher makes his listeners aware of the dangers and difficulties they have experienced in accepting and giving love, they will hear with understanding the story of God's love in Christ. The meaning of the human experience of love is brought into dialogue with the meaning of Christ's love for man; each is illumined and completed by the other.

I wish to make clear that I am speaking of the *principle* of dialogue, and am not concerned for the moment about the methods of dialogue. I am not advocating a particular method of communication. Any method can serve either a monological purpose or the dialogical principle. A monological method, such as a lecture, can serve the dialogical principle; and a dialogical method, such as a seminar, can be made to serve a monological purpose. An imperialist, for example, may use the seminar process as a way of forcing his views and purposes on others. A lecturer, however, honors the dialogical principle when he speaks to the meanings people bring to him. All of us have listened to lecturers and preachers who seem to draw us into an implicit dialogue with them in such a way that the meanings they bring to us activate the meanings we bring to our hearing of them.

The employment of the dialogical principle of communication would save us from the ridiculous tool loyalties to which some educators are otherwise subject. Some are loyal to group process methods, others are disciples of the lecture approach, and still others are devoted to the audio-visual tool; indeed the church is fractured by methodological schools. What would we think of carpenters who divided themselves into tool schools so that we had to choose between one who said that he would use only a hammer and another who would use only a saw? The structures built by carpenters who practice single-hearted devotion to only one tool would be no more ridiculous than the results of a teacher who undertakes to accomplish the educational task with the use of only one tool.

Our choice of tools should be made in relation to the task to be performed, the choice being made freer when the teacher is serving the dialogical principle. By this I mean that if a question needs to be asked, the methods should be used that will help people to formulate their question. This would seem to indicate something approaching the group process. If, however, the question has been asked and an answer is needed, some method should be used that would provide the answer in response to the implicit or explicit question, and this might indicate a lecture. In the service of the dialogical principle the teacher may hope to acquire a variety of tools and versatility in the use of them.

Returning now to a consideration of the nature of dialogue, I ask: What keeps communication from taking place? When the teacher is concerned only with the transmission of his own ideas and meanings and regards the student as the receptacle for them, he almost always strikes what I call a "meaning barrier." A meaning barrier is created whenever a communicator is unaware or unresponsive to what his students bring, and the students are unprepared to receive and respond to the communications of the teacher.

The teacher aims his communication in the direction of his pupils. They are present, presumably, for the purpose of learning, and possess within themselves certain meanings, including affirmations and questions, which are necessary if they are to receive the teacher's message. They may not be able to marshal these in ways that prepare them to hear their teacher, and he may not know enough about the learning process to realize that he must be responsible *for* his students in relation to their meanings as well as responsible *to* his students in relation to the subject matter of the curriculum. All too often the meaning barrier keeps the meanings of the students and of the teacher from meeting. There are leaks in the barrier, however, and sometimes the message of the teacher is met by the meanings in some pupil's life. We are delighted, but we may not be anymore aware of why communication occurred than we are of why it failed at other times.

We can always assume, I believe, that people bring meaning to every encounter. We may not recognize their meanings, we may not like them, and we may wish that they had brought other meanings, but the fact remains, meaning there is. But we cannot assume that the meanings people bring to educational encounter are available to them. The teacher, for example, may undertake to make clear to a group how dependent is the church on presence and action of the Holy Spirit. No matter how competent he may be in his Biblical and theological understandings of the subject, unless he makes available to his students understandings out of their experience, he will fail to make his point. On the other hand, if he reminds them how debilitated they are when the spirit of depression possesses them and how alert and energetic a spirit of euphoria makes them, they will begin to understand how dependent human beings are on spirit and, therefore, how dependent we are on the Spirit for Christian living.

If the teacher also reminds his students that they cannot be members of a school in a real sense until they have the spirit of the school, they are prepared to understand that the church as the Body of Christ is created by the Spirit of Christ and that we are made members by the Spirit. There must always be this dialogue between the meanings of the students and the meanings of the teacher. Only by dialogue can the questions that emerge out of life be correlated with the answers implicit in the Gospel, and can the message of the Gospel, in the process of education, escape from the classroom and find its destination in the affairs of the world.

The Christian teacher, therefore, has the responsibility not only of preparing himself for teaching the truth, but also has the responsibility of preparing his students to hear it. The proclamation of the Gospel has to be faithful to the meaning of the Gospel, but the hearing of the Gospel has to be faithful to the meaning of life. Furthermore, the meaning of each must inform the meaning of the other. In other words, the word of man must be in dialogue with the word of God in order to be judged, purified, and transformed. And the Word of God must be in dialogue with the word of man because it is the word for man, being born as it was out of the dialogue between God and man as it took place in Christ.

The kind of teaching that we are talking about is the kind engaged in by our Lord. All of his teaching was dialogical because his life was dialogical. Read the pages of the Gospel and note how he taught. Mark how he moved in his conversation with the woman at the well from a consideration of the water that quenches physical thirst to the Living Water, and from a theoretical discussion about religion to a consideration of the kind of life the woman was living.

Teaching of this kind calls for what I term correlative thinking. When we are studying doctrine in its propositional form, we should at the same time be thinking in terms of the life situation and the question that asks for it. Similarly, if we are studying the meaning of a human situation of any kind, we ought to think also of the ultimate meaning to which it points.

The cultivation of correlative thinking is indispensable to the Christian teacher and is a creative way in which we can practice the imitation of Christ.

The dialogical principle of communication with its employment of correlative thinking lies at the basis of our Lord's parables. We need to relearn the use of the principle in our own time. Recently I heard a teacher address a group of children and adults on the meaning of baptism. Instead of beginning on the side of the propositional meaning of the sacrament, he spoke from the people's side of the dialogue. He began by saying that some puppies had been born at his house during the past week, and that these puppies were fortunate because they had had a mother who was devoted to them, kept them warm and fed them, and in every other way that she could, cared for them. He went on to say, however, that not only had they been born into a good dog world, but that they had been born also into a good human world, and that this human world would not only help the mother dog take care of the puppies but would do for the mother and the puppies what the mother could not do by herself. And so it is with us in relation to the human family and God's family. Afterward, it was amazing how many adults said that this was the first time they had really understood what baptism was about, and the children in their classes were able to talk about the meaning of baptism in terms of their own lives.

That they were able to talk about baptism in their own terms is an important fruit of education, and the presence of that fruit is dependent upon the employment of the dialogical principle which is the foundation of education. One reason for the great gap in both clergy and laity between their theological formulations and their theological understanding of life is due to the neglect on the part of the church's teachers to make sure that their lessons are understood in the terms of the learner instead of in terms of the teacher. The purpose of education is that the truth shall be incarnate in the person and not held mentally as abstracted information or insight. This observation leads us, then, to our second point.

Incarnation: The Ground of Dialogue

Christian education has to rest on the phenomenon in history known as the Christ and the change that it effected in creation. Christ was the event of God's participation in human life that marked the beginning of a new creation. Because of him we live in a different world than did David or Julius Caesar, and have resources, if we will use them, that they did not have. The passage in II Corinthians, Chapter Five, beginning with verse 17, gives us a picture of the true basis of the Christian life, and therefore of Christian education: "Therefore, if anyone is in Christ he is a new creation. The old has passed away, the new has come. All this is from God Who through Christ reconciled us unto Himself and gave us the ministry of reconciliation, so we are ambassadors of Christ, God making His appeal through us."

Even as God was incarnate in Jesus of Nazareth, so now the Holy Spirit incarnates himself in those of each generation who would receive him. The spirit of Christ appeals to us, and, through us, appeals to others. Christian education, therefore, is more than communication about the work of God; it is in itself participation in that work. Christian education itself is a part of the Gospel action in our time.

In the new creation all true communication takes place in the saving dialogical relationship between God and man initiated by Christ and continued by his spirit. A young couple, for example, experiencing the stresses of estrangement, may now be assured that God is at work in the interests of their reconciliation and reunion, and that he wants them to take the risks of communication, to speak the word and leave the other free to respond, with the belief that out of this exchange will emerge a renewal of their relationship and, therefore, of themselves.

Likewise, the embattled teacher and student, instead of withdrawing for the sake of the proprieties of the relationship, may now recognize themselves as living in the hospitality of God's reconciling work, and are, therefore, free to speak the word of truth, in spite of frustration and pain, with the expectation that in response the word of truth may be returned. In other words, the truth becomes incarnate in the relationship between teacher and student and calls them both forth as persons. The purpose of Christian education should be the emergence of persons who appear in response to true dialogue.

The truth that I have just stated derives from our doctrine of creation, for God created man to be in relation with him and with one another. The vocation of persons is to enter in relation with other persons, but the act of entering into relation is not as easy as many people understand it to be. The invitation to be, which is necessary for the individual's becoming a person, must come from another person, and we must wait for that invitation. And we need to remember, as Buber has pointed out, that the invitation comes from a person who must inevitably stand at some distance from us. In order for there to be a relation it must have the quality of distance as well as the quality of presence.

Many young couples, for example, make the mistake of assuming that love requires only intimacy, that each must lose himself in the other. Such sensual appropriation of another destroys a relationship because the polarity necessary for dialogue does not exist, and polarity is what we mean by distance. The same polarity is necessary for a teaching relationship. Both presentness and distance are requirements in a relationship in which education occurs. Each must be a person independent and distinct for there to be a relationship in which dialogue makes education possible.

The appearance of a person is always in response to the participation of another person in his life. This is what I mean by the incarnational principle. The mother participates in the living of her child. If she seeks to live her child's life for him, the results are disastrous. If she does what is appropriate for a mother and leaves the child free to make his own responses, he will begin to appear as a person.

So likewise the educator participates in the learning, thinking, and growing of his students and leaves them free to make their own responses and decisions. If he succumbs to the temptation to do their thinking and make the formulations for them, he only succeeds in destroying them as persons. We are loved in order that we may love. We are taught in order that we may teach. Truth is more than subject matter. It is a quality of being. The truth of God's justification of us by grace can be treated as mere subject matter about the relationship between God and man, but it is meant to be the power enabling a man to accept himself because he is accepted. And he will endeavor to accept, love, and understand others.

Anything the Christian educator says about God will be spoken in the context of his life with God and expressed in his relation with his neighbor. He believes that the act of communication and, therefore, the act of teaching is more than a description of the truth, and should be an embodiment of the truth. In other words, human becoming and identity are founded upon the act and content of communication. When I talk about love, my talking must be an act of love. If I would speak of God, then God himself must make his appeal through my speaking about him. There can be no separation of the word and the life: this is a judgment that Christian education must accept.

Relationship: The Source of Curriculum

It becomes clear that what happens between persons is the curriculum of education. The dialogue between man and God produced the Bible, and the study of the Bible is concerned with the encounter that took place between God and man. Similarly, the dialogue between God and man produced the formulations of theology, and the study of theology should have as its primary concern the illumination of the relation between God and man. Unfortunately, however, many ministers have been trained to think theologically about theology and do not know how to think theologically about life. Likewise, the dialogue between God and man through the centuries has a history, but the study of that history should give perspective to the contemporary encounter between God and man. But many people who have studied the history of the church have no perspective to bring to the life of the church in our own time.

The abstraction of Biblical, historical, and theological thought and the life that produced it makes it difficult for us to accept the full religious meaning of contemporary dialogue. What happens now between man and man, and man and God, is also a part of the curriculum of Christian education. I remember an occasion when, in the course of a seminar for laymen on the meaning of the atonement for modern man, several members of the group became alienated as a result of feelings and opinions expressed during the discussions. When it was suggested by a discerning member of the group that the relationship between these members was the responsibility of the whole group and should be discussed by it, several other members protested that we ought to stick to the subject, namely, God's atoning work in Christ. Considerable time and effort was required before they could see that what was happening between them was a legitimate and relevant part of the curriculum of the conference. It is much easier to talk about atonement than it is to participate in God's reconciliation as accomplished in the concreteness and complexity of our human relations.

In a very real sense the contemporary dialogue between God and man is but a continuation of what we call the Scriptures. The Word of God and the word of man have to be kept in dialogue. To read the secular press thoughtfully and not read the Bible meditatively is a sin, and to read the Bible meditatively and not to read the secular press and participate responsibly in contemporary life is a sin. The Bible was born out of the meeting of the news of the day and the Word of God. Likewise, participation in contemporary life needs the illumination of the Bible just as the understanding of the Bible calls for participation in the making of contemporary history. Let us never forget that out of the meeting of history and the Word of God was born the Good News, and the Good News will continue to appear in our own time as men live responsibly *in* the world and *to* the Word of God. What happens therefore between man and man in dialogue with the Word of God is as much a part of the curriculum of Christian adult education as anything that is delivered to us by the theologians.

The Purpose of Christian Adult Education

One of educators' commonest images of themselves is as dispensers of answers to people's questions. The same image is common in most people who are authorities in any field. Have you not noticed that when a question is asked of one who is an authority, he often proceeds to answer the question instead of using his understanding and skill to help the person himself think and study toward an answer to his own question? And tragic it is that educators all too often use their knowledge and experience and understanding to give inquirers their own predigested answers to questions rather than to help the students use their growing resources in relation to their own questions.

Education that does not bring the full powers of both teacher and student into dialogue weakens a person rather than strengthens him, and it makes him more dependent rather than more resourceful. As a result of this kind of education, some ministers with whom I work are afraid to think independently and creatively; they are more apt to quote someone else than speak with authority themselves. And some of them would rather that I give them answers to their problems than help them do their own thinking. We may be turning out generations of scribes and pharisees rather than people who speak as having authority.

There is no reason at all why we should provide people with answers to their questions, although there is a great temptation to do so. The purpose of communication, instead, is to contribute to people's living in such a way that they will move toward answers. I am reminded of a session I once had with a couple. The woman had conceived a baby when she had had the measles, and the best medical prediction was that the baby would be born defective. They had three other children. Their physicians recommended that she have a medical abortion. The wife wanted it; the husband did not. They had not been able to make up their minds, the time when such an operation was possible had almost passed, and they had to make a decision within a week. They came to me asking what they ought to do. This kind of question can still panic me until I realize that answering it is not my responsibility. It was their responsibility to make the decision and mine to introduce information, to raise questions, to stimulate thinking, and generally to help them use every resource that would in turn help them come to their own decision. Apparently I was successful on this occasion, because when they left they thanked me for the help I had given them. I must accept their statement on faith; I do not know what decision they made, but they gave the impression they were ready to make it and make it together. In other words, our communication had brought them to the point where they were able to answer their own question, and it had not been my responsibility to give them the answer.

The comment I have just made does not mean that one does not supply essential information. One of the purposes of dialogical communication and, therefore, of education, is to provide content, as shall be elaborated later. If a question has been asked, it is only sensible that an answer be given. But our problem is that we often answer questions that have not been asked. We have witnessed an interesting shift in the teacher's understanding of his role. Some teachers, as a result of the emphasis on the group process of teaching, have moved from the old authoritarian role to the new permissive non-directive role, with the result that too many teachers now involve their people in an *ad nauseam* formulation of the question because they are afraid to provide the information their questions ask for. I hear clergy and others saying, when they do finally yield to this kind of request, "I feel guilty that I told them something that they needed to know." They have been removed from one horn of the dilemma and impaled on the other.

Teachers who employ the dialogical principle assume responsibility by deciding, insofar as they are able, what students need in the process of learning, whether it be to ask questions, contribute their own insights, or make their own affirmations. It is also their responsibility to decide whether to present their own formulated doctrine, contribute needed information, or summarize and interpret the insights that have grown out of the discussion. Under no circumstances, however, do teachers in the employment of the dialogical principle assume the learners' responsibilities for them; nor can they ultimately.

I wish now to state the purpose of dialogical communication which underlies education, and I do so in reaction to a common misunderstanding of its purpose. The common misunderstanding I refer to is that the purpose of communication is to secure consensus with the point of view of the educator. Instead, I suggest that the purpose of communication and, therefore, of education, is to help the person who is receiving it to make a responsible decision, whether that decision be a "Yes" or a "No" in relation to what is being said. Incidentally, this purpose is consistent with the necessity that each person in the dialogue be free to make his own response. In my estimation, the communication has been successful if either responsible decision has been made. I think we worry too much about the "No" or the negative response to communication. It is sometimes necessary for us to say "No" before we can say "Yes." Surely we see this in the life of children. A "No" may be a step on the way to saying "Yes." It should be observed also that a "No" to one thing means a "Yes" to something else, and that a "Yes" to one action means a "No" to another possible one. The purpose of communication, then, is to help people realize to what they are saying "No," and to what they are saying "Yes."

One of the weaknesses of church membership preparation, for example, is that people are allowed to say "Yes" to being a follower of Christ without realizing what it means, and without knowing the attitudes, values, and loyalties to which by implication they have said "No." Church members, as a result, are ambiguous in their loyalties and are like trumpets that blow an uncertain sound when the call to battle is heard. The loyalties and issues of Christian profession need to be made clear. Apparently we are afraid to make them clear, and may, therefore, use communication to promote premature and superficial assent. Apparently our Lord was equally concerned that our "Yeas" should mean Yea, and our "Nos," No. He also told the parable about the man who said "Yes" and did not go into the vineyard, and the man who said "No" and did go. The latter man made the better response, and his "No" led eventually to his living a "Yes."

The failure to leave men free to make their own responses can be tragic. I know a man who prides himself on the number of young men he has persuaded to enter the ministry. They had given assent to his decision for them without having opportunity to consider alternatives. Their preparation for the ministry required that they reconsider their decision in order that it might become their own. Many of them discovered that they had been pressured into a commitment for which they were ill suited, and they wisely left the seminary.

Likewise, in the nurture of the young in Christian fellowship we should try to help people within their capacities and understandings to know what it means to be a Christian in the world today, and to know the alternatives in order that they may make and maintain an authentic choice. Some ministers say they are afraid to present such a choice because they fear that young people will make a wrong response. But is it not wrong for them to make a response that is no response, or to choose a way of life that they do not know how to follow?

Another purpose of education is to bring the forms of life back into relation to the vitality which originally produced them. The original vitality of a marriage, for example, produces customs and rituals which serve important purposes. When communication between the partners breaks down by ceasing to be dialogical, the forms become separated from the vitality and finally become substitutes for the vitality of relationship. The same thing happens to the church. The forms of worship may become substitutes for the vitality of the spirit which can be renewed only when the church returns to its task, namely, living for its Lord dialogically with the world. The purpose of the church and its ministry of education, therefore, is to maintain the creative tension between vitality and form.

A final purpose of dialogical communication and education that I wish to identify is to make available to people the knowledge and skill that has accumulated from the study and experience of generations of men. Communication is not primarily or exclusively concerned with contemporary experiences between persons, but is equally concerned with the acquisition and assimilation of knowledge about the world of persons and things, and with the ultimate meaning of them. But let us not forget what we have already considered in this lecture: that content is the product of the living and thinking of men. The propositional formulations of life and thought must be studied and held in responsible relation to the requirements of life. Content separated from experience becomes lifeless form, but experience separated from the disciplines of content become formless life.

In summary, I would say that education founded on the dialogic principle has some clearly identifiable characteristics:

1. It is concerned not with transmission of meaning from one person to another, but with the meeting of meaning between all participants in the educational enterprise.

2. It is incarnational and not merely propositional, that is, there must be mutual participation on the part of teachers and learners in the meaning of one another's thinking and living.

3. Because truth must be embodied eventually in persons, persons are basic to education. Ideas and systems of ideas are but the coinage in the exchange between persons in the search of truth. Educator and educated alike engage in the work of self-actualization, and should seek and help one another find his own special form and task. Thus, the educator accepts the independent "otherness" of the learner and does not wish to impose upon him his own relation to truth.

4. The purpose of education is responsible decision on the part of learners in relation to one another and, therefore, to God.

5. Christian education thus conceived understands that implicit in dialogue between man and man is a meeting between

God and man. And the educator knows that if a person is to speak to God he must really speak to his neighbor, that if he would love God, he must love his neighbor, and that in loving his neighbor he will be found of God and loved by him.

6. And, finally, dialogical education produces learners who can recognize and participate in truth as they encounter it in the world of human relations as easily as in its propositional forms in the classroom. In other words, they are as much at home in the world as in the classroom, and are thus prepared to be members of the church whose mission is to the world.

11. The Significance of Christian Theology for Adult Education

ROGER HAZELTON
Dean, Graduate School of Theology
Oberlin College

I UNDERSTAND THIS TOPIC as an opportunity for indicating some of the recent developments in Christian theology which have significant bearing upon the enterprise of adult education in the churches. Where possible I shall attempt to make explicit connections, but my main concern will be to sketch the salient features of the theological terrain itself. I hope, however, that these reflections may be useful in stimulating discussion regarding both content and methodology in the teaching of theological material to Christian adults.

The Theological Revival

I do not think it is sufficiently recognized in the church-at-large that there has been a decided revival of theological interest, a veritable reformation, taking place over the last thirty years. At any rate, one has the feeling that the services and activities of local churches on the North American continent do not reflect this fact in anything like its full magnitude and potential importance. Sermon topics, worship programs, and group meetings proceed as if nothing radical or startling had happened in the realm of theological effort. At the local level the main accent still seems to be on what Will Herberg calls the religion of togetherness; God is regarded as a resource for personal and corporate ills, and the Christian message as giving needed answers for the problems of everyday life. Prayer and spiritual discipline, while highly valued, are prized more as techniques guaranteeing a kind of mastery or success rather than as means of opening the self to the promptings of God's spirit and the upward gravity of his grace. In brief, religion and not God, justification by works and not by faith, appear to be the order of the day in the mind of the average church member. And all this stands in utter contrast to the thinking and writing of the more creative, forceful theologians of our time. It is almost as if there were a kind of bottleneck in the churches which despite years of seminary teaching, ecumenical advance, and top-level conferences and study programs, continues to reject the truth in what our theologians have been trying to tell us.

For the entire bent of contemporary theology, with very few exceptions, has been in quite the opposite direction. The accent has been put upon the priority of God, upon what he has done and is still doing for the redemption of his world. It has been upon the actual, eventful character of God's mighty works in history and creation. It has been upon his unique and absolute self-disclosure in Jesus Christ, not as teacher or example only, but as the very deed of God within our human time and space. It has been upon the church as a community called into being through convenant with God, continuing the saving work of Christ within the world, and awaiting the final consummation of his victory over sin and death. And it has been upon faith, not as a problem-solving or a peace-producing experience, but as the gift of God for which the only condition is man's obedient doing of God's will. These and other stresses, it is clear, define a movement very different from the anomalous, amalgamated, activistic tendencies which are evident in present-day American Protestantism.

What Truman Douglass calls "the radical estrangement between the ministry and the world" has its counterpart in the estrangement between the theologian and the church. Perhaps church people have always looked askance on theology, as most of them do now, regarding it as the preoccupation of an intellectual, remote from situations in which Christian living must be done, and offering little positive guidance or illumination. It may even be that the widespread reputation of theologians for contentiousness, aridity, and irrelevance is in part deserved. However, recent theology has been far more church-conscious and church-oriented than it has at any period in the past 200 years. Theologians have been doing their thinking explicitly on behalf of the whole church, and much of their work has been devoted to understanding the nature of the church. Yet what the theologian calls "the church" bears little obvious resemblance to the organization to which lay men and women belong; and they frequently conclude that he and they are simply not talking about the same thing.

There are some signs that this unfortunate gap is being bridged. On the one hand, there is considerable evidence of what can only be termed a hunger for theology on the part of increasing numbers of lay people. By such a hunger I mean a desire to learn the elemental truths of Christian faith, the basic convictions by which Christian conduct and character should be guided. The adult curricula of the denominations in recent years reflects this, as does the pattern of lay retreats and conferences around the world. In part this is a hunger for identification and support, and I am convinced that it is also one for deeply Christian anchorage and perspective. It has, of course, been intensified by the extreme mobility and rapid change to which life in the church has been subjected—rootlessness and short-term membership and democratic pluralism—but it remains true that whatever the causes, the form this interest takes is theological.

And on the other hand, it can be pointed out that professional theologians are getting more and more involved in the preparation of church school curricula, study courses, and other similar projects. Handbooks of doctrine and Biblical interpretation, as well as brief, succinct statements of the meaning of such corporate churchly actions as baptism or the communion service, come from the press at an increasing rate. Theologians, instead of writing only for each other, are beginning to take seriously the theological vacuum and are trying to fill it. They are being drawn more carefully and responsibly into the orbit of denominational and cooperative effort. From both directions, therefore, we have indications that the long-continued rift between theologians and the laity is in process of being spanned.

Some Contemporary Tendencies

I turn now to a consideration of some of the more influential trends in contemporary theology which have pertinence for Christian adult education. In each case I shall be thinking of this pertinence in potential terms, not so much recognizing a *fait accompli* as attempting to indicate avenues of fruitful exploration and endeavor. And I shall be thinking of adult education not simply within the framework of the church or church school, but as part of that whole dialogue between the church and the world to which I believe we are most urgently called at the present time.

Theology today around the Christian world is marked by several distinctive characteristics. It is Biblical in content and outlook, ecumenical in reach and purpose, lay-minded in conception, and world-redeeming in orientation. I shall spell out each of these in turn, dwelling upon those features which seem to me to be of special interest in the present context.

Biblical Theology. Ever since Karl Barth rediscovered for himself "the strange new world of the Bible" as he preached to his Swiss congregation during the first World War, contemporary theology, very largely through his influence, has become profoundly saturated with Biblical motifs and categories. What has happened is not merely that theologians have studied the Bible with particular care, trying to understand and interpret its key passages in a coherent manner, but also that theological language and method have been altered as a result of this exposure to the Bible. Instead of using the Bible as "resource" or "raw material" for theological reflection, or as possessing merely "historical" interest, theologians have found within it their own standing ground of faith and life. Rather than something to be explained to a theologian's rational satisfaction, the Bible has become the very perspective in which theological thinking is to be carried on. Thus it is widely held today that all theology is Biblical theology.

Just what this means will, I hope, become clearer as we proceed. For one thing, it means that the language of theology has shifted from the abstract, definitional framework into one of concrete acts, events, and personal or corporate experience. This is always the language of story and myth, calculated not so much to describe situations as to evoke responses, though the inescapable factual element is always present. So the great archetypal figures of the Old Testament have a larger-than-life dimension, representing as they do stages in the long divine-human encounter recorded in the pages of Scripture. So too the narratives of military prowess and defeat, or of the rise and fall of kingdoms, take on full theological importance as revealing within human history the mighty acts of God. There is a kind of resonance in Biblical speech, arising from the fact that it finds God speaking and working in the sights of earth and the deeds of men, and also perhaps from the fact that in the Bible there is always the possibility of a divine breakthrough in even the commonest of circumstances and the most "natural" of happenings.

Thanks to this Biblical exposure, theology has once again become acquainted with the whole dimension of the mysterious in human life and the surrounding universe. "Let God be God" is one of its chief tenets, borrowed from Luther. For contemporary theology the Bible does not consist of puzzles to be solved or ideas to be organized, but rather of truth about life lived in the sight of God. The task of theology is then that of expounding this mystery—of creation, revelation, and redemption—from within the Biblical perspective itself, and with as little dependence as possible upon alien principles of interpretation coming from purely rational sources.

Another feature of Biblical theology is that the Bible is read and understood as a whole. Whereas we used to be taught that Scripture is a whole library of documents thrown up in varied periods and for different purposes, we are now being reminded that it does after all display a most impressive continuity despite these real differences. Its many styles and forms, from straight historical narrative to personal meditation and communal praise, make up a complex unity. They constitute the record of God's revelation of himself to man through his choice of a particular people to serve and witness to his will. So conceived, the Bible is the word of God as spoken to the people of God, and through them to the whole created world. And by the same token, theology must become the theology of the Word which unifies the entire library of Scripture; thus Christian theology reads the Bible forward and backward, so to speak, from Christ. As the Old Testament awaits his coming, so the New announces it; the law is fulfilled in the Gospel; the old order of judgment is decisively transcended by the new economy of grace. Thus the unity of Scripture is a primary assumption of present-day Biblical theology.

A third feature has to do with the relation of the Bible to the church. According to Biblical theology, there is a real sense in which the church is a part of the Gospel, that is, a part of God's plan of salvation for mankind. But it is also true that the norms of life within the church, the ordering of the sacraments, for example, or the directives for social action, are always Biblical. One of the most significant discussions between Roman Catholic and Protestant thinkers is going on in this realm of Biblical authority and church tradition, and some surprising convergences are already becoming evident. Suffice it to say that the Bible, while it judges the church, is also in large part the product of the apostolic Christian community, and as such it can truly be called "the pit from which we were digged."

Thinking in terms of the needs of Christian adults at the present time, we could rightly say that such an understanding of the Bible-Church relationship is one of far-reaching significance. As Professor Nelson points out, "In the New Testament the people of God are the church; without the society of believers there would be no Gospel of remembered acts of the Apostles. The letters of Paul were written to congregations about the common problems of the church." [1] That is emphatically true; and it means that adults ought to study the Bible, in particular the books of the New Testament, not for private reasons, not for light on the ancient past, but for the purposes of corporate edification and mutual understanding. The Bible should be read and studied, and it can be, for the benefits of very practical wisdom about interpersonal relationships within the church itself. There is a wealth not only of information but of fruitful suggestion touching upon issues of church order, common worship, stewardship, social stratification, evangelism, and missionary outreach in the New Testament; and such a study booklet as that prepared for the New Delhi Assembly of the World Council of Churches shows just how these Biblical patterns and principles may be clearly aligned with contemporary church life.

Ecumenical Theology. Like the Bible, the church has become in recent years not merely the object of careful theological inquiry, but also the framework within which it is carried on. Today's theologians wish to do their thinking as responsible churchmen, on behalf of the whole church, and in light of its great doctrinal traditions. This is largely due, of course, to the almost unprecedented movement toward reunion of the denominational churches which has been taking place over the past quarter-century. Organizational mergers, however, like the growth of local, national, and world councils of churches, are

---

[1] See page 276.

not sufficient to account for the ecumenical emphasis in theology. There is an increasing dissatisfaction with denominationalism as a vehicle for expressing the nature and purpose of the church; and this has led to much self-criticism and a kind of internal reformation in which theologians have been taking a considerable share of leadership.

The root of ecumenical theology lies in a concern for the wholeness of the church, for its "catholicity" in the original meaning of that term. It is true that this concern is frequently misunderstood. It has little to do with the Church of Rome, one of the larger denominations in the ecclesiastical complex of our time. And yet Protestant thinkers have been discovering, often reluctantly, how much they have in common with the Orthodox and Roman branches of Christendom; just as these other branches have been emphasizing more and more some features of Christian faith and worship for which Protestants have traditionally stood. Not only do the two sides in this ecumenical encounter express a growing willingness to learn from each other, but also a determination to include what is significant to each other. Thus Protestant theologians have given attention to the sacraments, and Catholic theologians have turned with new interest to the study of the Bible. It is now clear that the wholeness of the church requires such openness and hospitality between the diverse ecclesiastical traditions operating within present-day Christianity.

In ecumenical thinking there is also a strong emphasis upon the universal elements in the church's life. This is by no means identical with mere bigness, but it has much to do with the plain fact that the church in its wholeness does manage to transcend those natural and social barriers which play so demonic a role in modern institutions. To be sure, there are national churches, racially segregated churches, churches under various political regimes; but in so far as these reflect to some degree the wholeness of the church, they are more than examples of mere divisiveness and discord in human affairs. They express also, however hesitantly and imperfectly, the oneness of mankind seen in the perspective of Christian allegiance to the one God. The church, to the degree to which it really is the church, is international, interracial, interclass; and even within the limitations imposed by history and contemporary life this essential, universal character of the church succeeds in manifesting itself. Some words of Daniel D. Williams are relevant here:

The Christian Church in essence is the one universal community which answers to the deepest need of men. It is not a substitute for family, nation, trade union or club. But it differs from all of these because it relates men to eternal destiny and holds up the one loyalty to God above all other loyalties. The community of the church unites personal freedom and a shared life in one social organism. . . . It is just this community of reconciliation and eternal life which no secular order by itself can bestow . . . the Church as the "new people among the people" can bear in its own life a practical witness to hope for a new, decent and peaceful order for the peoples of the world. In spite of manifest failures, the churches show signs of a renewal from within to achieve a more adequate demonstration of this possibility.[2]

This, I think, is clearly true; and it deserves attention because Christianity is so often held up to scorn as riddled with denominational fragmentation and isolation. Without wishing to blink the obvious facts, it needs to be pointed out that the church is basically a form of human community which cuts across other forms and judges them all, by virtue of a power and a standard peculiar to itself.

Contemporary theology has had much to say regarding the grounds of this universality and wholeness in the church. What gives to the church its distinctively transcultural witness is allegiance to its common Lord. The Pauline figure of the church as the Body of Christ has fascinated ecumenical thinkers. It has held before them the hope of organic union over and above organizational alliances. But at the same time it has been useful in showing how even the *disiecta membra* of Christendom may demonstrate something of the fullness of the common life in the Body of Christ. Among other things, this has meant that

---

[2] *What Present-Day Theologians Are Thinking* (New York, 1959), 151-52.

within the major denominations there has been a determined effort to express more completely the common heritage in worship and doctrine, order and action. If no denomination can rightly claim to be the whole church, every denomination can make its own unique contribution to that wholeness and be nourished by it.

Perhaps it goes without saying that adult learners greatly need to become acquainted with this ecumenical understanding of the work and character of the church. Particularly in the United States we tend to think of denominationalism as the *status quo,* and it comes as a bit of a shock to realize that this is a peculiarly American phenomenon. Nor are we as aware as we should be of the real progress that is constantly being made in the direction of a form of church life more expressive of our real unity in Christ. It must be plain that a divided church is no match for a tragically broken world. It must also be clear that continued disunity in the church is a kind of treason to its Lord, who prayed that all might be one.

Current Theological Accents Upon the Laity

It remains to discuss the current theological accents upon the laymen and the world as these bear upon our theme in this paper. Only the briefest account can be given of each of these areas of interest.

Theology of the Laity. In Dr. Bertholf's paper we are given a full and balanced description of the various lay movements which are a noteworthy feature of contemporary church life. I shall confine myself to indicating something of the parallel theological endeavor to interpret the role of the layman within the household of faith. Before doing so, however, it is well to remind ourselves of the extent to which the Christian churches, both Roman Catholic and Protestant, had until recently become infected with a clericalism or professionalism in the conception of the ministry which left the laity in a decidedly secondary role. It should be remembered, too, that in Protestant churches today the minister has necessarily assumed managerial or administrative functions unheard of in the Reformation, which again has left the laity in the position of supporting the program planned and executed by the clergy. All this has greatly diminished, in practice if not in theory, the role of the layman in the church. Indeed, the very word "layman" in its broader connotation signifies the non-expert who follows another's lead.

Now the rationale which lies behind the notable increase in lay activity within the churches at the present time looks in a very different direction. We are being told by theologians and Biblical scholars alike that the conception of the church as the *laos* or people of God forbids any separation, except a purely functional one, between clergy and laity. Indeed, speaking theologically, laity and ministry are interchangeable terms. "There are varieties of service, but the same Lord." The clerical office is but one such kind of Christian service. Indeed, laymen are to be thought of as making those decisions and exerting those influences which in the long run make the most significant Christian difference to life in the world. They stand closer to the centers of power and authority than the professional clergymen. The minister may provide needed vision and encouragement, but it is laymen who must bear the brunt of choice and conduct in the light of the Gospel. There cannot be, and must not be, a double standard in the church. The church itself is a ministering community in which clergy and laity share responsibly, each bringing their special talents and training to the service of the other.

This reinstatement of the layman at the center of the church's life has many theological implications. One such implication is that of the priesthood of all believers, a cherished Protestant conviction. This does not mean that every man can be his own priest, for priesthood by its very nature is something done for another. Rather, the stress is clearly upon mutuality, upon the intercessory character of common work and worship within the church. Protestantism is not equivalent to individualism.

The bundle of life into which we are bound by Christian faith means that in belonging to the church we also belong to each other.

Another implication of this theology of the laity is that action and devotion in the name of Christ are fundamentally one. Worship is no longer thought of as a mere incentive or resource for the betterment of Christian character and conduct, nor as a respite from life's stern demands. On the contrary, worship is itself the highest form of Christian action, since it is something done deliberately and corporately, representing the offering of the common life to God for judgment and for blessing. And social action becomes not a mere consequence of personal discipleship, but rather the very meaning of that discipleship. There is a necessary alteration or rhythm between action and devotion, but no schizoid disjunction. The layman is worshipper and worker; his obedience and fidelity to the Gospel demand that he be both.

A third implication is that upon the power of the local congregation as the expression of the visible church. One does not have to go halfway around the world to top-level ecumenical conferences to gain this sense of the congregation as the people of God engaged in his service. It may happen in every regular meeting of the church for worship, in so far as worship is able to reflect a congregation's deepest and most common needs and aspirations. Viewed in this light, there is no division between the minister as actor and the layman as spectator, but a mutual corporate involvement and responsibility.

These implications suggest, it seems to me, a totally new orientation for adult education in the church than that which has recently been most in evidence. The whole conception of the church as providing services for the layman, giving him instruction, counseling, and the sense of belonging is radically called into question. Ministers are not called for the purpose of doing things for laymen, but in order to enlist them in common effort and ever-renewed dedication. This awareness of the laity as God's people makes possible and necessary a rethinking of the role of the minister, who becomes on these terms not so

much a professional leader as a representative servant, symbol-
izing in his office the very meaning of stewardship and church-
manship. To be sure, the minister's office frequently frustrates
as well as facilitates this representative function. Nevertheless,
his task and call remain clear. He may well conceive himself
as the teacher of his congregation, but this need not mean
that the congregation is to be passive and receptive only. Actually it means that the forms of adult education in the church
must be made flexible enough to make room for genuine dialogue and encounter; small groups in face-to-face relationship,
emphasizing study and discussion rather than what is often
termed the "didactic stance" on the part of the clergyman, seem
best suited to these ends.

The World in Theological Perspective. The last of the new
stresses in contemporary theology which I wish to discuss is the
changed conception of the world. Perhaps I may best make my
point by mentioning two book titles, twenty-five years apart in
date of publication. The first is *The Church Against the World;*
the second and later, by one of the same authors, is *Christ and
Culture.* In the intervening quarter-century, as these titles indicate, a decided shift of emphasis had taken place. Instead of
suspicion and hostility toward the secular order, theology today
is engaged in a full-scale exploration of that order with a view
to its ultimate redemption by the power of the Gospel. Thus,
for example, there are theological penetrations into the alien
and once forbidding territories of art, science, philosophy, education, and technology. It seems fair to say that theology is re-
discovering the world, after a long process of shrinking somewhat defensively from it.

So one often hears today, in quarters which cannot be
suspected of deviation from classic doctrinal positions, that
"the goodness of creation" must not be forgotten, that "secularism" is a misleading word, and that there is a proper Christian "love of the world" which ought to motivate Christian
witness and evangelism. This is a genuinely new accent when
compared with theology of the recent past in Europe and
America. It means that the church is now thinking of itself not

so much as the ark of salvation or a repository of truth, as a task force or vanguard of God's world-redeeming purpose. The emphasis today is upon witness, mission, service to the world.

This may come as a surprise, it is true, to those who have been overly impressed by the middle-class, complacent character of American Protestantism. While it cannot be denied that there is considerable self-satisfaction and a depressing dearth of self-criticism in many of our churches, it also needs to be said that there are notable instances of what may be called experiments in cultural rediscovery and responsibility as well. Studies of the churches' response to rapid social change, particularly with reference to social mobility and the population explosion, are already under way. A strategy for the inner city, from which Protestantism has tended to withdraw, is being mapped by many denominations and inter-denominational groups. Seminary courses reflect a new concern for off-beat ministries, the various chaplaincies, and church-supported social work. All this, again, adds up to a decided change in outlook and endeavor, and the measure of this change is being taken earnestly by an increasing group of Christian thinkers.

To put it as concisely as possible, it is the conviction of these thinkers that the church is in the world for the sake of the world. The church must not seek to preserve its own life, lest it be lost. God so loved the world—not the church, but the world—that he gave his Son for the world's salvation. The church testifies to this gracious self-giving act of God in Christ. And not only its preaching but the very form and style of its life should bear this same witness. The church is not in the business of conserving faith but of giving it away to those who need it most; not in the business of housing God but of making way for him. Christianity, as D. T. Niles observes, is "chiefly one beggar telling another beggar where to get food." Techniques of indoctrination and manipulation have no place in such a conception of the church's mission to the world. Only as the church can learn how to live alongside the world, sharing its treasure in the earthen vessels of Scripture, sacrament and active service, can it become truly obedient to the vision and demand of its own Lord.

In terms of Christian adult education this means several things. First, it means that a purely sectarian Christianity is a betrayal of the Gospel. The sect-type of Christian church, as Ernst Troeltsch showed, emphasized the importance of being different, of setting oneself against the world, of seeking right-eousness through withdrawal and distinctive separation. This is often the first phase in the history of Christian groups, and a significant one. But it cannot and must not absolutize itself. After a measure of cohesion and self-consciousness has been at-tained, such groups are called to move out again into the world. For them the divine imperative becomes that of mission and witness rather than of purity and preservation.

Second, this perspective on the world means that the world is in the church quite as much as the church is in the world. It is emphatically the case that church life is ordered, or dis-ordered, by the invading principalities and powers by which men and women outside the churches live. Religion becomes, as Whitehead said it should not become, a "research after comfort." Forces of discrimination and segregation enter church life and are all the more terrible for being sanctified. Christian adults should be made more aware that the churches to which they belong are essentially social clubs frequented by people of similar tastes and interests, given to fellowship and together-ness, and run by organization men. In them the vision of a world groaning and travailing toward personal and corporate salvation is often tragically absent. One might even suggest that exhibits of modern art or study courses in contemporary drama have more relevance to their condition than do lectures on the letters of Paul, unless the probing and radical bearing of these latter are honestly set forth with reference to the kind of life we know best.

Third, this theological perspective means that the education of Christian adults must not be understood and carried on as if it were all of one piece, a kind of conditioning process or a set of answers. Far too often the very use of the words "Christian" and "Biblical" suggests that what is being conveyed is a sort of propaganda or ideology which must be learned in order that one may talk as a Christian should. It needs to be insisted that the language of faith is not shop talk or club talk. The creeds of Christendom begin not with "We believe" but with "I believe," thus calling attention to the indubitably personal decision that is always involved in Christian faith. There should be more questioning, more two-way dialogue, more exposure to positions other than what is assumed to be the Christian one, than is customary in most adult study groups and Bible classes. Only in this way can the truly existential nature of faith become plain to those who claim to have it, as information gives way to appropriation and allegiance.

12. Christian Adult Education and the Ecumenical Movement

A. WILSON CHEEK

Associate General Secretary
World Council of Christian Education

and

EVERETT M. STOWE

Editor
World Christian Education

I

A New Dimension of the Church's Teaching

THE ECUMENICAL MOVEMENT is not an end in itself. Rather, as the word "movement" implies, it is the striving of the churches to move from the invisible unity which we have in Christ to a visible unity; from the state of disunity among the churches to the unity of the church. Like any other dynamic process, the ecumenical movement is resulting in new and growing concepts. If not wholly new, these represent a rediscovery and fresh application of basic truth so radical as to be new to our present confused generation.

In updating the definition of the word "ecumenical," the Central Committee of the World Council of Churches (WCC) said in 1951 at Rolle, Switzerland: "The word *ecumenical* is properly used to describe everything that is related to the whole church to bring the Gospel to the whole world." This was a clear recognition that mission is an integral aspect of unity; the one cannot exist without the other. In the Second Assembly of the WCC, at Evanston, Illinois, a third key term was added, namely, "renewal." This implies a continuing process, for renewal cannot be static. The Third Assembly, at New Delhi, will give careful study to "witness" and "service" in relation to "unity." These terms not only require redefinition of the meaning of ecumenical; they may well require rethinking of the meanings of Christian education.

These are the slow but sure steps by which the churches are struggling to become the community of those who are called. Dr. Visser t' Hooft, General Secretary of the World Council of Churches, has said: "The unity of the called is realized as they live up to their calling. . . . There is no way for churches which are neither fully united nor fully separated to arrive at real, concrete, manifest unity except the way of common obedience to the common calling. The ecumenical task is to go forward together in making a common response to the one calling." [1]

The ecumenical movement, therefore, must claim our deep involvement as it "helps the existing churches in process of renewal to become the one missionary Church." This calls for ecumenical education, yet not in the limited sense of a study of the history of attempts to reunite the churches, nor of the growth of ecumenical organizations. *Ecumenical education essentially means fostering the understanding of, commitment to, and informal participation in the whole ecumenical process.* This means that ecumenical education cannot remain an isolated segment of Christian education, but must indeed become a dimension of the life and teachings of the churches. Christian

---

[1] Visser t' Hooft, *The Pressure of Our Common Calling* (New York, 1959), 26.

education falls short of its task and is incomplete if ecumenical education does not permeate its total philosophy and the scope and design of the curriculum. This is especially true for Christian adult education. Adults have the capacity for insight into meaning, and the influence to effect change.

It is significant to note that these developments are not coming from an ecclesiastical hierarchy. Rather they are part and parcel of lay commitments to the renewal, unity, and mission of the church. Similarly, Christian education as we know it today was preceded by the Sunday school movement, which had its origins and direction through laymen concerned with finding more adequate ways of teaching the Gospel than the churches then afforded.

Christian education, in discharging its full responsibility to the churches, can help individual Christians. They need not be Christians who live between the churches (sometimes known as "ecumaniacs"). Instead, they can be denominational Christians who are helped to grow into new ecumenical commitments within their own churches and in association with other churches through councils dedicated to the striving after visible Christian unity.

The greatest danger to the ecumenical movement, however, is self-delusion on the part of the existing churches. One form of this comes from the supposed sacrosanct character of some particular denominational doctrine, polity, or tradition, or a combination of these. Such differences may be exalted to a degree that makes common obedience to a common calling an impossibility. Pious affirmations about unity, whether from laity or clergy, mean little unless backed with deep intent to give concrete meaning to the professed desire to have the whole world know the glory and oneness of the Father and the Son.

Another self-delusion is to mistake and confuse cooperation among the churches for true unity. Cooperation may hinder the ecumenical movement by creating a false or superficial sense of togetherness. This means not that churches should cease their cooperative activities, but that they go forward with painful awareness of our divisions and with a determined effort to heal them. For this we have the imperative from the Gospel itself: "that they may be one." Such effort will mean conscious, deliberate confrontation of the matters on which there is disagreement, hence disunity, in full recognition that there can be no common direction without common orientation.

A specific instance of need at this point comes in relation to the purpose of cooperatively planned curriculum materials. This cooperation may signify little if it means simply better denominational materials. But it may mean much if such an effort has the result that we speak with a common voice of our common Lord and our obedience to him.

Some Visible Signs of Existing Oneness

There are already many points of visible unity among Christians and among churches. These encouraging signposts along the road toward unity give Christian educators clear clues for emphasizing, expanding, and enriching areas where agreement already exists. Here are some of these present signs of visible unity.

The Term Christian. The non-Christian world has only derision for the various labels within Christendom. This ignorance of the fine shadings of our divisions is nearer the truth than the elevation of denominational or confessional labels above the name "Christian." It is our common acceptance of this term, not our denominational or confessional labels, which drives us to seek Christian unity.

The Cross. The symbol of the cross, whether on church spire or coat lapel, is universally recognized as a symbol of the central and essential fact of the Christian faith—the crucifixion of Jesus Christ. Whether or not this powerful symbol is fully understood, wherever it is seen it testifies to the bonds of unity among those called by Him, and who in turn call on His name.

Holy Baptism. Baptism is recognized by all Christian churches as the sign and seal which incorporates all Christians in the visible body of Christ. No division at other points can destroy for Christians the fundamental and visible unity of the baptized.

The Bible. There is universal acceptance of both the Old and the New Testaments as a main expression of the visible unity of the church. Max Thurian states it this way: "The knowledge of the Lord's name, of His being, of His existence, and of His will, is given to us through His Word. Uttered in the Old Covenant, incarnated in the New Covenant, this Word is embodied in the Scriptures. The Scriptures are the fixing in concepts and in words of the Eternal Word of God to His people. In this sense the Scriptures are a visible and audible body . . . an institution set up for the sake of unity." "All Christians," he continues, "universally acknowledge the inspiration of the Scriptures, whatever meaning they attach to this term; they acknowledge the essential faith of the Church to be expressed in the Scriptures. . . . The Bible as a whole is therefore a visible institution of the Church, and an expression of its unity." [2]

Classic Expressions of Christian Faith. These are found notably in the Lord's Prayer, in the Psalms, in the Apostles' and Nicene Creeds. "Thy Kingdom come" and "Thy will be done" are but two of the majestic expressions in the Lord's Prayer used by Christians the world over as a real prayer for unity. So are the prayers in the Psalms the common heritage of all Christians and the visible mark of their unity. The two historic creeds, the Apostles' and the Nicene, have not been integrated into the liturgy of all churches, yet they stand as the historical testimony of an undivided church, expressed through genuine ecumenical councils. They are precious signs of unity of faith in the visible unity of the church.

Striving for Broader Human Unity

The ecumenical movement, as already indicated, is not an expression of full unity, but it is succeeding in creating temporary institutions which are visible signs along the road to unity. The most obvious of these is the World Council of Churches. It is soon to be merged with the International Missionary Coun-

---

[2] Max Thurian, "The Visibile Unity of Christians," *The Ecumenical Review,* 13 (1961) , 318-19.

cil. Other ecumenical bodies have supporting and complementary roles: the World Council of Christian Education, The World Student Christian Federation, and the world organizations of the Y.W.C.A. and Y.M.C.A. It is the World Council of Churches which, without assuming to be a structure for the universal church, has revived the work of the ecumenical ministry within the churches and between the churches. This is essential for their universal communion and for local renewal, and it has gone far to evoke the reappearance of one sign of the visible unity of the church, that is, the ministry of catholicity.

The Ecumenical council called by Pope John XXIII, for some future date, has contributed to the striving to accept the full unity of the Church Universal which broods over all Christendom. This too contributes to the ministry of catholicity. Visits to the Vatican such as those of the Archbishop of Canterbury and the Moderator of the Church of Scotland betoken glimmers of the ultimate reunion of all Christians, which is inevitable. Only so can there be a visible fulfilling of the prayer, "Thy kingdom come, on earth as it is in heaven."

The striving for unity is characteristic of our times. This is true whether we speak of the individual or of groups in communities, nations, or groupings of nations, although it is also true that regionalism may be a necessary intermediate step to full unity, whether in the ecumenical movement or in the world generally. Our society has become one in a physical sense, yet it is without values strong enough to die for (or live for), without a sense of direction. The result is, we are frequently reminded, a great restlessness, rootlessness, and a loss of a sense of identity. All of this is doubtless true. But it is in this very state of futility, emptiness, and longing that we may discover our greatest hope.

The feelings of right and wrong, high standards of ethical and moral behavior, are no longer attached to stable institutions —the home and the church. This only intensifies yearning and discontent. These conditions make understandable the great prominence of psychoanalysis in the twentieth century. One writer, however, contends that while analysis could uncover an identity, provided such were hidden, it cannot create one that is lacking, and this is not likely to be found in the unconscious. [3] Perhaps there is in the organic psyche that which is even more significant and promising. Ira Progoff contends:

What seems to be primary is not one's own self, not one's individuality, but the wholeness of being of which one is an integral, inseparable, indistinguishable part, as the waves of the ocean are integrally united with the ocean. The feeling is of fusion, of being part of and participating actively in the interior consistency and power of an encompassing reality.

Now what does such an experience mean for man in the modern world? It gives him a new kind of perception and a new way of knowing. We might call this *integral cognition* (or the Christian might call it faith) for it is a way of knowing that is based upon an experience of unity with the wholeness of life rather than upon separateness and differentiation.[4]

Also there is a search for political and economic unity. Instances of the former are the struggles for national unity in Asia, Africa, Latin America, the Union of Soviet Socialist Republics, the United States and, finally, in the United Nations. The search for economic unity is instanced in the building of the common market and in efforts to gain for all men at least minimal living needs. Christian churches may become so identified with national aspirations that these become as divisive influences as are doctrinal differences. But if true ecumenical unity is to be achieved, these barriers must be transcended.

In my judgment we are on the threshold of responding to the call of God for unity, supported by these innate drives within the restlessness of mankind. And in this surging toward unity is to be found new purpose and meaning which will be in keeping with the dawning space age. The ecumenical movement, then, is not a passing fancy, but rather is related to the ultimate reality, and has cosmic implications. The created sons of God will

---

[3] Allan Wheelis, *The Quest for Identity* (New York, 1958).

[4] Ira Progoff, "The Depth and Magnitude of Human Nature," *Main Currents in Modern Thought*, 16 (1960), 101.

participate more fully in the continuing creation with the Creator.

The time is especially propitious for the adult, who in past history has not felt keenly the need for a continuing learning experience. Today he faces so much that seems unknown and uncertain in the midst of confusing and changing situations that he is ready and eager to learn. In short, it is the church's greatest hour with adults in its undertakings in Christian education. How shall we meet this challenge? I doubt that anyone of us, or all of us together, really know.

—A. Wilson Cheek

II

In the preceding section, primary emphasis was given to the church and its meanings for the ecumenical movement, with special reference to adult life and growth. Yet the church is to serve the world. As the extension of the Incarnation, its tasks are conditioned by the developing life of the world. "Ecumenical" means "the whole inhabited world"; its special significance in light of the Christian faith must include the fact that those who do not share this faith are also integral constituents of this world. The specific attempts of the churches to carry on new tasks of Christian adult education need to be seen in the world setting.

Indeed, as one reads of thought and action of secular groups concerned with adult education, the close kinship of these concerns with those of Christians is striking. Consider, for example, world conferences on adult education held under UNESCO. The first of these was held at Elsinore in 1949, the second in Montreal in 1960. At the first of these, a characteristic remark came from Torres Bodet: "When you are discussing adult education you are in fact discussing no less a matter than the future of our civilization." In the 1960 UNESCO meeting in Montreal, the first speaker described "man's spiritual loneliness, his unpreparedness for an understanding of his surroundings, his feeling of not belonging" and even "his never-ending stupidity"!

There was no less emphasis, however, as one participant noted, "on the brotherhood of human destiny, on the task of educators to put men and women back on the road to freedom, to teach them to appreciate their responsibilities in the world, to overcome their complexes of insignificance, and to turn them into beings capable of decision and choice." [5]

The World Setting of Adult Education

It seems clear that the critical need for adult education in this era is felt as keenly in secular as in church circles. To be sure, there is a trend to redefine its meaning and to speak of it as "life-long education." This is in contrast to earlier usage which was slightly condescending to adult education efforts, from the supposition that it was to make up for deficiencies in school education. Life-long education, however, becomes a necessity in a world whose change is succinctly expressed by Margaret Mead: "No one will live in the world in which he grew up; no one will die from the world in which he grew to maturity." That we live at the watershed of the epochs is suggested by the fact that perhaps 90 per cent of all the scientists who have ever lived are alive today. Whatever the churches may achieve in the field of Christian adult education, it can be assumed that relating Christian faith to the lives of the growing number of informed adults in our world will be a task of enormous proportions. In the church is enshrined belief in the "faith once delivered to the saints." Those who come to this faith will necessarily share the changing conditions of living, and the experience and expectation of change must form part of the mental equipment even of a child if in adult life he is to be able to make a swift and accurate transference from former experiences to newer experience.

The swiftness of change possible, even in terms of secular effort, is proved by what happened in the Union of Soviet Socialist Republics in the period 1928 to 1938. No less than forty million persons learned to read and write in that period. The stress

---

[5] *International Journal of Adult and Youth Education* (UNESCO) 13 (1961), 5-14, 34-47, *passim.*

upon the education of adults today in the Soviet Union continues to be strong. Employees who are successful in their studies may have from one to two days off per week, with pay, for pursuing their studies; and the fact of avid reading on the part of common workers seems almost universal. In the world as a whole it remains unfortunately true that nearly 50 per cent of the people cannot read or write. But that so swift a change in this respect has come to one region suggests the same possibilities for others, with all the consequences which follow or which are potential to informed minds.

And other facts coming from the pressures of modern living have ominous aspects. What form will life take for "mass man" living in ever greater numbers and with ever decreasing living space? One response in our time may be seen in the vast changes which have come within a brief period to the fourth of humanity that is China. The reconditioning of the mentality of multiplied millions living there under the inescapable duress of a totalitarian regimen indicates one possibility. The process of bringing about these changes is not as yet fully known, but enough is apparent to indicate what can result from determined control and the use of all available information media.

That this new world is "ecumenical" is made clear at least in biological terms by data from the increase of population. A net increase of about fifty million per year—nearly one hundred forty thousand per day—suggests not only the inevitable pressure on food supplies, but other pressures resulting from the social consequences of such plenitude. Among the causes of this rapid growth in human numbers is the greater life expectancy, now reaching to more than seventy years in many Western countries, where not many decades ago this expectancy was not more than about thirty years. A by-product of this fact, with many educational implications, is the greatly lengthened period of adolescence with the tensions resulting from persistence in present control by "those least qualified to live in the present."

A further fact of world-wide importance for adult education is the agglomerations of people who live in cities and must depend increasingly on technological developments for making a living, indeed for their very survival. The trend to urban living seems universal. The consequences are suggested by Lewis Mumford in these words: "The positive functions of the city cannot be performed without creating new institutional arrangements, capable of coping with the vast energies modern man now commands." [6] In this one sentence is suggested a vast array of human problems and possibilities, flowing from the "institutional arrangements" necessary to urban existence.

One institutional arrangement of greatest antiquity is the family. It persists as an essential fact even in the most urbanized conditions of living. Yet its form, and the changing mores of sex attitudes and relationships, constitute a focal problem for adults in the widest spread of cultures. The relation of urban living to the powerful impulses centering in sex and the social institution of the family is characterized in a sociological study of a fashionable Canadian suburb.[7] The authors point out that in the ultra-mechanized and formalized style of living of the suburb, sex is the one remaining live touch with organic nature. At the opposite end of the social scale, in the slums, extreme disintegration of familial relationships often is found. This chaos comes at a moment when empirical fact and social analyses confirm anew the basic and integral relationship of parents to growing children. The most critical form of adult education, many would maintain, is that for parents.

Some Ecumenical Responses of the Churches

Certain responses being attempted or projected by ecumenical organizations serving the world-wide church may be briefly outlined. They are reported in full recognition of the truth of the dictum, "To make a thing real, make it local." It is in face-to-face relations that the essential meanings of *koinonia,* of *diakonia,* of *marturia*—fellowship, service, witness—are most truly realized.

---

[6] Lewis Mumford, *The City in History* (New York, 1961) , 571.

[7] John R. Seeley, R. Alexander Sim, and Elizabeth W. Loosely, *Crestwood Heights* (New York, 1956) .

In the World Institute on Christian Education, held in Toronto in 1950, the Commission on Christian Education of Adults reviewed the situation: "In our world the Christian education of adults takes on new urgency. There are more adults than ever before. They are confronted with a crisis in human affairs of the greatest gravity. There are powerful new currents of desire for freedom. There are competing systems of thought which seek to claim the minds of men. In the midst of this crisis stands the simple and compelling power of the Gospel of Christ which is for all people." Studies made in preparation for this World Institute made two facts clear: that work with adults was in many instances markedly inadequate, and that there was a growing sense of its critical importance, yet with little clear notion of first steps to take (except for stress on home and parent education).

In the years since this meeting, the World Council of Christian Education has come to the place where at last Christian adult education is officially recognized as integral in the work of the organization; its importance is fully equal to the education of children and youth, and indeed basic for effective Christian influence on those who are younger. The World Institute and World Convention, held in Japan in 1958, laid strong stress on family and home in their programs. The universality of problems in this area was there strikingly evident—as well as their great particularity. For example, polygamy (concurrent in form, not tandem as in the West!) proved a burning issue for delegates from Africa.

A fundamental feature of the work of the W. C. C. E. is aid, on request, in the development of indigenous curriculum materials. Major undertakings are now under way in Latin America; in India; in Africa, south of the Sahara; in the Middle East; in Pakistan, East and West; in the Caribbean area; and for the Chinese in southeast Asia. In most of these, an integral place has been made for adult work and study, or for family religious education. Thus the editor of the Caribbean materials has sought help from social scientists as well as educators in making an approach to the highly unconventional arrangements on the family in the subculture of that region, whose distinguishing mark is "faithful concubinage," or disregard of formal marriage relationships.

The International Missionary Council is another ecumenical body which has pioneered in one form of adult work, notably, the matter of Christian home life and family education. The Council was initiated by Dr. Irma Highbaugh, and great encouragement has been given to Christian Home Movements in various Asian countries. In Manila, November 2-16, 1952, a conference was held on The Christian Family in Changing East Asia. In early 1958 a three-month Workshop on the Christian Family was held in Chiengmai, Thailand, with Dr. and Mrs. David Mace as resource persons, sponsored by the I. M. C. to work with some twenty highly selected Asian leaders. Findings of this workshop have proved influential in Christian home movements in many Asian countries, reflecting as they do the basic conclusions of Asian leaders themselves.

The World Council of Churches is perhaps most closely related to adult work through the Department on the Laity and the Department on the Cooperation of Men and Women in Church and Society. In the period since 1954 the Department on the Laity has concentrated on the development of ideas rather than on the setting up of channels and relationships. *The Laity Bulletin* has been a printed organ of information.

The W. C. C.'s Department on the Cooperation of Men and Women in Church and Society has conducted various studies to show Biblical bases for partnership between the sexes; a leading concern has been with marriage and the family. One study in this area has been on marriage liturgies, so that vows may be honestly taken. Other studies have been concerned with the single man and single woman, celibacy, responsible parenthood, and employment of married women. A woman's ecumenical team worked in West Africa, April 1959 to April 1961. The report on this significant venture includes this statement: "The churches have been called upon to undertake a vast effort of self-examination and self-criticism, in order to cope with the challenge of the world's social revolution. . . . The irony of the situation is that Christian missionaries have helped bring about the upheavals in Africa, Asia, and Latin America, but the churches have given little attention to the study of the ethical and spiritual forces at work in national political movements." [8]

In conclusion, the phrase, "Christian Education and the Ecumenical Movement," suggests correctly that we have pitched our tents on the new shores of a vast continent, still to be mapped and explored. Let us never forget that this is crucially important territory. Our ultimate concerns, spiritual and secular, are involved in the relation of Christian faith to the effective Christian education of adults in a period which can occur but once in the history of mankind.

—Everett M. Stowe

[8] World Council of Churches, "The Women's Ecumenical Team in West Africa," Progress Report of the First Two Years, April 1, 1959-April 1, 1961 (Geneva, Switzerland, 1961), 9.

13. Some Reflections on the Current Status of Adult Curriculum Materials

MARVIN J. TAYLOR
Associate Professor of Religious Education
University of Pittsburgh

Two studies of adult curriculum were conducted in advance of the June 1961 Workshop. The first focused upon the procedures followed in the production and use of curricula. The second involved an analysis of the current status of adult materials which were then being used by the various denominations. It is this latter analysis which is here reported.

Invitations to participate in this survey of existing materials were sent to thirty-seven denominations. Each was asked to contribute complete sets of the adult materials which it had published for use during the calendar year 1960, including everything which it identified as "adult curriculum materials." Twelve denominations did not reply to the letter of invitation. Two declined to participate for quite opposite reasons, comments about which will appear later. Twenty-three sent some or all of their curricular output, and seventeen of these were also represented in the personnel of the Workshop.

The first reflection on the current status of adult materials grows out of this process. There appears to be considerable confusion as to what constitutes "adult curriculum materials." Although all publications in this category were requested, some denominations sent only the International Uniform Series. Other alternative graded materials available on an elective basis were ignored in a few instances. It became necessary to send additional requests in which the omitted publications were specifically named. Thus, there appears to be a tendency to equate "adult curriculum materials" with the Uniform Lessons even among some of the denominational leaders who are producing these publications.

But conversely, other denominations omitted the Uniform Lessons in the packet of 1960 publications. In each of these instances it took specific mention of titles to obtain copies for inclusion in this study. Letters of explanation almost unanimously reflected the conclusion that Workshop personnel would hardly be interested in this type of material.

A third evidence of confusion came from the response of still another denomination. It had ignored our original request, and a follow-up letter had been answered with the statement that no adult educational materials were being published, adding "at least none of a dated nature." It had apparently been assumed that only those publications issued for use by adult groups on a specific date corresponded with the anticipated Workshop "image" of adult curriculum materials.

A final element in this confusion is the fact that only one denomination among the twenty-three sent or even mentioned men's and women's organization publications. To be sure, our letter of request did not specifically mention them, and we obtained only what we requested. But this curious fact merely serves to indicate the extent of our predicament. As a woman's society officer once told me: "This is a woman's organization, and we have our job to do in the church. You educators leave us alone. We don't have anything to do with Christian education!"

In summary, the very process of collecting the materials for analysis was quite revealing. Even those persons who are professionally involved in publishing are somewhat uncertain about

what constitutes "adult educational materials." This may help
to explain the dilemma in which many of us find ourselves as we
work with adult groups in local churches concerned with the
quality of their corporate experiences yet desiring to remain
within the scope of the "approved" curriculum established by
the denomination.

Another writer has already indicated the extent to which the
several denominations depend upon the Uniform Lessons in
actual local church practice. Perhaps I can enlarge upon this
analysis of the extent of use by a few comments focused upon
the extent of publication. Only two of the twenty-three denominations sending materials do not publish lessons built around
this series. Both carry on a rather extensive publication program for adult education, and one issues numerous Bible-
centered elective materials, but neither uses the uniform format
and outlines. Twelve of the twenty-one which do publish International Uniform Lessons limit their program exclusively (or
virtually so) to this series. None issues denominationally graded
alternatives, although a few publish lists of additional resources which are often no more than undated reissues of former
Uniform Lesson units, published books, or pamphlets; they
are listed and recommended without study guides or other aids
to the group.

Among those publishing Uniform Series, there is the widest
variety of practice and scope, both of which are probably correlated positively with the size of the denomination and its economic problems. The most limited publication was a thirty-two-
page quarterly (which was a considerable hazard to the eyes!)
issued for students and teachers of every age group from children to adults. No other piece of literature is issued by that
church. The opposite range encompassed a 128-page booklet for
the student and an additional 160-page volume for teachers,
both appearing quarterly. Only two churches supply Uniform
Lessons on a monthly basis, in both cases as supplements to
other quarterlies dealing with the same lessons. Both use different writers, and there is no apparent effort to unify the parallel treatments. Several denominations use different writers

for students' and teachers' publications regularly, and at least one issues the Uniform Series in five different publications designed ostensibly for varieties of students. Such variation on the same theme appears to be rather unnecessary and considerably above and beyond the call of duty.

Comments on the Uniform Series Publications

In an effort to gain data on the lessons for this survey, I decided to use the first quarter of the year 1960 as my basic sample, supplementing it with later units. Without attempting to do a content analysis in detail, I read and analyzed the lesson for the first Sunday of each month, later adding other first Sundays for the second and third quarters. The research included the reading and study of both pupils' and teachers' publications for the selected dates in every denominational curriculum available to me. The comments which follow grow directly out of this program of reading and analysis.

Concept of the Curriculum. As the Commission on General Christian Education (N. C. C.) committee has indicated, the purpose of the outlines is to provide "a plan for studying the Bible which will help growing persons increasingly to know its content and to understand its message in the light of their own experiences and relationships." It is clear that this is central. The point of focus is the Bible. Even in the lessons where topics with a current flavor are selected, the Bible remains the point of origin. The purpose of the lesson always starts with what the Bible says, even though it frequently branches out into contemporary emphases and applications. Two illustrations from the first quarter will perhaps sharpen this idea. The initial Sunday's topic was "Pioneers for Christ." Virtually every writer developed this in a manner designed to produce more adequate understanding of the early church, specifically in Antioch. Applications to the modern church were relatively brief and general. In contrast, the first Sunday in February stressed the theme "Persistent Evangelism." Its starting point was Paul in Corinth, but many writers did not dwell long in that city. Clearly, here was a theme with great possibilities. The transition to the twentieth century came quickly. The Bible passage served to give authority to this mission, but it was the modern understanding of the mission that dominated the discussions, rather than an exegesis of the passage for the goal of Biblical competence.

These examples have been included merely to illuminate the conclusion which I shall now state. The lessons tend to be subject-centered, with the subjects first explored on the basis (usually unspoken) of the Bible's authority, followed by an application to life. These are often introduced under headings such as "The Lesson in Life," "Lessons for Us," "The Lesson for Today," "Our Task Today," "The Lesson for Our Day," etc. The applications were seldom overdrawn; I was impressed with the exegetical integrity observed in the reading. But despite this, there was a lack of personal involvement in the process. I was interested, for after all it is the Bible; but the concerns dramatized in these materials were not necessarily my concerns. Malcolm Knowles's comment, which appears elsewhere in this volume, seems valid here: "A need is not a need unless felt by a learner."

Learning Theory. The 1958 Workshop on Christian Adult Education framed a proposition on the nature of learning which I shall quote. It defined the process of Christian learning as "a series of events beginning with the learner's awareness of a need or a tension." It went on to add that learning "requires personal effort at appropriation of the resources of the Christian Gospel, goes on to a transformation of his [the learner's] perception of and dealing with his life situation, and a consequent reduction of this tension. . . . The tension may arise spontaneously from the learner's experience of his own inadequacy or from his encounter with some aspect of the Christian gospel relevant to his personal situation." [1] This is not the total statement, but it is sufficent to indicate the emphasis.

My analysis of the selected lessons raises some doubts about their validity when examined in the light of such a criterion. If

---

[1] Lawrence C. Little, ed., *Formulating the Objectives of Christian Adult Education* (Pittsburgh, 1958) , 58, 59.

the presence of learning is contingent on the learner to the extent that the above statement implies, then too little attention was given to him in the lessons examined. Only in two or three publications were needs considered; and these, incidentally, were rather well done. The nature of the Gospel provided the imperative, and though the need may not have been brought to the lesson by the learner, the injection of some particular concept from Christianity enabled the leader to stimulate awareness of need where none may have previously existed. To be sure, many adults exposed to this motivation may have acquired none of it, and to the extent that this was absent, just to that extent, the lessons lacked relevance within the framework of this personal equation. Unless one felt a need for the acquisition of this particular subject matter, the real purpose of the lesson becomes vague to the pupil, and the quality of the learning questionable. It is doubtful (and hardly debatable) that we can assume the pupil's presence in the class to be an evidence of need for the lesson. His agenda may be quite different from that of the lesson writer, and may well be altogether unrelated to the purposes of the group or the church. It was my considered estimate in the reading of these materials that many of the millions exposed to these particular lessons may have had other immediate needs standing in the path of those selected for attention. If this be correct, then the learning outcomes of the group experience were surely limited and probably only tangential to, or even quite different from, those assumed. It would appear that more attention could be directed toward this personal dimension in learning. Or stated in another way, International Uniform Lessons could profitably give much more consideration to assisting learners in gaining a need to acquire the learning offered rather than starting with the content and moving on—hopefully—to acceptance of value and implementation in personal experience.

As a corollary to this a comment about the pupil activities recommended is needed. In comparison with a similar survey done several years ago, I observed a definite trend toward more direct and frequent learner involvement than previously.

Though the structures of the groups addressed remained undefined—and the size undoubtedly varies from a handful to a hundred or more in each denominational instance—lesson writers have not only recognized the validity of the principle of learner involvement, but almost every publication recommended to the leader that he vary class session practices. Lecture was assumed in most instances as the basic technique, but additional alternative procedures were advocated too. Discussion, use of buzz groups, projects by individuals and committees, role playing, use of resource persons imported for a particular task at some stage in the study, use of audio-visuals (projected and otherwise), etc., were recommended. However, the potential value of these discussions was often vitiated by "canned" questions, rather than allowing the full play of real interests aroused by the formal presentation. But even this type of suggestion has its merit for improving the traditional Bible class use of Uniform Series. It was interesting to note that in several instances where small group discussion was recommended, suggestions for managing this in sanctuaries with fixed pews were added. The frequency of this is perhaps enough of a commentary upon the handicaps under which so many of our congregations seek to carry on adult learning programs. This survey is focused exclusively on materials, of course. It would be most interesting to conduct a similar survey of their use to discover the extent to which these recommended teaching procedures are becoming operational. No extensive survey of this kind has come to my attention. We can hardly claim that Uniform Lessons are being improved merely through the printing of descriptions of these newer techniques unless corresponding changes in procedures are occurring in the class sessions.

Evaluation. We have spent considerable time considering the possibilities of measuring the learning that adult groups may exhibit. On the one hand, there is the contention that the practice of the presence of God is such a personal, internal, even esoteric experience that attempts to reduce it to measurable terms must necessarily be complex if not actually impossible. On the other hand, there is the position that Christian learning and experience are not totally unlike other experiences and learnings. When learning does transpire, some type of change has occurred, and however internalized its basic focus may be, it will possess some behavioral dimensions which can be subjected to measurement. These discussions are usually most helpful and challenging to the educator.

Perhaps the most startling thing about these possibilities has been their virtual absence from the materials surveyed. In the first place, objectives were seldom specified. About one-third of the quarterlies did include some comment on the "purpose of the lesson," or similar terminology. This was almost always phrased in terms of the mastery of a particular body of Biblical content. The others remained silent on this important aspect of the lesson and its relationship to the pupils for whom it had been prepared. In general publications for teachers, some interesting contrasts appeared. In one denomination which uses Uniform Series with children, youth, and adults, this contrast on objectives was sharpest. In almost every exposition for teachers of children and youth, the first heading dealt with purposes in the use of the lesson; but this emphasis was almost totally absent from the expositions for teachers of adults. One is tempted to speculate on the meaning of this omission. Does it mean that adult education is aimless, that its focus is so lacking that nothing—even of a general nature—can be said, or does it mean that no real attention has been given to this? In defense of the materials—and in fairness—I must admit that a considerable variety of general articles on the goals of Christian education of adults did appear. But I found much less of an attempt to reduce these generalities into specific categories of objectives which could be related to week-by-week lesson writing. Thus, the first step toward evaluation, i.e., attention to goals, was often lacking in the varieties of quarterlies examined.

At the other end of the evaluative process the silence was even more striking. There were occasional articles on improving the adult class, and these usually placed their emphasis upon stressing pupil preparation—reading the materials in advance—and more adequate pupil participation, including the whole range of techniques to which reference has already been made. But I found only one instance in which a teacher was urged to engage in any activity which could be called evaluative within the framework of our use of the term. In this instance the materials had centered on a study of the book of Acts, and the teacher was encouraged to develop a content examination—paper and pencil test—for administering to the class. The suggestion was made that data derived therefrom would help the teacher to discover his effectiveness in dealing with the Bible and promoting pupil comprehension of it. The avoidance of even this rather elementary type of measurement probably stems from a general hesitation to offend, a fear that such procedures might be disruptive. Basing my observation on this limited survey, I would suggest that we have little to fear. Only the teachers of adults in one of our moderate-sized denominations were urged to engage in this program on one Sunday in 1960. This could hardly be disruptive. Unfortunately the result of this omission is an all too frequent substitution of the techniques of head counting for measurement of outcomes in Christian learning. In the absence of any other evidence, we are willing to settle for the unspoken, but very real, assumption that the size and continued or increased attendance of the group is an evidence of religious growth. As we all know, and it need not be stressed, it may mean nothing more significant than the fact that the teacher is entertaining, or that the parents feel a need to have their children in the morning church school program and this is a good place to wait for them.

Similarities and Divergences. The analysis of these varieties of Uniform Lesson materials produced some observations about their similarities and differences which are revealing.

1. There does seem to be a considerable amount of learning from each other taking place in the production of the Uniform Series. There is a tendency for the same features to appear in most quarterlies. The text is explained, the background analyzed, the emphasis for today stressed, suggestions to the teacher enumerated, class discussion questions posed, and a preview of next week included. The major differences between these items

lie in the extent to which each is developed and the degree to which it is given specific status. The size of the publication usually dictates the decision in each case, since space is an unrelenting taskmaster. This leads me to the conclusion that on the basis of surface features, there are great similarities and few significant differences in the publications of the Uniform Series.

2. Having reached this conclusion about similarity, I returned to the publications again seeking some other justification for their multiplicity—justification other than denominational pride, that is. I reread the lesson expositions for the previously identified weeks, this time to discover what was distinctive about each. Quite frankly, my hypothesis at the outset was that we have entirely too many Uniform Lesson expositions, that a few could serve the twenty-one denominations just as effectively. This idea was by no means original. The Evangelical and Reformed branch of the United Church of Christ and the United Presbyterian Churches do combine efforts in producing these materials. And the Presbyterian Church in the United States and the Moravian Church possess a similar working arrangement. I was curious to discover potentialities for other merged efforts of this kind.

My second reading identified two types of distinctiveness, one theological and the other ecclesiastical. In the first place, the major families of denominational groupings showed considerable theological similarity, at least to this reader. And it is my judgment that perhaps half a dozen sets of uniform materials could cover the range of theological interpretation that the survey revealed. To be sure, in some instances varieties of interpretation would be essential, but within this framework of differences in minor detail, there could be general agreement. The second type of differences, the ecclesiastical, would probably be more troublesome. There were numerous instances where denominational particularities had been woven into the exposition of the Book of Acts. One church used this set of lessons at several points to reinforce its concept of the church with a particular form of polity. Another found occasion to stress a church-wide fund-raising campaign as a legitimate goal of the church today, basing its conclusion on a study of the church in the first century. A third found support for its reluctance to engage in ecumenicity. Other examples could be cited, but these are sufficient to illustrate the nature of the differences. These might well prove to be more of a deterrent to interdenominational Uniform Lessons than the theological variations.

3. A third observation grows out of, and is informed by, these two. My analysis also revealed a tendency in the Uniform Lessons to see adults as a kind of blurred composite of all conceivable varieties of mature persons. Individual differences in age, education, socio-economic status, need, etc. are largely ignored. Such homogeneous materials tend to be so general in nature that they speak clearly and sharply to no one. It is my observation that given the similarities and the differences outlined above, it would be possible to pool our resources and efforts, producing fewer publications and these across the denominational barriers already noted. Perhaps this would permit more attention to varieties of learners. This observation may be too naïve, and it may emanate from tools of analysis too blunt to discern the important distinctions which require our separation. It may well be true that the differences are so significant that my suggestion is unrealistic; but I did not find adequate or clear evidence of this in the analysis of the materials submitted for our investigation in this survey of adult educational materials.

4. A fourth observation grows out of contacts with individuals professionally engaged in this field. There appears to exist considerable general dissatisfaction with the Uniform Lesson concept and the quality of the publications. In response to our request for cooperation in the survey, one denominational leader sent his elective publications but omitted the Uniform Series. When reminded of this, he responded with these words: "We don't have much confidence in these, and it never occurred to me that a Workshop on 'Adult Education in the Church of Tomorrow' would have any use for them." Another editor also ignored the request, stating later that their only publications were Uniform Lessons, and "We aren't very excited about them or their use." Still a third declined to permit us to examine his

denomination's materials, saying, "We wouldn't want to be judged by what we are now doing." A fourth person wrote, "We aren't very happy about these publications, but we continue issuing them because we would be certain to drive many churches to independent publishers if we stopped." All of these comments were taken from correspondence received in response to the invitation to participate.

The logical observation seems to be that no one loves Uniform Lessons except the public. There is clear evidence that in almost every denomination they continue to remain by far the most popular selection, even in those churches presenting the widest range of offerings. This is a rather curious dilemma. On the one hand, these materials prove to be quite unpopular with the educators, even with the editors who are employed to produce them. At the same time the local churches continue to select the Uniform Lessons, ignoring other choices available to them. I know of no extensive research on the factors involved in the making of these choices. Perhaps this is an area in which further research is especially needed.

Comments on Additional Materials

The balance of the adult materials provided for the survey are one of two types: (1) denominationally graded, dated lesson series, and (2) electives, undated, usually comprised of study books and leaders' guides. I shall comment briefly on each type.

Denominationally Graded. These are materials provided by churches to parallel the Uniform Series in structure. They are ordinarily issued in quarterly or monthly form, with assigned weekly topics and readings. There is usually much more freedom in these curricular efforts to focus on the needs of particular groups within a specific series. The United Presbyterian *Crossroads* is a good illustration. Included are adult lessons built on the Christian Faith and Life theme for the year, graded for adults. Another series, The Christian Round Table, provides weekly resources for young adults designed to help in the resolution of problems in Christian living of this age group. Still a third series for Parents' Discussion Groups appears, although weekly topics continuing through the entire quarter are not included.

The Methodist Church offers a variety of dated electives. The Adult Bible Course provides an intensive study of the Bible on a much more systematic basis than uniform outlines and themes permit. The Adult Fellowship Series is a lesson program built chiefly around current life problems, although an occasional unit which hardly corresponds with this image sometimes is encountered. (For example, the unit for July-August 1961 was a study of personalities in the early church.) The Advanced Studies Series selects significant books for use in discussion groups. Curriculum writers prepare guides for class members and leaders, and these guides are published in the dated monthly curriculum pieces. The assumption is that all class participants will read both the published book and the dated guides in advance of individual class sessions. Recent examples of the volumes included are William Hordern's *Layman's Guide to Protestant Theology* and Jaroslav Pelikan's *Riddle of Roman Catholicism.*

Other denominations are also engaged in the publication of dated electives of this type, and they are readily available from the publishers for examination. Although I was not able to examine every sample in detail, selected reading in them revealed much greater concern for the practical problems of Christian living encountered by adults. Even materials which focused primarily upon blocks of subject matter (the Bible, doctrine, church history, etc.), tended to consider these in the light of adult needs. In a very real sense all of these graded materials exist only because of the inadequacies encountered in the use of the Uniform Series, and almost all have profited from this previous experience. With the exception of the Methodist Adult Bible Course, they are constructed around the needs of adults in contemporary society.

Electives, Non-dated. The second type of elective material represents a more recent activity on the part of several denominations, one in which much interest is being aroused. The Christian Discipleship Series is a good illustration. Composed of six courses, preceded by an introductory study on Christian learning, the series proposes to engage adults in a study of their faith and the demands made by this faith on their lives in every facet of experience. The Christian Board of Publication is issuing this set of materials. The Methodist *Basic Christian Books* will contain, when publication is concluded in 1964, a dozen volumes consisting of a kind of "core of adult Christian learning" including faith, life, the church, ethical behavior, other faiths, and themes of this nature. The Church and Home Series of the United Church of Christ is similar in nature; it is planned to cover the significant areas of the Christian faith. Books written especially for the series are being published for reading by class participants. Leaders' guides are also made available.

In addition to these specific series of elective courses, many denominational boards of education compile and issue lists of their own and other publications which have been screened and are "approved" for denominational use. Frequently study guides are available to groups and leaders using these materials. At least one denomination confines its entire adult curriculum to resources of this elective nature. Perhaps for primarily personal reasons I found these non-dated elective materials to be the most attractive and stimulating. Numerous electives stand squarely in the areas of my current interests and concerns. Short-term, small-group study and discussion experiences focused on these themes seem to hold the greatest promise for effective Christian learning. The leaders' guides examined revealed a generally good grasp of the newer, more effective techniques of classroom methodology which are being presented in the literature of adult education today.

One word of caution does seem necessary, however. While it is probably true that adults respond best when stimulated by their own interests and needs, a purely elective curriculum runs a dangerous risk of imbalance. The Christian gospel may well make demands upon us which are not consciously felt by the learner, however conscientious or interested he may be. Hence, elective patterns would appear to be the most defensible when set within some kind of overall pattern which assures balance; and further, both the need for and the nature of this balance should be clearly indicated to local church groups making selections. This feature is present in both the Christian Discipleship and the Church and Home Series, and other similar study units. It is absent in almost all others which limit themselves to the issuance of study lists of approved materials and leaders' guides. Since the latter elective scheme was found in several denominations, some attention to this need for balance seems indicated.

The Church and the Home

Having been convinced for years that the effectiveness of the church's program of nurture is directly correlated with the quality of the learner's experiences in his home, I quite naturally examined the materials submitted with this bias. Two types of emphasis were discovered, although certain sets of publications fell into a third category which I shall identify first. This was the category in which the home was largely ignored as an educational institution. The implication seemed to be that the church is the agency of Christian nurture. I doubt if any editor would agree, yet numerous materials imply this by the absence of the home from their concerns. This was especially true with some denominations relying solely on the Uniform Lessons. Here the home seldom appeared except for daily home Bible readings.

By far the most prevalent curricular material which recognized the home saw it as an ally in the church's teaching. Efforts were made to inform parents about the program their children experienced in the church, with a view to enlisting their support in reinforcing the desired learnings. One family magazine devotes two pages monthly to a rapid, but fairly complete, description of the subject matter and activities to which children will be exposed. Supplementary activities within the family group are encouraged. The help required by the youthful pupil as he does his "home work" is described. The major emphasis upon the home encountered in this survey was of this type.

It was not the only emphasis, however. One other infrequent, but nonetheless quite important, idea did occur. This treated the home as an educational agency having a distinctive function not paralleled by any other agency, including the church. It sought much more than a mere repetition and reinforcement of the church's teaching techniques. Non-technical theoretical articles discussed the family matrix as an educational institution; articles and discussion materials implemented this concept with examples from specific families. Unfortunately this theme is not treated very often. To this observer it holds the greatest promise.

A further unhappy circumstance is the fact that almost all of these church-home materials appear only in specialized magazines. They are seldom found in the regular adult publications, and as a result they tend to be omitted from the regular curriculum for adults. This would seem to be a major weakness in almost every denomination. We must come to a clearer understanding of the educational function of the home; and once this has been sharpened and defined, we should include the emphasis in the main stream of materials reaching adults, rather than relegating it to special purpose publications.

Needed Research on Curriculum Status

The foregoing analysis has been based solely upon a survey of materials published for use in a single calendar year. It leaves many questions unanswered. In conclusion I offer the following areas in which research is needed if we are to find answers to the dilemmas which confront us in Christian adult education.

1. Little is known about the factors operating within the local church influencing the selection of curriculum materials. Analyses of local church practices in decision making would be useful in planning the future production of the materials.

2. A similar gap in knowledge exists in the area of adult

classroom procedures. The past decade has witnessed rapidly growing interest in newer instructional methods, but studies are lacking on the extent of their adoption and implementation in the churches. If our understanding of consumer usage is to match editorial expectation, research of this nature is needed.

14. Pooling Our Efforts in Building a More Adequate Curriculum of Christian Education for Adults

J. BLAINE FISTER

Executive Director, Department of Adult Work
Division of Christian Education
National Council of Churches of Christ in the U.S.A.

An EXCELLENT EXAMPLE of the pooling of efforts in the building of a more adequate curriculum of Christian education for adults is the series of workshops held at the University of Pittsburgh in June 1958 and 1961. This was the first occasion on which denominational leaders took so long a time to consider so many aspects of curriculum for Christian adult education. In these workshops they pooled their efforts not only across denominational lines, not only along functional lines within denominational structure, but across the lines of foundational disciplines. The educator, the social scientist, the theologian, the program director, the editor sat down together in an attempt to see their tasks in a totality that augurs well for the future. It was a significant step in a direction that should set patterns for future endeavor.

The pooling of efforts in developing curriculum materials for adults in the church has been going on for a long time—almost one hundred years. Before looking to the future, we might do well to look at what has been done and what is happening now in pooling efforts.

There is wide acceptance of the definition of curriculum as "the total organized provision made by the churches to guide and enrich the experience of those who take part in their activities." Under such a definition, the words "total organized provision" imply a way of operating in the development of curriculum that is frequently non-existent, though lip service is given to the concept. All too often curriculum development has been the exclusive concern of the development of "curriculum materials." However, we must recognize a significant trend toward the inclusion of "program" in curriculum matters.

First of all, it is necessary to realize that Christian education boards and committees do not have a monopoly on adult education in the church. In the National Council of Churches there have been many significant educational enterprises sponsored by units of the Divisions of Christian Life and Work, Home Missions, and Foreign Missions, as well as United Church Women and United Church Men. Within the Division of Christian Education, the major concern of the Department of Administration and Leadership has been training of adults for specific tasks or skills; the Departments of Children's Work, Youth Work, Family Life, Audio-Visual and Broadcast Education have sponsored major projects within their areas of specialization. But their work has been with adults, and therefore a form of adult education. The mission study books published each year by Friendship Press, through the Commission on Missionary Education of the Division of Christian Education of the National Council of Churches, represent another significant example of cooperative efforts in developing study materials for adult groups.

However, for the purpose of this paper we shall concentrate on the cooperative developments through the Department of Curriculum Development of the Commission on General

Christian Education of the National Council of Churches. There are three committees that deserve our attention: The Committee on the Uniform Series; The Committee on Graded Curriculum; and, more recently, the Cooperative Curriculum Project.

Two historic policies have guided the committees in their cooperative curriculum endeavors: "The desirability of cooperation among the denominations, and the prerogative of each denomination to determine the product which goes to its home churches." [1]

Committee on the Uniform Series

The "Uniform Lessons" were officially born on the occasion of the National Sunday School Convention in Indianapolis in 1872, by the passing of a resolution establishing a Lesson Committee, "to select a course of Bible Lessons for a series of years not exceeding seven [this was later changed to six], which shall, as far as they may decide possible, embrace a general study of the whole Bible, alternating between the Old and New Testaments semiannually or quarterly, as they shall deem best." [2] Thus began the work of the International Lesson Committee, made up at that time of five clergymen and five laymen from the following denominations: Baptist, Congregational, Methodist Episcopal, Presbyterian, and Protestant Episcopal.

Changes in committee structure, procedures, and sponsoring body have taken place through the years—from the International Sunday School Association to the International Council of Religious Education in 1922, and to the Division of Christian Education of the National Council of Churches in 1950. Improvements have taken place along the way, but the emphasis upon Biblical content has not changed.

The present Uniform Lesson Committee is made up of ap-

---

[1] From a report of the Committee on Lesson Policy and Production to the Commission on Educational Program, February 9, 1940, quoted in *A Guide for Curriculum in Christian Education* (Chicago, 1955), 113.

[2] George Herbert Betts, *The Curriculum of Religious Education* (New York, 1924), 126.

proximately one hundred members, representing thirty denominations in the United States and Canada. *The Handbook of Principles and Procedures,* which has undergone numerous revisions since its initial preparation in 1948, specifies that the committee should have persons directly appointed by their cooperating denominations, that these are to be representative of all age groups, but that members are to be selected only by denominations proposing to use the Uniform Series and such other general resource persons as may be desired.

The Handbook thus defines the objectives and scope of the series:

> The Outlines should be developed with the purpose of providing a plan for studying the Bible which will help growing persons increasingly to know its content and to understand its message in the light of their own experiences and relationships. . . . The outlines should plan to cover all portions of the Bible fruitful for group study in churches using these lessons, but some portions should be recognized as affording more teaching value than others and they should be given larger place. . . . Topical studies should be included, such as temperance, world peace, problems of civic responsibility, Christian family life and so on; such topical studies to be related directly to biblical content but not limited to Biblical content. . . . The outlines should include provisions for adequate Bible study on a literary, historical, psychological, sociological, and ethical basis.[3]

In spite of the fact that the Uniform Lesson Series has been under criticism from the day of its inception, it still persists. There is evidence that the lessons based on the cooperatively developed outlines are the most widely used curriculum materials in adult groups within the Protestant churches today. In 1924, George Herbert Betts wrote what sounded like a funeral oration for the Uniform Series: "The day of the Uniform Lessons is past. The ungraded uniform type of lesson, with its lack

---

[3] Committee on Uniform Series of the Commission on General Christian Education, Division of Christian Education, National Council of Churches, *Handbook of Principles and Procedures* (Mimeographed document, December, 1960) , 1.

of adaptation in material and organization, with its stress on subject matter and its neglect of the child, with its indifference to the educational progress of the age, with its face resolutely set toward the past instead of the future—in short, with its tragedy both of theoretical and of practical inefficiency, is without excuse in this day of educational and religious enlightenment." [4] That was thirty-seven years ago, but the end is not yet in sight, although with the coming of closely graded and cycle graded materials, the use of uniform materials with children and youth has greatly decreased, especially in the larger denominations. Not so in adult groups. Even though denominations have produced other materials for adult study, the Uniform Series remains the most widely used.

In addition to the adult materials based on Uniform Lesson outlines available from denominational publishing houses, the lessons find their way into the churches and homes through syndicated columns in over 860 newspapers throughout the country, through seven published volumes of commentaries, and through lesson materials published by many non-denominational and commercial publishing houses.

Anyone who has seen the Committee on the Uniform Series in action must testify that this "pooling" effort is very much alive. The hub of the Committee's procedure is its Cycle Committee. In its March 1961 meeting, the first draft of the 1969-1974 Cycle was submitted for review and revision. The Quarterly and Age Group Subcommittees were putting into final shape the 1965 outlines, taking into account criticisms submitted by denominations; the 1966 outlines were prepared in tentative form to be submitted for denominational review and subsequent completion in 1962.

There is no evidence that the Uniform Series will soon be eliminated. And we need to ask seriously, "Should we be working toward that end?" Efforts to improve the Series have continued through the years. Many of the early criticisms have lost their potency; others persist. Even though excellent writers are

---

[4] Betts, *The Curriculum of Religious Education*, 134.

used and the most creative methods suggested, there is uneven-
ness in the quality of printed materials produced from the Uniform outlines. We still need to ask, "Does the Uniform Series
offer an adequate curriculum for adults?" In any event, we
cannot ignore this Series.

We need to know more about the reasons for the continued
widespread use of Uniform lessons. It is easy to understand this
use in denominations where the Uniform Series is the only
study material being published. But what about denominations
where other material is available? What part is played by tradition, familiarity with the format, resistance to change, insistence
on a particular type of Bible-centered material, limited variety
of teaching methods, lack of adequate leadership training, and
the financial investment of publishing houses? An understanding of all the factors involved will help us to understand the
problems and find solutions.

Committee on Graded Curriculum

In addition to the Committee on the Uniform Lesson Series,
three sub-committees of the Committee on Graded Curriculum
are conccerned with adult materials: The Adult Committee,
The Home Committee, and the Older Youth-Young Adult
Committee. At one time the Adult Committee and the Home
Committee produced cooperative outlines for study units for
adults; they no longer perform this function. Their meetings in recent years have provided a channel for sharing adult
and home curriculum concerns, insights, and trends across denominational lines.

One subcommittee of the Committee on Graded Curriculum,
however, has been busy producing cooperative materials, the
Older Youth-Young Adult Committee. The main task of this
subcommittee has been the planning of a series of elective
courses for use by persons of post-high-school age (18-28), designed to be used in situations in which young adults may come
together for study and discussion. The series is called "Faith
for Life Series," and deals with the essentials of the Christian

faith. The content of study courses is decided by the subcommittee, descriptions are written, and writers are selected. Defining the areas for study, writing descriptions of the courses, and making suggestions for writers are all done cooperatively through the subcommittee. The courses are published through the Cooperative Publication Association. This is an organization of denominational publishing houses which coordinates the publication of vacation, weekday, and leadership education texts, materials for use in the home, camp materials, and the young adult electives mentioned. For those denominations that are advocating the use of electives by adult study groups, this series is making an excellent contribution.

Joint Study

Perhaps the most significant cooperative effort in curriculum development in recent years has been the joint study sessions sponsored by the various curriculum committees of the Division of Christian Education of the National Council. During the last decade a number of denominations have been engaged in their own curriculum studies, many of them using the same resource persons, specialists, and consultants.

In the spring of 1957 a concern among denominations for intensive joint curriculum study became evident. Under the leadership of a Steering Committee for Curriculum Studies, attention was given to the question, "What kind of curriculum is needed by our churches in the task of Christian education?" Six study sessions were scheduled: four at the time of the regular March meetings from 1957 to 1960 of the Committee on Graded Curriculum and the Committee on the Uniform Series; and two special study sessions in December of 1958 and 1959. The themes discussed during these four years of study reveal the direction and progress:

1957—What is the relationship of theological foundations and psychological insights in Christian nurture?

1958—Philosophy of curriculum, with the use of the Bible and the problem of "progression" as basic considerations.

1959—Study of objective, scope, organizing principle, and learn-
    ing theory.
1960—What learning sequences should be included in the cur-
    riculum of Christian education?

The study papers prepared in connection with the sessions
gave direction and content to the exploration of curriculum
concepts. Following the 1960 joint study session, the Steering
Committee asked D. Campbell Wyckoff to report the results
of the study, and this has been done in a published book.[5]
No one can really estimate the results of this joint study
project. Certainly the individual participants have benefited by
going through the process, and the denominations they represented have profited by a new vision of what cooperative study
can achieve. According to Wyckoff:

The chief findings of the studies might, then, be summarized in
terms of the context, scope, purpose, process, and design of Christian education. There appears to be something of a growing consensus on these matters. The context of Christian education is seen
as the worshiping, witnessing, working community of persons in
Christ. The scope of Christian education is the whole field of relationships in the light of the gospel. The purpose of Christian education is awareness of revelation and the gospel, and response in faith
and love. The process of Christian education is participation in the
life and work of the community of persons in Christ. The design of
Christian education consists of sequences of activities and experiences by which the learning tasks may be effectively undertaken by
individuals and groups.[6]

The Cooperative Curriculum Project [7]

A most significant outcome of the joint study process has
been the emergence of the "Cooperative Curriculum Project,"

---

[5] D. Campbell Wyckoff, *Theory and Design of Christian Education Curriculum*
(Philadelphia, 1961).

[6] *Ibid.,* 79.

[7] Described in a special background paper prepared for the Constituting Conference for the Cooperative Curriculum Project, December 12-14, 1960, St. Louis,
Missouri.

which hopes to achieve a curriculum designed to accommodate the entire life span of the individual, and therefore includes adult curriculum. It seems appropriate to describe the project briefly.

In the spring meeting of the 1960 joint study session, decisions were reached: (1) to organize a Cooperative Curriculum Project that would implement insights garnered from the study and (2) to organize a vigorous program for continued curriculum study that would involve representatives of the many agencies of the churches concerned with Christian education. Denominations were invited to send representatives to an exploratory meeting later that year. Twelve denominations sent delegates, and two expressed interest but were unable to send representatives. The delegates agreed to proceed with the project, and at a later meeting the Cooperative Curriculum Project was officially constituted by duly authorized representatives of the denominations. It has become a project of participant denominations cooperating through the Division of Christian Education of the National Council of Churches for the development of curriculum for Christian education.

Specified conditions for partnership in the Project involve such matters as the assignment of staff time, continuity of personnel, and financial underwriting. It is anticipated that "the design will make possible the development of supporting materials for use not only in the educational settings of the Sunday church school, vacation church school, camp and conference settings, and leadership education enterprises, but also in the wider range of educational opportunities which are served by denominational agencies in their ministries to the home, the church, the community, and the world."

A time schedule and program of work extend to March 1964, when it is expected the project will be completed. The following tasks or stages have been delineated: (1) agreement on curriculum design; (2) delineation of scope; (3) development of guides to areas of curriculum; (4) development of guides to themes or topics (subdivision of areas of curriculum); (5) development of possible sequences across the life span (delineation of the spread of areas, themes as they might relate to a plan of sequences and emphases) ; and (6) development of descriptions of units for teaching-learning experiences.

At the present time, sixteen denominations have agreed to partnership. That this project has come so far is evidence that denominations are realizing that they can work together at much deeper and more fundamental levels than previously was thought possible. Fresh approaches to curriculum development are going into the project. Undoubtedly, this is the most significant venture to date in a cooperative curriculum endeavor, by virtue of its comprehensive nature and the intensive joint study which preceded it. The project is not far enough along for us to know how the curriculum for adults will be handled. It may be that some adult materials for local use will be produced cooperatively and others separately by the denominations themselves. Nevertheless, we can be sure that those who have been at work in the development of the design are conscious of the importance of adult education.

We have seen that the pooling of efforts in building curriculum for the Christian education of adults is active in two major enterprises: one of long standing, the Uniform Series; the other new and just begun, the Cooperative Curriculum Project. In many quarters new and fresh approaches to adult study in the church are being suggested. There are designs and programs for adult education in the church coming from many sources: university centers, denominational bodies, local churches, lay academies. There is ferment abroad in curriculum development in general, and in adult work specifically. We are being forced to evaluate and to clarify. The climate is right for us to do this together.

Directions for the Future

What are some directions as we pool our efforts? Here are only a few suggestions:

1. *We must develop a clear understanding of the cooperative projects that are already under way, and if possible join in the*

processes of their development—to give as well as to get. It is only in this way that doors are continually open to re-examination of goals, purposes, theory, design, the actual materials produced, and the way they are used. As mentioned previously, the Uniform Series will not be wished out of existence, even in churches of denominations that de-emphasize their use or do not publish the materials themselves. The materials find their way into the churches through other means: nondenominational publications, volume commentaries, syndicated columns, etc. The Committee on the Uniform Series has not been rigid and inflexible with respect to change; at each meeting real criticisms are faced and improvements made. We are all aware of the importance of Bible study in adult groups. This has been one of the strengths of the Uniform Series. It should certainly be possible, using our combined efforts, insights, and understandings, to produce a study series for adults that will embody the best approaches to Bible study. There are churches that now use selected units of the Uniform Series as Bible study electives.

The Cooperative Curriculum Project is in its infancy. It is not too late for denominations to join in the development. It is a significant and important project because it represents the outgrowth of intensive joint study by denominations of the theological, psychological, and educational foundations essential to a good curriculum. What evolves in terms of materials and program for adults will be determined in large part by the spirit, scholarship, and workmanship of those guiding the process.

The Uniform Series and the Cooperative Curriculum Project, then, offer established channels for sharing new insights and improvements, and are worthy of our interest and support.

2. *We should provide for a continuation and increase in the use of adult study electives.* Most denominations have published lists of elective study units for adult groups, and it is interesting to note that their lists include units and courses published by denominations other than their own. This represents a spontaneous pooling effort, and perhaps we need to explore this avenue for cooperative exchange of electives in a more systematic way. Not nearly enough adult groups are willing, and some-

times they are unable, to deal with elective units; but they can be equipped to do so through appropriate leadership development programs.

3. *We must plan an increase in leadership development programs for adults.* An adequate curriculum for adults demands this. Leadership education and adult education have been growing closer and closer together; they are inseparable. New understandings of group procedures, leadership-membership roles, emphasis on small groups, and creative methods have been finding their way into adult programs and have been the reason for the greatest change.

We have found that process and content are equally important if learning is to take place. The lecture method continues to hold sway as the predominant teaching method, but it is well to remember that interaction within a group does not take place automatically. When adults participate actively in self-direction for study, and leadership is shared, effective learning can take place; but it presupposes experience and training. This must go hand-in-hand with curriculum plans; otherwise we shall find ourselves in the peculiar position of having printed materials and resources, perhaps good ones, but with little understanding of what they are and the lack of ability or desire to use them effectively.

Denominations and councils of churches are sponsoring a variety of leadership development programs: how-to-teach workshops, laboratory schools, short-term leadership courses, and weekend institutes, among others. Such training events are held not only under Christian education auspices but under the direction also of committees on social action, evangelism, stewardship, men's work, and women's work.

The National Council of Churches sponsors an annual Laboratory on Personal, Group, and Organizational Effectiveness, at Green Lake, Wisconsin, which has become a training center for professionals in denominational and interdenominational work. Four hundred thirty-four persons have participated in this experience during the past six years. The Leadership Education Curriculum of the National Council is still serving local councils of churches and some denominations through guidance in planning leadership enterprises. If we are honest, however, we must recognize that there has been no real coordination of effort; each sponsoring denomination or committee has carried on its own enterprise independently of what others in adult education are doing. Of course there have been occasional consultation and sharing of information, but not on the level of basic philosophy and goals.

4. *There should be coordination of the adult program on all levels.* This does not mean coordination for the sake of greater efficiency or "calendar clearance," but because wholeness and unity are basic to our concept of the church. We must start with the local church. There are men's groups, women's guilds, Bible classes, weekday study classes, prayer meetings, social action groups, missionary societies, and many others. The disaster is not that they exist, but that they exist unto themselves for their own edification and self-interest. And the national boards of our denominations, and the divisions of the National Council of Churches, are similarly divided.

Has not the time come for us to take a long hard look at our structures? Are they helping or hindering us in fulfilling the mission of the church? Certain denominations have done this, and radical changes have occurred. In the summer of 1960 the Committee on Adult Work of the National Council sponsored a Conference on Coordinating the Educational Program for Adults in the Local Church. The delegates were representative of the variety of adult work interests in the church. While the conference did not result in pat solutions, it sharpened the sense of necessity for greater understanding and communication between all who work with adults in the church. The conference sought to identify the many "barriers to effective adult programming": physical barriers (time, distance, equipment) ; barriers resulting from lack of awareness; ideological barriers; organizational barriers; personal barriers. An attempt was made to define principles of coordination that would aid in breaking down the barriers. It is not the purpose of this paper to repeat what was said at this conference, but rather to suggest that many more conferences such as this should be held.

Workers with adults in various aspects of the church's program have held varying images of each other: Christian education versus social action, for example, or men's work versus women's work. Through the years the forces of Christian education have had particular difficulty because of the nature of the early Sunday school movement. Starting outside of denominational structures, the Sunday school eventually became integrated into the total church program and became the church school. Still later Christian education recognized its task as involving more than the church school.

But this does not mean that others have seen Christian education in this broader light. When sponsors of a specific program begin to think in terms of the total church, there is the temptation to become imperialistic and to say, "It's all Christian education"; or "It's all evangelism"; or "It's all stewardship." The very fact that this can happen emphasizes the need to explore together the mission of the church and how we can fulfill it.

It is significant that this particular workshop on curriculum was not aimed exclusively at editors, but at program personnel as well; not only at the adult Christian educators, but at all builders of adult programs in the church. This means that Christian educators are seeing their mission to the total church more clearly, their relationship to social action, evangelism, stewardship, family life, men's work, women's work. The pooling of efforts is going forward with a new sense of unity and mission. Adult work in the church is being seen whole.

It is worthy of note that the joint curriculum study sessions in the Division of Christian Education of the National Council of Churches, which gave birth to the Cooperative Curriculum Project, are being continued in a new locale, not among the editors alone in a setting of curriculum committee meetings, but in the setting of the program meetings of the Commission on Missionary Education and the Commission on General Christian Education. This is a beginning step. It is envisaged that representatives from the wider areas of the life and work of the church might join in this cooperative study: social action, men's work, women's work, and all the rest. We are on the road toward the unity we seek.

5. *There are many experiments in lay education today that deserve our study and evaluation.* Much is being said about the "renewal of the church" and the "ministry of the laity." We are called to re-examine the nature of the church and its mission. If we are to build a more adequate curriculum for adults, it should reflect what we believe the church to be and what we believe it should be doing. A telling criticism is given by Hendrik Kraemer in his book, *A Theology of the Laity:*

> The church does not primarily exist on behalf of itself, but on behalf of the world. Strange to say, this elementary trust, which finds ready intellectual assent, is nevertheless absent in the church. Even the deeper feeling of evangelistic responsibility and the many kinds of work which are done by the churches as a contribution to the general need of society do not change the striking fact that the church as such is introvert, and considered as such by public opinion. . . . Without entering into a discussion of the many reasons, good and bad, valid and invalid, which have caused this situation, the upshot of it is that the mind of the churches is bent, above all, on its own increase and well-being. It is church-centered. It is self-centered. The interest in the world is at best a side-issue.[8]

As we plan a program-curriculum for adults, are we aiming at preparing them for church work, or for doing the work of the church? And this is a question that comes to all of us, not to any one denomination but to Christians, and we must face the question together. We must listen with sharp awareness to what the lay movements are saying to us, both here and abroad. Franklin Hamlin Littell describes the rise of the lay academies and the Kirchentag in *The German Phoenix*,[9] and he includes a special chapter on "What America Can Learn?" There are brief descriptions of some of the movements in this country such as Parishfield, Michigan; The Faith and Life Community,

---

[8] Hendrik Kraemer, *A Theology of the Laity* (Philadelphia, 1958), 127.

[9] Franklin Hamlin Littell, *The German Phoenix* (Garden City, N. Y., 1960).

Austin, Texas; the Ecumenical Institute, Evanston, Illinois; Kirkridge, and others. Informal consultations take place between most of the lay institutes in this country through what has come to be known as The Columbus Group. We must know about these movements; we must hear what they are saying; whether we agree or not, we can only be helped in our task at curriculum building. And perhaps what we do together will have some relevance.

6. *There must be continuing study and research in adult education.* The study conference held at the University of Pittsburgh in 1958 was a milestone in adult Christian education. The volume which resulted has been an invaluable resource and aid to all persons working in this area.[10] In addition, the joint curriculum studies of the National Council of Churches have contributed to our deeper understanding of total curriculum problems, needs, and procedures. We are encouraged by the growing number of universities that are offering opportunities for advanced study in adult religious education and by the availability of scholarship grants to make this possible. There are a multitude of problems and questions facing us in adult education that present challenges to further study and research, and represent possibilities for future cooperative projects.

One example of an area needing further exploration is the use of educational radio and television. What is the contribution that these media of communication can make to our total adult curriculum? Rather than leaving religious programming to chance or to the spontaneous enthusiasm of individuals, is there not a real opportunity before us as Christian adult educators to cooperate in setting standards, defining goals, planning for distribution and use?

We must become aware of the vast amount of research and study that is going on in adult education; as the findings and insights are shared with us, they will contribute to our work toward more effective curriculum development for adults.

---

[10] Lawrence C. Little, ed., *The Future Course of Christian Adult Education* (Pittsburgh, 1959).

There is a strong desire on the part of churches to explore their educational task. The history of cooperative Christianity is a thrilling one to read; we have moved a long way in our quest for Christian unity on all levels and in a variety of ways. There was the day when the criteria for interdenominational cooperation was, "We do only those things together that we cannot do separately." Other voices now say, "We do only those things separately that we cannot do together." We are aware more than ever that an agency such as the National Council of Churches is not an end in itself, but exists only because of the divisions within the Christian church. God does not will disunity; Christ's prayer "that all may be one" is not an empty petition; no one denomination can be the whole church. The National Council of Churches is not the whole church. There is a more basic unity which is above and beyond any of our many separate structures. It is the unity that God wills for all His people.

The introduction to the book, *Protestantism Faces Its Educational Task Together* concludes with these words: "And thus, this holy urge that makes all things one, through these many fields in which it has been at work, has constantly lifted the vision of Christian education to the years-to-be, for it is only those *who ask the question together* who can find a wise answer to the query, 'Whither goest thou?' " [11]

The italics are mine. The basic questions that need to be asked, that will help us in the building of our Christian adult education curriculum, are questions that belong to all of us. No one denomination can find the answers alone. We are not "pooling our efforts" because it is more efficient, economical, or practical, but because of belief in a unity that exists regardless of what we do together. But working together is evidence of our awareness of this unity, and our desire to make it real.

[11] William C. Bower and Percy R. Hayward, *Protestantism Faces Its Educational Task Together* (Appleton, Wisconsin, 1949), xi.

15. Behavioral Outcomes of the Christian Education of Adults

PAUL B. MAVES

Professor of Religious Education
Drew University

I

FUNDAMENTALLY, CHRISTIANITY is the response of sinful, finite men to the God who has encountered them as infinite love in the events of their lives through Jesus Christ. It is a quality of response which is characterized by faith, hope, and love. As a response it is behavior. The response that is demanded is that of the whole person, first to God and then to neighbor.

There are many clear statements in the New Testament about the relation of love and faith to behavior. James may be the most direct and explicit about faith: "My brothers, what use is it for a man to say he has faith when he does nothing to show it? . . . if it does not lead to action it is in itself a lifeless thing." [1]

John is equally explicit and even more vehement about love. "My children, love must not be a matter of words or talk;

---

[1] James 2:14, 17. *The New English Bible.*

233

it must be genuine, and show itself in action. This is how we know we belong to the realm of truth." [2]

The Apostle Paul devotes an entire section of his letter to the Romans to Christian behavior.[3] This contains nothing less than exhortations to observe certain duties and to avoid certain kinds of activities as befitting faith. Likewise in Galatians, called forth to refute those who insisted that the new Christians were bound to observe the Jewish ritual laws, Paul again abjures the Christians to be responsible in their freedom and to let themselves be guided by the Spirit which produces the fruit of peace, love, joy, patience, kindness, gentleness, self-control, and fidelity.[4]

Love in the New Testament is not mere sentiment or feeling. It is not something that happens to persons automatically when "the chemistry is right." It is a way of relating to others. It is responsible action with reference to God and in obedience to his commands. It is not the means to justification but the witness to it, the indication of the presence of the Holy Spirit. Love calls persons into community and makes them responsible for their actions, even as it frees them from the fear of death and from anxiety about their imperfections in their relations.

To be a Christian is to acknowledge and to affirm that Jesus is the Christ, the Lord of life, and the Savior of men. To be a Christian is to be progressively transformed by the love of God as shown forth in Jesus Christ. To be a Christian is to participate in the nature and work of Christ, and to be increasingly governed by the Spirit of Christ. Participating in Christ means belonging to, identifying with, and taking part in the life and work of the Body of Christ, which is the church.

The church is an historical community of persons, bound together and identified by a common memory, a common hope, and a common mission. In this community Christians remember and recite what God has done to create it, preserve it, and redeem it. In this community Christians hope for the final

---

2 I John 3:18, 19. *The New English Bible.*
3 Romans 12:1-15:13.
4 Galatians 5:16-26.

triumph of God's sovereign purposes over all of life and for the full redemption of the whole creation, because they see here a foretaste of this future. Through this community Christians minister to the world with the message of reconciliation and administer to those who accept the means of grace.

The church is the people of God, those who have been called out from among the people of the world by God through Jesus Christ, brought into fellowship with Christ, and given a commission. They constitute a royal priesthood which proclaims the Word of God, confesses its faith, worships its creator, and witnesses to the world what God has done. In the words of H. Richard Niebuhr its purpose is "the increase among men of love of God and neighbor.[5] In this relation with God lies man's highest good, his eternal life, and his ultimate destiny.

This love of God and neighbor is expressed cognitively through its statements of faith, its creeds, and its theologies. The Christian is one who studies the history of the community to which he belongs, reflects upon it, and articulates his own faith in the language of his day in order that he may witness more accurately to God's love. This love of God expresses itself aesthetically through art, architecture, drama, liturgy, and the language of devotion as worship. This love expresses itself in ecclesiastical organization, which structures the community institutionally, in such a way that it may minister most effectively. So organizational and administrative activity in the Spirit of Christ is a way of loving God and neighbor. This love of God and neighbor is expressed socially in terms of the groups it gathers and the relationships between persons it fosters and makes possible.[6]

Karl Barth has often been charged with downgrading ethics and moral living in the contemporary theological scene. There is no question but that he challenges the confusion of a code morality, or a conventional piety, or a petty moralism which

---

[5] H. Richard Niebuhr, *The Purpose of the Church and Its Ministry* (New York, 1956), 31.

[6] These ideas were suggested by Paul Tillich in his lectures on "The Church and The Kingdom of God," given at Harvard University Divinity School in 1957-58.

elevates local mores and customs into an absolute, with the Christian faith. He rejects the notion that the "teachings of Jesus" are a new law and the Christian merely a more zealous Pharisee, or that the Bible is to be regarded as a set of rules, or that the word of God is discovered by man and imposed upon others as a code of action. An ethical thinker cannot substitute for any other man or speak for God to him, since both are free. According to Barth, "ethical theory is not meant to provide men with principles to be interpreted, applied, and put into practice. Ethics has to make clear that every single step man takes involves a specific and direct responsibility toward God, who reached out for man in specific and direct encounter." [7]

This is to say that the future is always open in light of the fact that God may enter a man's life at any point. A man's history can be traced, but his actions cannot be predicted with any great precision on the basis of it. A man who is open to the call of God cannot close the future by his own planning or bind himself irrevocably in advance by being committed absolutely to any rigid habit, absolute rule, or set program.

Barth has maintained that faith and love are dynamic, personal relationships. He has insisted that our obedient and joyful response to God as revealed through a person may become hardened and institutionalized into a religion which then stands as a barrier to the receiving of revelation, for religion may become the expression of unbelief and human pride rather than faith in God. He has emphasized that even when justified by faith, man is still a sinner, living only by the daily renewed mercy of God. As a sinner, man's understanding and will are distorted; as a finite being his freedom is limited so that he cannot, even when he intends it, do what is right. It may be relatively easy on the basis of superficial reading to believe that Barth has no concern for ethics, and it may even be that the extreme emphasis upon God's initiative and man's helplessness reduces the tension which drives a man to work out his salvation with fear and trembling.

---

[7] Karl Barth, *The Humanity of God* (Richmond, Va., 1960), 86.

However, in his Prolegomena to *Church Dogmatics* he has a long section on "The Life of the Children of God." There he states clearly that "if we think of the life of the children of God as a creation of the Holy Spirit we have to do with a determinateness of human life understood as *being* and *doing* . . . the Christian life regarded . . . as the being of a man, does not subsist of itself, but only in a specific doing on the part of the subject." [8] For Barth, being is thought of as the inward nature newly created, while doing is thought of as "the outward aspect, the social nature of the Christian." In his view, these correspond to two actions: the love of God and the praise of God. Love, which is the essence of the Christian life, "consists in a definite being, relationship, and action." The praise of God breaks out in love to neighbor. To love the neighbor is to be a witness of Jesus Christ in word, in deed, and in attitude. For the forgiven man the neighbor takes on a sacramental significance, for he illuminates our own need for forgiveness and the meaning of God's grace. This in no way supports the notion that faith is a mere intellectual affair or that behavior is unimportant, although, again, Barth's use of such terms as "proclamation" and "witness" may be read as indicating verbal behavior solely. There is, however, a distinction between surface conformity to social norms, and behavior which is an authentic and creative expression of the total orientation of the person. Furthermore, action may not always be discerned as the expression of love to God by the onlooker, especially if he is a man of unfaith. Not even the actor can be sure that what he does is an act of love, for only God can judge whether it is or not. We act in faith and not in knowledge.

Barth has been quoted at length because of his commanding position in the contemporary theological world, and because he is often used to support a disinterest in Christian action. However, while he emphasizes present decision on the part of men made free by the Word of God, and while he gives no comfort to those who are concerned with morality as the observance of

---

[8] Karl Barth, *Church Dogmatics* (Edinburgh, 1956) , I, 369.

rules and the discharge of duties made by man, he certainly makes it clear that faith cannot be separated from behavioral outcomes. This is in keeping with his commitment to the Hebraic view of man as an organic whole.

Brunner similarly holds that obedience to the will of God means loving the neighbor. He affirms that the content of such love is not a law or a program that can be laid down before-hand, but simply responsiveness to the needs of others in their particular circumstances. Even more emphatically he points out that it is morality itself which is evil and legalism which is the worst form of corruption because it makes man confident in himself as not needing God. The Christian, though, knows that all men sin and fall short of the glory of God, even though they sometimes may do good.[9]

II

If we have established the fact that faith, hope, and love are ways of behaving in relationship in obedience to God's will, let us look more closely at the nature of this behavior. What kind of behavior does Christian faith produce?

Paul Ramsey affirms that "The central notion or 'category' in Christian ethics is 'obedient love'—the sort of love the gospels describe as 'love fulfilling the law' and St. Paul designates as 'faith that works through love.' " This is in contrast to mystical love or aspiration for a vision of God. This "obedient love" leads to an ideal of character derived from that which is seen to exist in Christ. As a life filled, illuminated, and governed by "obedient love," it can be said that the object of the Christian is to attain a more Christ-like character, possessing the virtues which are found in Christ, the virtues which find their unity in love. This, however, is sought not as an end in itself, nor in hope of self-fulfillment, but "faith working through love is concerned only to show what *love* is and to discover the neighbor's needs, not to demonstrate that it itself is faithful." [10]

---

[9] Emil Brunner, *The Divine Imperative* (Philadelphia, 1957) , 59 ff.
[10] Paul Ramsey, *Basic Christian Ethics* (New York, 1950) , xi, 136.

Ramsey enters another qualification at this point: "Love of neighbor which is a Christian's obedience to God and the source of his virtue, is never *itself* a 'habit,' 'stable character pattern,' or 'fixed personality trait.' It is always a 'present decision.' However many times repeated, it does not become easier or more assured. Such obedient love is never a virtue; it *has* virtues." [11] I believe that here he is overemphatic, perhaps because he misunderstands the concept of trait as generally used.

George Thomas takes a similar line of reasoning when he says that the "virtuous life is not primarily a stable set of habits imposed on the natural impulses by reason; it is an expression of aspiration for a perfect good that is grasped by faith and clung to with hope." Nevertheless he takes a more liberal attitude toward moral education: "Moral education is usually concerned above all with inculcating those dispositions which are called virtues. This is due in part to the recognition of parents, teachers, and elders in general that the root of moral conduct is *character*. The concern for character is accompanied by instruction in what are regarded as duties. But this instruction is not thought to be successful unless it leads to the formation of virtuous habits which makes the performance of duties spontaneous and in a sense natural." He defines a moral virtue as a "*habit* or *disposition* of the will . . . *a flexible habit adaptable by intelligence to changing situations.*" [12]

Professor Thomas is able to accept this because he sees that a moral habit or virtue does not need to prevent further growth or deprive a person of freedom of will. Virtues are not habits of routine, but habits of control over emotions, so the will may be freed from subservience to the passions and be able to determine the response in light of the needs of the situation. For him "Virtues are aspects of *character*," which is "the relatively *permanent structure* which underlies the moral conduct of a person as a whole," and which also involves "an *attitude* toward his environment." As he sees it, at the base of character is an

---

[11] *Ibid.*, 219.
[12] George Thomas, *Christian Ethics and Moral Philosophy* (New York, 1955), 98, 484, 492 f.

ethical ideal. Personal examples are crucial in the development and inculcation of moral character. Moral virtues grow out of a transformation of the self by God's love. They are stable and dependable ways in which the new self, controlled by love, seeks to serve God and to fulfill the needs of persons. At the same time, they are the results of the new self's aspiration for perfect goodness.

Thomas makes clear that the goal can never be fully attained, but it can be progressively approximated. Also, development toward Christian maturity depends upon moral effort. It is acquired by acts, in struggle, by exertion of the will. He seems to meet the qualifications raised by Barth and Ramsey that the Christian life is a life of decision in freedom and at the same time leaves open a place for moral education in the Christian life.

III

If love as relation and as action is the main characteristic of the Christian, we need then to come to grips with the concept of "character" and the way in which character can be described and developed. If we cannot describe Christian character with some degree of precision and if we do not know how it develops, we can have little confidence in any program of Christian nurture or education. The problem cannot be avoided by saying that our sole responsibility is to witness what God has done for us, for obviously we cannot witness responsibly unless we know what its effect is upon those who hear it.

Within the field of Christian education the terms "character education" and "moral training" have become suspect, smacking of justification by works, and identified with liberalism. These have been relegated to the public schools, to be associated with "education for democracy" and the concern for "spiritual values." Perhaps it has been not only the association of character education with liberalism but also general discouragement over the possibility of defining and devising measures for attitudes and traits which contributed to the loss of interest in it in the church. For these reasons we now state our objectives in the most global and ambiguous terms. Or else we take the easy road out and measure our success in terms of increase in membership, giving, and attendance, in the size of our salaries, or the amount of building that is going on, or the number of meetings that we have had in the past year.

Where do we now stand with respect to the concept of character and ways of describing it?

Allport believes that character is "an ethical concept. . . . Character is personality evaluated, and personality is character devaluated." He believes therefore that this is an unnecessary concept for psychology.[13] However, the educator needs to make some judgments about what is valuable, and therefore the concept of character as a particular kind of personality is useful to him.

Cattell says:

Character or character integration refers to the manner in which the drives are organized in relation to one another. By many persons it is also understood to mean the consequent relation of the total system of drives to some set of external principles—e.g., religious or moral beliefs, a social code, or a philosophical system, or even only to the particular code in which they themselves believe. It happens that good dynamic integration, on the one hand, and good orientation to the moral code of the culture in which one is brought up, on the other, tend strongly to go together. But the psychologist, who is not in a position to judge moral values or weigh the relative goodness of cultural patterns, defines character simply as *good integration of dynamic traits*—i.e., perseverance and freedom from maladaptive impulsiveness—*in relation to the attainment of those cultural goals which the individual has accepted, whether or not they are in his own cultural pattern.*[14]

Peck and Havighurst define character as "a persisting pattern of attitudes and motives which produce a rather predictable

---

[13] Gordon Allport, *Personality: A Psychological Interpretation* (New York, 1937), 52.

[14] Raymond B. Cattell, *Description and Measurement of Personality* (New York, 1946), 202.

kind and quality of moral behavior. To be sure, there are some inconsistencies within the moral behavior of just about everyone. Some individuals are markedly inconsistent. . . . Such a pattern has its own kind of 'consistency,' though. It is an enduring, predictable kind of pattern that sets the person off from other people of different character." And they conclude that 'if character be defined in terms of powerful, emotion-laden attitudes, as well as action patterns that tend to become habituated, the evidence indicates that there is indeed such a thing as individual character, and that it tends to persist through the years." [15]

Brunner finds no difficulty with the concept of character, although he does not dwell upon it to any extent:

Man does not only consist of distinct acts; his life is also characterized by what one may describe as 'settled conditions' or a 'state of being.' . . . We do not merely live in acts of decision, but in life there is also a region of the habitual. . . . There does exist what we call *character*, which can be described in empirical terms, the permanent element. . . . There is a relative constancy, an attitude, a certain stamp, whose external sign is the fact we are in the body. And faith extends its influence into this region of the factual, habitual state—just as much as sin does. There does exist something which can be described as a 'Christian character.' [16]

IV

There are two main ways of describing character in empirical terms. One way is to use the concept of character types. The other is to use the concept of traits or dimensions. The concept of character type emphasizes elements of discontinuity between groups of persons. Type is a global concept in which a particular person is used as a prototype to whom others are compared. Religious writers, as we have seen, talk about "Christlike character," or of a Christian character as contrasted with a "worldly" character. Most contemporary typologies

---

[15] Robert F. Peck and Robert J. Havighurst, *The Psychology of Character Development* (New York, 1960), 164, 165.

[16] Brunner, *The Divine Imperative,* 168.

are based on the attempt to analyze character defect, such as Karen Horney's four types or David Riesman's three types. Similarly, H. S. Sullivan describes syndromes which are either diagnoses of personality pertaining to uninterrupted career-lines, or descriptions of disorder representing episodic changes in directions.[17]

Since types are global terms designating dominant tendencies or outstanding or particularly striking aspects of behavior, it is usually necessary to describe them further in terms of traits. Thus, a Christlike character is described in terms of the Christian virtues. For example, H. Richard Niebuhr talks about virtues which Christ exemplifies and communicates to those who participate in him and his work. He calls attention to the fact that each of these virtues has been emphasized as paramount by some group. Religious liberalism magnifies the virtue of love of God and neighbor. Eschatological interpretations underscore the place of hope in God's triumph. Existentialism focuses upon radical obedience to God's will. Orthodox Christians prize faith. Monasticism, he says, is taken by the virtue of humility: "Thus any one of the virtues of Jesus may be taken as the key to the understanding of his character and teaching; but each is intelligible in its apparent radicalism only as a relation to God."[18] These virtues could be, and often have been, fixed upon as the objectives of Christian education and the marks of Christian character.

It has been observed that particular cultures tend to produce particular character types. Each culture is more favorable to persons of a particular disposition than to others. Each tends to develop certain potentialities of personal growth and to sacrifice others. Attempts have been made to describe these.[19]

---

[17] Karen Horney, *Neurosis and Human Growth* (New York, 1950); David Riesman, Nathan Glazer, and Reuel Denny, *The Lonely Crowd* (Garden City, N. Y., 1950); Harry Stack Sullivan, *Conceptions of Modern Psychiatry* (Washington, 1947).

[18] H. Richard Niebuhr, *Christ and Culture* (New York, 1951), 27.

[19] Ruth Benedict, *Patterns of Culture* (New York, 1934); Gregory Bateson and Jurgen Ruesch, *Communication: The Social Matrix of Society* (New York, 1951); Erich Fromm, *Escape from Freedom* (New York, 1941); Erik H. Erikson, *Child and Society* (New York, 1950).

Peck and Havighurst conceived of five main character types, each of which represents a stage on the ladder of psychosocial development.[20] These were correlated with six cluster-traits arrived at by factor analysis. The universe studied consisted of 120 children who were born in 1933 and who were living in Prairie City in 1943. Their hypotheses were tested through case studies made of thirty-four children over a period of seven years. The types representing degrees of Maturity of Character were designated according to the kind of conscience as Amoral, Expedient, Conforming, Irrational-Conscientious, and Rational-Altruistic. The six clusters of traits were designated as Moral Stability, Ego Strength, Superego Strength, Spontaneity, Friendliness, and Hostility-Guilt.

A correlation was found between Maturity of Character and Moral Stability, Ego Strength, and Superego Strength. These also correlated with Moral Reputation. Friendliness was significantly correlated to Maturity of Character but not to Moral Reputation. Spontaneity was found on the extremes of the Maturity scale among those with high mature characters and those with poor or immature characters. Hostility-Guilt was negatively related to good character. Failure to develop through the stages is attributed predominantly to inadequacy within the nurturing family during the early years of the child.

While exceedingly useful, the statement of development of conscience is descriptive of a process and is almost entirely lacking in ethical or religious content. That is to say, it probably could describe as well the development of an Islamic, a Judaic, a Buddhistic, or a Shintoistic conscience.

It is interesting to compare this construct of the development of the conscience with Emil Brunner's description of the "principles" or "stages" to be found in the moral understanding of the self. He discerns seven stages. He designates them by the terms Immediacy, Custom, Intelligent Purpose (which is the bourgeois Philistine stage), Sensible Infinity (which is the masterful robber baron expansiveness), Aesthetic Element as a

---

[20] Peck and Havighurst, *The Psychology of Character Development.*

Form of Life (which is characteristic of the intellectual), and the Moral Man. In this discussion he points up a dilemma which is too often smoothed out in empirical studies or humanistic approaches. This is that "the more deeply the sense of the Holy penetrates a people, the more morality is burdened with a priestcraft which has no ethical influence or significance . . . [while] the more that morality severs its connexion with this system of taboos, the more it becomes 'humane' and rational, the more also it becomes secular and tends to approach the borderline of mere utilitarianism or of bourgeois decency. . . . The rational purification of morality always seems to be connected with a loss of moral sentiment and of reverence for the law as such." [21]

In many ways this analysis fits remarkably well into a model of personality development worked out by Erik Erikson. Jahoda's definition of the healthy personality as one which actively masters its environment, shows a certain unity of personality, and is able to perceive the world and himself correctly, is accepted. Certain inner laws of development are assumed which "create a succession of potentialities for significant interaction with those who tend" the infant and that such interaction "must remain within the proper rate and proper sequence which govern the growth of a personality as well as that of an organism." [22]

This also introduces the concept of developmental task which is here applied to the total life span. Here we have a list of certain central traits which describe a type of character according to certain attitude-trait-vectors which emerge according to an order laid down in the organism's constitution and which are cumulative in their effect so they add up to a mature healthy personality, but which are also recurrent at every age.[23]

Ernest Ligon, who has been one of the most persistent ad-

---

[21] Brunner, *The Divine Imperative*, 31.
[22] Erik H. Erikson, *Identity and the Life Cycle* (New York, 1959), I, No. 1.
[23] See Robert Havighurst, *Human Development and Education* (New York, 1953).

vocates of the trait analysis and scientific measurement of
Christian character in the last three decades, has derived eight
dimensions of character from the Beatitudes which characterize
the personality of Jesus and presumably that of his followers.
These he has called Vision, Dominating Purpose, Love of Right
and Truth, Faith in the Friendliness of the Universe, Sympathy, Desire to Help Every Man Achieve His Maximum Potential, Magnanimity, and Vicarious Sacrifice. The first four of
these he clusters under the heading of Faith, and the last four
under Love. The similarity to Niebuhr's list is marked. It
might be wondered if another cluster designated Hope could
be found.

In addition to these dimensions of character derived from a
so-called "Christian Hypothesis," Ligon posits six other variables, derived from a factor analysis of trait descriptions; these
six—two ethical, two social, and two personality variables—
are (1) sense of ethical values; (2) moral consistency; (3) social
effectiveness; (4) breadth of temporal and social orientation;
(5) extent of personality integration; and (6) expression of
maximum potential behavior.[24]

Other categories of traits have been derived from concepts of
health and maturity. Gordon Allport, for example, has compared lists of qualities or dimensions of maturity and has found
six categories which seem to be common to all of them. They
are (1) ego extension, or the capacity to take an interest in
more than one's body and one's own material possessions;
(2) self-objectification, which includes a sense of humor or
perspective and the ability to relate the feeling tone of the
present experience to that of a past experience when the present experience is in fact determined by the past; (3) a unifying
philosophy of life, which provides a frame of meaning and of
responsibility into which life's major activities fit; (4) the
capacity for a warm, profound relating of oneself to others;
(5) the possession of realistic skills, abilities, and perceptions

---

[24] Ernest M. Ligon, *Dimensions of Character* (New York, 1956), 208-66, 274-76.

with which to cope with the practical problems of life; and (6) a compassionate regard for all living creatures.[25]

Traits, characteristics, or dimensions of personality are abstractions or conceptualizations, perceived as consistencies or patterns in the stream of human behavior, and given a name. They are mental constructs, not physical entities, and what is looked for and what is perceived depend to a large extent upon the interests and the frame of reference of the observer. As with all behavior, traits represent modifications of the original organic response patterns by the environment through learning. Statistical methods are merely ways of determining the extent of agreement between observers or the extent to which the named categories are actually discrete or the extent to which they regularly are observable.

One of the major problems in personality study is the multiplicity of trait names and the lack of correspondence between various models of personality. Gordon Allport has made one of the most careful studies of the philosophical-psychological problem of trait theory. He concludes that no one "doubts that underlying the conduct of a mature person there are characteristic dispositions or traits. . . . they are here accepted as biophysical facts, actual psychophysical dispositions related —though no one yet knows how—to persistent neural systems of stress and determination." He concedes the difficulty of determining the traits since they are not directly observable but are inferred from behavior. He faces up to the question of trait-names and holds that they are "symbols socially devised (from a mixture of ethical, cultural, and psychological interests) for the naming and evaluation of human qualities." In his view, "their common usage establishes a presupposition that some human beings possess actual dispositions or traits roughly corresponding to these symbols." Hence his caution, in "scientific work no single trait-name can be accepted with assurance as

---

[25] Gordon Allport, "Personality: Normal and Abnormal," an address delivered to the Fifth Interamerican Congress of Psychology, Mexico City, December 18-23, 1957.

applicable to a given personality until its correspondence with a true trait has been experimentally or clinically established. Traits cannot be called forth by fiat: they must be discovered." [26]

A rigorous proponent of trait theory who has done some of the most definitive work to date on the subject is Raymond Cattell. He concludes:

1. Personality is concerned with and deduced from all the behavior relations between the organism and its environment. It is that which predicts behavior, given the situation.

2. The attributes by which it is described and measured are traits (structures or dispositions defining potential behavior) which may be considered properties of the organism, but which can only be defined in terms both of the organism and its environment—i.e., as relationships between the physiological organism and its environment.

3. Traits are functional unities manifested in the case of common traits by covariation with respect to individual differences and also, in the case of individual traits, with respect to occasions. . . .

4. Common traits are defined not only by the organism and the environment, but also through the group or species to which the organism belongs.

5. Complete description of personality may also require truly unique traits, measurable in attributes (dimensions) of behavior not found in any other individual.

Cattell believes that psychology has avoided the problem of exact description which must be solved before measurement can be made. Until this is done we cannot predict or control, because, "personality research like any other research, deals with changes, under certain influences, of known entities." [27]

Cattell set out to examine and compare syndromes of behavior which are derived from clinical observation, behavior rating, self-inventory data, and objective test measurements. He scrutinized some two hundred and eighty-six studies. Initially he concluded that there are three primary forms of traits: dynamic traits which result from the molding effect of environ-

---

[26] Allport, *Personality: A Psychological Interpretation*, 339, 310.
[27] Cattell, *Description and Measurement of Personality*, 566-67.

ment on constitutional dispositions; temperament traits which are also molded by experience; and ability traits, the way in which capacities have been molded into acquired skills and information.[28]

Trying to break these down more specifically, using correlation analysis, in a survey of fourteen independent studies, Cattell found 130 nuclear clusters of traits. He believed that this gave him some sixty-five reasonably well-confirmed surface traits which are behavioral descriptions. He then brought these together in twenty psychological and topographically distinct sectors. Probing further for primary source traits, which he believed were more useful for predicting behavior, he found twelve through factor analysis. They combine temperamental, dynamic, and ability elements in a holistic factor.

In reflecting upon these various attempts to find descriptive entities which are reasonably secure, it would seem that what is called "obedient love" is a global term for a generalized tendency to respond in a particular way. It would come under the heading of what Allport has called a "cardinal trait," or McDougall a "master sentiment," which in itself is the integration of a great number of other traits.[29] What various religious writers have called the Christian virtues are what Allport would label a "central trait," or a dominant predisposition to respond in a particular way in a particular kind of situation. The idea of "obedient love" sums up an orientation which involves dynamic, temperamental, and ability traits. For a person to possess or to be controlled by such a cardinal trait, a high degree of integration would be indicated; there would have to be some ruling passion which would override all other passions. Most of us only approximate the complete integration which seems to be called for by writers in the field of theological ethics. We respond lovingly in selected relationships or on occasions. In most of us there is both inconsistency and looseness of integration.

---

[28] *Ibid.*, 74 ff.

[29] *Ibid.*, 341; William McDougall, *An Introduction to Social Psychology*, 2d Rev. Ed. (Boston, 1928).

"Obedient love" is difficult to define with precision. In II Corinthians 13, the Apostle Paul describes the kinds of relations that result from it. H. Richard Niebuhr turns his hand at a similar lyrical description of love. He recognizes that if the purpose of the church is "the increase among men of love to God and neighbor" it is important to be clear about what it is we are talking about.[30]

Since the existence of "obedient love" must be inferred from the quality of the relationships that obtain between persons, and since there is a variation in the quality of such relationships, and in the extent to which such relations approximate the norm of "perfection," it might be helpful for purposes of more effective measurement and description to adapt a research instrument invented by Carl Rogers. In order to measure the progress of a client toward health during therapy, he developed a scale of health using several continua of behavior and related these to stages in the process of therapy. This scale measures the quality of relationship which exists between the therapist and the client in terms of (1) Feeling and Personal Meanings; (2) Manner of Experiencing; (3) Degree of Incongruence; (4) Communication of Self; (5) Manner in which Experience Is Construed; (6) Relationship to Problems; and (7) Manner of Relating. Seven stages in the relationship have been described. The highest stage represents an ideal which has not been observed in the therapy situation. The scale has been tested with a high degree of reliability and of validity on a sizable population of persons in treatment.[31]

What is suggested by all these studies of traits is the need to attempt the construction of a scale of behavior which would describe various approximations to "obedient love." The value of such an attempt would be to sharpen our understanding of the meaning of a key term in Christian vocabulary and to

---

[30] H. Richard Niebuhr, *The Purpose of the Church and Its Ministry*, 35.

[31] Carl R. Rogers and Richard A. Rablen, "A Scale of Process in Psychotherapy," Mimeographed paper, University of Wisconsin, 1958; and Carl R. Rogers, "The Process Equation of Psychotherapy," an address given at the University of Pennsylvania, December 11, 1959.

provide some markers for the measurement of progress, as we forget what lies behind and strain forward to what lies ahead, pressing on toward the goal for the prize of the upward call of God in Jesus Christ.[32] It would also enable us to ascertain more accurately whether our clumsy attempts at Christian nurture are actually helping or hindering the process.

V

It is to be noted that Carl Roger's study of behavior (mainly verbal) took place in a special role-relationship. This suggests further that the concept of social role provides another useful tool for the study, description, and measurement of behavior. Scales of behavior would have to be constructed for the various roles which we sustain. Therefore we need to consider briefly the meaning of social role in the development and expression of personality. According to Donahue, Orbach, and Pollak,

Objectively, a role is constituted by a collection of patterned sequences of behavior which forms a meaningful unit and consequently usually can be given symbolic identification through a name. . . . Normatively, a role is characterized by a set of rules or norms of behavior which are deemed appropriate to the particular position in the social order or in interpersonal relations which its name signifies. . . . Thus a person is identified as having a given role to *enact* in terms of a position he *occupies* in social life. . . . Subjectively, the enactment of a role represents a personal interpretation and unique integration of normative and behavioral elements.[33]

Ralph Linton has said that when a person "puts the rights and duties which constitute [his] status into effect, he is performing a role. Role and status are quite inseparable." [34] So we see a role as a meaningful unit of behavior which is identifiable; it is a patterned sequence of acts which is influenced or

[32] Philippians 3:13, 14.

[33] Wilma Donahue, Harold L. Orbach, and Otto Pollak, "Retirement: The Emerging Social Pattern," in Clark Tibbitts, ed., *Social Gerontology* (Chicago, 1960), 332-34.

[34] Ralph Linton, *The Study of Man* (New York, 1936), 113-14.

shaped by cultural teaching and social pressure. It has to do with rights and duties in relation to a particular social position. As enacted by an individual it is a unique interpretation of what is expected from him, of how he intends to act. Obviously it would be styled in terms of his unique integration and development of psycho-motor abilities.

John Spiegel adds another dimension to our thinking about the nature of social role when he suggests "that no role exists in isolation but is always patterned to gear in with the complementary or reciprocal role of a role partner." [35] To take a role is to enter into a relation. Some of the pairs to be seen are husband-wife, parent-child, teacher-pupil, friend-friend, lover-lover, citizen-government, clergyman-parishoner, seller-buyer, physician-patient, and many others.

In the Kansas City Study of Adult Life, nine rating scales were used to measure performance in eight common roles. A role was defined as "a socially defined and prescribed pattern of behavior . . . learned or internalized by an individual so that it becomes a self-expectation." [36] The roles studied there included worker, parent, spouse and homemaker, citizen, church member, friend, and association member. These tended to fall into clusters. Under these headings it is possible to find a variety of paired roles or reciprocal relationships, which, in a manner similar to that between therapist and client which Rogers studied, could be measured against a norm of love.

To carry the analysis further, we have the role as conceptualized or pictured in the mind of the person taking it, his perception of how he is actually doing it, and the role as it is really enacted. We also note that the way this role is to be played may change subtly or dramatically in the course of aging. This concept has some similarities to that of the "orders" employed by ethicists such as Brunner.

---

[35] John Spiegel, "The Resolutions of Role Conflict within the Family," *Psychiatry,* 20 (1957) , 3.

[36] R. J. Havighurst, "The Social Competence of Middle-aged People," *Genetic Psychology Monographs,* 56 (1957) , 303.

The concept of social role helps to explain the molding effect of the cultural environment upon personality in encouraging the development of particular traits and particular types of character. The theory explaining the situational determinants of personality as set forth in social psychology and cultural anthropology has been summarized admirably by John Gillin:

> In general these studies have taught us at least two things. (1) There is a definite correlation between the socio-cultural constellations to which the child is exposed and the type of person he becomes as an adult. (2) The fact that human groups have developed so many ways of producing so many different types of adult personalities suggests that the possibilities of planned and manipulated personality development are very real.
>
> If we speak of these matters in terms of learning theory, we may say that the socio-cultural system creates for the infant and child a series of patterned stimulus situations. The system more or less consistently endeavors to elicit responses considered appropriate to such situations by the group as a whole, and to establish such responses as habits in the individual. It provides a constant drumfire of punishments for disapproved responses plus rewards for approved reactions. It tends to create within the individual a system of tensions, inhibitions, and acquired drives or motivations similar to and consistent with those of other members of the group or social category. It tends to force the internalization of all these patterned experiences through the use of symbols common to the group. And it molds this material into an internal organization and maintains it by a facade of customary pressures surrounding the developing child. Thus a child in any society is encased in a sort of "Iron Maiden" of socio-cultural pressures and channelized satisfactions which are intended to make him into the kind of person the members of the group want and expect him to be.[37]

To become a person is to be an actor playing a succession of roles before an audience. These roles are taken by the most accomplished players in the light of a commitment to a master

---

[37] John Gillin, "Personality Formation from the Comparative Cultural Point of View," in Clyde Kluckhohn and Henry A. Murray, eds., *Personality in Nature, Society, and Culture* (New York, 1949), 168.

role or a paradigmatic way of viewing the self.[38] The audience consists of those persons who are significant in one's life, whom one strives to please, upon whom one depends for satisfaction and fulfillment. The paradigms are supplied by the heroes and high status persons with whom a person identifies. They are known through their demonstration by the nurturing persons in one's world or as they are encountered in the love of a living tradition.

To become a Christian is to place oneself within the context of a community and a culture which embodies Christ. The Incarnation provides the paradigm for our relation to God and to neighbor. Entering into Christ, Christ enters into us. We put on Christ and, reflecting his glory, are transformed into the image of his maturity. The members of the Christian community are the nurturing persons.

VI

And so at last, after all of this, we may have arrived at the place where we could begin work on what was the original assignment for this paper, namely, a description of what might be expected by way of behavioral outcomes from a program of Christian education for adults. The next step might be to develop a design for research looking toward the construction of a scale of maturity in terms of "obedient love," as this might be expressed within the major role relationships sustained by individual persons. The neighbor is my wife, my child, my student, my employer, my father, my secretary. What does love mean in these relationships with respect to the concrete decisions which confront us daily? What are the dominant motifs of these relationships? How are they to be integrated into a Chris-

---

[38] I am indebted to my colleague, Sam Banks, Jr., Drew University, for this insight. The general thesis was reinforced by Norman O. Brown in a paper entitled "Symbolism of Personality," read to a colloquim on "Dynamic Psychology and Theological Meaning" at Drew University, on February 13, 1961. Another colleague, Carl Michalson, has called attention to Colossians 3:1-8, where the imperative "put on" can be interpreted as an injunction to take the role of a Christian.

tian character? The process of growth toward maturity might be plotted in stages, making use of the concept of developmental tasks. But always it should be borne in mind that it is by repentance and commitment, and not by achievement, that one is justified before God.

VII

So we have concluded that Christian faith does have behavioral outcomes. We have noted that these outcomes are not to be described or looked for in terms of conformity to mores, rules, regulations, or codes of conduct, or in terms of particular sets of actions. Rather, the behavioral outcomes of Christian faith are seen in a responsiveness to the neighbor's particular need in particular circumstances which is the expression of love in response to the way God has met us. We have concluded also that God's love transforms us and leads to a dynamic state of being or central tendency which can be designated as "Christian character." This character can be described only by naming its dimensions or patterns under such headings as virtues or traits. I have indicated that I believe it would be possible and fruitful, though not easy, to construct a scale of Christian maturity which would help us to clarify our much too facile speaking about Christian love, and to measure more precisely growth in Christian character.

However, two words of warning need to be said. The first is that the rational, analytical approach to personality is only one mode of knowing. Furthermore, it is a mode of knowing that is susceptible to an ossification of constructs that may prevent the emergence of creative insights, that is tempted often to mistake the part for the whole, and that may repress an awareness of the mystery of the self. One may know much about a person and not know him as a person. In making an analytical, objective approach to persons, too much of the self may be withheld to allow for the deepest kind of knowledge.

The second word of warning is that our teaching may become manipulative or that we may try to force persons into restrictive molds which represent our own finite conceptions of what ought to be, rather than to allow what is there to emerge, or to permit the person to respond in his own way to the world which is presented to him. In Christ there is an infinite range of possibilities, room for an infinite variety of expressions and reflections of the divine love. To reflect Christ is not to diminish individuality but to add luster to it. In him differences cohere and are transcended, not blotted out. If our commitment is to Christ rather than to our image of him, our prejudice, our objective, and our mold will be favorable to freedom, autonomy, and authenticity of response.

In all honesty, we need to admit that we do have models or prejudices in mind when we teach and that we do use our influence to reproduce them. These models must be subject to the judgment of God in Christ, who eludes exactness of description, who is beyond slavish imitation, and who transcends our attempts to measure up to him. We point not to ourselves and our understandings but beyond ourselves to Christ. Our models are to be pointers to, or line drawings of, that which we hope each of us can meet personally and come to know better.

Therefore, we hold the experimental, analytical, scientific approaches to the descriptions of the behavioral outcomes of the Christian witness in a tension with the existentialist, phenomenological, and even mystical approaches, hoping that such tension may be creative. We seek to clarify the image of the fullness of the stature of Christ which lies behind our statements of objectives, but we stand ready to let the image be reformed and transformed in the process of communion with our living Lord.

16. Criteria for Judging the Quality of Christian Education for Adults

C. ELLIS NELSON
Professor of Christian Education
Union Theological Seminary

Developing criteria for judging the quality of a Christian adult education program presents certain formidable problems at the outset. We cannot judge without a basis of judgment, so we are immediately faced with the problem of making explicit our conception of Christianity and its relation to the modern world.

For example, if one believes that Christian education is primarily the inculcation of correctly held beliefs, then his criteria will probably inquire about standard topics such as God, man, Christ, Bible, and church. He will then examine the church's program to see that proper balance and interrelation exist between these subjects, and also to appraise the effectiveness of the teacher in communicating these concepts.

Or, if one believes that Christianity is primarily a religious experience with a God who is immanent, then his criteria will probably pay little attention to formalized statements of belief. His interest will center more in human conduct, in the quality of interpersonal relationships, and in the ability of the educational program to help a person actualize his self-potential.

In addition to these two common points of view, many other variations of the concept of Christianity could be cited. This matter is further complicated by the denominational character of the Christianity we know. The officially held beliefs, especially those related to polity, create different settings for Christian adult education programs. Some denominational polity automatically excludes about half of the adults (the women) from positions of leadership, although their influence may be felt indirectly in the affairs of the church. Other denominations practice pure democracy whereby all adult members have the opportunity to participate. Some denominations use a representative democracy so that the effective decision-making body is only a small portion of the congregation. These official means of managing the institutional life of the church and the way in which they are used are, in themselves, a training technique that quietly but surely develops initiative or chills enthusiasm for the affairs of the church. These attitudes naturally permeate the Christian adult education program, since the officers of the church are also adults in the congregation. Methods used to take official action in the congregation have the status of being "right" and often govern the way the Christian education program is planned.

Our problem is further compounded by the purpose of evaluation. We could seek to evaluate the structure of the program: the equipment, facilities, formal standards and procedures that are used for Christian adult education. Although all of these are important, they will not be dealt with in this paper. We could seek to evaluate the growth of persons who participate in the program. This is perhaps the ultimate test of any program and may be the only fair basis on which to decide the efficacy of the program. However, to do this properly would involve research techniques far beyond the ability of the average minister or director of Christian education.

Even the program does not leave us without uncertainty. Surely the program for adults includes preaching, worship, and to some extent the administrative practices of the church. Yet if these are included, we go beyond what the adults can effectively control. Also, denominational policies or programs of the church formulated on the regional or national level in areas such as higher education and missions impinge on the work of the local church. Without overlooking these matters, let us think of criteria designed primarily for the local church and pertaining to those areas in which the adults have a large measure of jurisdiction. We shall therefore attempt to work out criteria for the total adult program of a local church by centering our attention on certain qualities that should characterize it. Moreover, we shall attempt to set forth the list of items in the criteria in such a way that they can be used by lay people who are attempting to evaluate their Christian education program for adults.

Each item in the list of criteria is stated as a question. The answer in many cases may be difficult to supply; yet some answer, even a tentative one, is necessary. The discussion following each item is designed to show the importance of the question and, in some cases, to indicate ways one can gather data in order to answer it.

Having indicated the inadequacy of using subject matter or experience as guiding units in criteria, what would be manageable units? For our purpose here, let us use as units of analysis those that help reduce the complexity of the problem by having fairly discernible boundaries—building blocks, if you will, that are interrelated yet, when put together, form a structure that is larger and different from each part.

The units suggested are: (1) conception of the role of education in the communication of the Christian faith; (2) the church in the community; (3) primary groups; (4) the family; and (5) the person. There is a certain artificiality about these units, but any set of units would be subject to the same criticism. These units have one virtue: each unit can be described in a semi-autonomous way and each is compounded of knowledge and experience, the basic ingredients of a theory of Christian education.

The Role of Education in the Communication of the Christian Faith

1. *What is the operating conception of the Christian faith?* Note that the question asks about "operating conception." If the church under analysis is a part of a creedal denomination, the answer might be given in formal theology. Yet "operating conception" does not mean formal theological statement, but rather the basis on which the church actually makes decisions. For example, do the decision makers have as a guiding image the "success" religion of popular Protestantism? If so, they will tend to plan their activities in such a way as to produce discernible, measurable results, such as an increased membership or an expanded budget, regardless of their formal theological creed. Or do the decision makers model the church on the pattern of a service institution that provides good constructive activities for all age groups?

Again, do the decision makers attempt to conform to an ecclesiastical model, such as the church being the place where "the word of God is preached and the sacraments rightly administered"? Another motif might be the church as "God's colony," a beachhead in a hostile environment. Some decision makers would want to make worship central and perhaps give special attention to the personal spiritual needs of the individuals in the congregation.

These conceptions are not mutually exclusive. Most churches will function with parts of these conceptions or develop others. Although we cannot say with certainty just what the operating conception is, we should attempt to write a tentative statement. This could be done by simply asking decision makers, ministers, and officers to give their ideas or by asking them to formulate a statement in a meeting called for that purpose. Other data can be obtained from a study of various areas of a church's life.
(1) An examination of the physical property, the use to which various buildings are dedicated, and the type of leaders employed for the various units of the church's program will indicate what that local congregation considers important and

worth supporting. (2) A critical analysis of the budget will often reveal the operating conception of the church. Jesus' words can be paraphrased, "Where a church's budget is, there is its heart also." (3) Next to budget, the clearest picture of the actual operating conception of the church is the list of characteristics desired in a new minister as formulated by the pulpit committee. Here is the church's real self-image. Here is what the congregation thinks it is and wants to be. Indeed, the formulation of the pulpit committee is a self-conscious effort to represent the current conception of the church, because that committee is usually carefully selected to represent proportionately all of the concerns and pressure groups within the church.

2. *What is the purpose of the Christian adult education program?* Unless the adult program is deliberately fashioned to some purpose, it will automatically be a tool of the operating conception. Fortunately, it is possible in many churches to have a class or group of adults existing for a purpose different from that of the decision makers. If there is a clear purpose for the Christian education of adults or for any unit of adults, it should be recorded. It is also fairly normal for adult groups to become institutionalized around a leader or a program. We must, therefore, record the purpose of all of the functioning units of adults. When this is done, we may find that we do not have a coherent program but rather a widely divergent number of groups with nothing in common but their adulthood.

Apart from the purposes of various existing groups, what is the purpose of the adult program as far as the church is concerned? Has the adult program been considered by an official group and has a purpose been formulated? If so, one can judge its adequacy in the light of local conditions. If not, one can then say that the adult program appears to be unimportant. We simply do not allow important matters to go unnoticed or unexamined.

Another way to approach the matter of purpose is to describe what the church expects from the educational venture. Some would consider the continued education of adults as unnecessary because attending worship and living exemplary lives are all that is expected. This notion also contains the idea that adults should be expected to teach children but not each other. Why is this attitude so common in American Protestantism? It may be that it is not primarily because the church has not heard of adult education; rather, it may be because many churches do not really want Christian adult education.

The minister may, unconsciously, fear the conditions that might arise if adults become deeply concerned about the nature and scope of the faith. The minister may have built into his personality the middle-class desire for order and control, with a distaste for events that appear unexpectedly or that disrupt established procedures. Moreover, his ego may be involved in maintaining a position of "expertness" in knowledge of the Bible and of skill as a church leader. If laymen become too concerned and articulate about procedures in the church or problems of faith, they may threaten the minister's values or his image as a leader. This is not a wholesale accusation against ministers; but it is a condition clear enough to explain why some ministers lack enthusiasm for, or fail to support, a well-rounded program for adults.

Also, let us not overlook the situation of the adults. Although they can learn about as efficiently up to age forty as they could in their youth, they don't need to. Adults already have a repertoire of learning that carries them through their regular responsibilities at their station in life. To engage in learning is to take on more work, of a difficult and uncertain nature. The average adult wants a social association more than education, so he does not often respond with excitement to learning opportunities that may cause him to change his life style.

There are also theological components related to purpose. On theological grounds, some would say that education can only prepare for the work of the Holy Spirit. Others would say that education is the development of understanding after religious experience; or, that education and religious development are so interrelated we cannot safely have one without the other. Any one of these positions may be influential in establishing, or citing as reasons for not establishing, a vigorous program of Christian adult education.

3. *Is there a plan for developing the program according to the purpose?* Perhaps at this point we should disassociate ourselves from the idea that a program is a highly organized, beautifully integrated arrangement of activities. Program just means that there is a plan consistent with a desirable purpose. It is possible, even desirable, that the program contain different kinds of units serving a variety of purposes. Program does not mean uniformity, and plan does not mean regimentation. To have a plan for Christian adult education, however, does mean that it is an important task in its own right—so important that a committee or board has the assigned responsibility of working out an overall strategy.

Along with the need for a plan is the need for a constant review of the program. Perhaps this is a good place to test the church's seriousness in adult education by asking if there is a committee or board regularly appointed and specifically charged to oversee the adult program. If so, does this committee also assay the various parts of the program regularly and have the authority to recommend modification of purpose and program to suit shifting conditions?

4. *Are adult communicant classes regularly held?* The way a church initiates new members is an important clue to its conception of the church. If the members believe the church is a club, they will encourage the "right people" to join and discourage all others. If the church leaders believe that the church is composed of the "saved," they will admit members on the basis of their statements of conversion.

We must first note that the practice of having communicant classes for adults is a recognition of the necessity of understanding the nature of the church. This conviction is tested by the length of time given to the classes, the type of leader supplied, and the seriousness with which the whole task is planned and carried out. The content of instruction in the communicants' class for adults gives a clear picture of what the church considers important. If the class discusses only matters related to the budget and the services available in the building, then the orientation is mainly to improve the performance of church-manship. If the occasion is used to open afresh the meaning of Christ for the individual and the church, then we might conclude that the effort is concerned with religious truth.

We must also note the way the church differentiates between adults who are joining the church on confession of faith and those who are transferring membership. The person who is transferring membership from another denomination or congregation is often handled in a very perfunctory way, as if the total meaning of the act were the shifting of his name from one church roll to another. When a person comes into a new community and a different church, his whole being is alerted to new relations, new ways of doing things, and fresh opportunities for expressing himself. We must exploit this opportunity to help the person understand the spiritual reality of the church or else he will assume that the church he is joining is a carbon copy of the church he has left. Therefore, some form of adult communicant class should be a requirement for every classification of adult membership.

The Church in the Community

5. *What is the guiding conception of the relation of the church to the community?* The church is intimately related to the immediate surrounding area. This may be a clearly defined geographical area, such as a village, a section of the city, or a more vaguely defined group of people living within commuting distance of the church. In any case, the community means the social matrix within which the church is located and carries on its ministry.

Again, we are not interested in a formal statement of theological principles but rather the actual operating conception utilized by the church under consideration. The following ideas are listed as illustrations. The church may be considered to be (1) an adjunct to the community; (2) an agency that personifies and inculcates moral virtues; (3) the conscience of the community, approving good and exposing evil; (4) a refuge from the conflicts and temptations of the world where the individual believer can be strengthened and encouraged; (5) the institution that by ceremony and instruction confirms the social values and blesses the means whereby the community gains its livelihood; or (6) the institution that identifies the problems men have and then brings to bear on these problems an intelligence that is informed by God's previous revelation of his Word.

Obviously there will not be unanimity among members of the congregation as to what the church's relation to the community ought to be. Our interest is in two facets of the problem: (1) how the various conceptions are handled within the church itself and (2) characteristics of the church's program developed as a result of its operating conception of the relation of the church to the community.

Assuming different conceptions within the congregation, how do they handle these conflicting claims? The official body probably sets its operating conception by a series of decisions based on matters that press for decision. For example, will the church allow its equipment to be used by the Boy Scouts? Another way of looking at the operating conception is to examine the type of people selected for leadership of the church. Are the leaders truly representative of the actual congregational membership, or are they all carefully screened so that a person cannot be a leader of the church unless he is an approved type of person, one who embodies the community virtues. It is extremely important to note also the areas where the church officials do not exercise decision, because this also defines the idea of the church's role in the community. For example, has the church taken a stand, made a declaration, budgeted money, or engaged in any action about juvenile delinquency, gambling, or racial inequalities?

By an examination of these areas one can derive a clear but tentative statement. However, it is also important to note how the divergent views of the church's place in the community are handled. When members of the congregation question official action, are these members allowed to express themselves or are they shunted off to places or leadership where they cannot be effective in changing the church's policy? Another way is to ask the question, "Is there a process whereby the adults can study these matters, form considered opinions, and convey their opinions to the official board of the church?"

6. *What is the role of adults in the ministry of the church?* The conception of the church's place in the community may determine in part the role of adults in the ministry of the church. The congregation, for example, could interpret its function prophetically but could expect only the ordained minister to proclaim the word of judgment. Congregations probably expect the minister to be the one who ministers since he is trained, has the time and equipment and, sometimes, the staff to do so. This idea leaves the laity as a fellowship to enhance the reputation and expand the influence of the institutional aspects of church life.

Against this common view must be placed the notion that the laity are also a priesthood. That is, laymen should minister to each other, not just in visiting the sick, but in sharing problems and temptations. Perhaps the way Alcoholics Anonymous functions in a mutual ministry wherein members support, guide, and suffer with each other is nearer to the New Testament conception of the church than the common Protestant expectation of a differentiated and trained set of professional leaders.

These two views make for different kinds of adult programs. In the first, the minister functions for the congregation so that adults become an audience and custodians of institutional well-being. In the second, the minister's approach makes the congregation the active participants in the real struggle of the soul and society.

7. *Is there a plan for coordination of the congregation's program within the community?* The adults of the church are the adults of the community, a simple fact often overlooked by the church. If the church views itself as different from the community or as an institution to be nurtured for its own wel-

fare, then both the program and leaders of the congregation will overlap and be in competition with the community. If the congregation has a self-image of service, then some elements of the congregation's program for adults will be coordinated with those of the community.

Perhaps the most serious aspect of this matter relates to leadership. Does the congregation have a process of allocating leadership? That is, do the adults make a matter of deliberation the way they will spend their leadership? With money, the matter is self-evident: the budget is spent according to need and policy. Why not budget leadership according to need and policy? Perhaps the best service for Mrs. A is to be free of all church assignments the year she is P.T.A. president, so that her energies might go into improving public education. And during the year that Mr. B is a member of the city council or public library board he might be freed of church assignments in order to spend his energies there. An act like this on the part of the church will not only support Mrs. A. and Mr. B., but it will demonstrate that some of the work of the Christian is to be done in the community for the general welfare.

8. *Is the congregation concerned with national and world-wide problems?* Parochial interests are relatively easy to develop and maintain because their importance is self-evident. Today the world is so interrelated that we cannot avoid the demand for Christian witness everywhere. Contrariwise, we must not overlook the meaning of events that happen elsewhere for life as we know it in a local community.

Group Life

9. *Are primary group experiences provided?* For our purposes here, let us define a primary group as one large enough to contain a variety of people, small enough to allow for a considerable amount of discussion and sharing of experience, and homogeneous enough to give stability. Groups may range from twelve to twenty in size, although other sized groups may work

equally well. These groups must meet regularly enough, usually once a week, to develop a quality of interpersonal relations marked by honesty and spontaneity.

Such a definition does not imply that large Bible classes, men's brotherhood meetings, and the like are without merit. Rather, such large, infrequent, formal groups can fulfill only a limited purpose. The primary group can give an intimacy of concern and flexibility of programming that is virtually impossible in a larger group. For example, a primary group may not need the traditional lecture-type leader, for members can work in small committees on various projects. In this way, the leadership can be delegated to various members according to ability.

Such a definition implies a theory of education: that change in goals and motives will be faster when a person has an opportunity to participate in a group sharing common purposes. Unless such a group experience is provided, an adult will not have a regular place to test his own developing theology or to experience the stimulation of others who are struggling to make ethical decisions.

10. *Are primary groups provided for all adults?* Women whose children are in school or college represent a vast leisure class in America, and the church often unwittingly has patterned its adult program to fit their needs and time schedule. Men's Bible classes or occasional brotherhood meetings are fitted into the men's time schedule and usually consist of lectures or discussion. More recently young adult groups have been formed around their need and time schedule. Congregations will often consider their adult work healthy if several of these groups are in operation when actually many adults are overlooked (older adults) and some groups (medical doctors) are not considered at all. But if we are concerned to provide groups for all, schedules can be made to include older adults and even doctors.

11. *Are primary groups involved in a cycle of Christian learning?* We must face at once the human propensity for ease, especially in the matter of religion. The Christian faith demands

of us that we use our minds to interpret the Bible and our lives to express the meaning of God's will for us today. This is difficult. This requires disciplined attention to the task and a humble, teachable spirit as well as remarkable courage. On every hand there are obstacles. We prefer comfort for our spirit, just as we do for our bodies. One editor of church school curriculum has said that the story of the Prodigal Son showed up so many times in so many different lessons about such a wide variety of topics that he had to give instructions to his editors to suggest to writers that other Biblical material be used. Selecting stories of this type illustrates our exaggerated concern with what God does for us without the corollary of our responsibility to God.

We have already implied in other questions related to the nature of the church that our culture presents several pressing problems. In American middle-class society, which largely makes up our churches, the virtues of success and achievement, of respectability and morality by code, of the image of individual man overcoming all obstacles by will power dominate the groups within the church.

We are therefore faced with personal reticence to venture into anything that disrupts and disturbs our hard-won psychological equilibrium. We are also faced with social pressures that perpetuate the middle class style of life. These two conditions explain why most church people want a Christian education curriculum that gives them something they can discuss cognitively rather than a full cycle of Christian learning that will expect them to act as well as to think in a Christian way.

To ask the question, "Are primary groups involved in a cycle of Christian learning?" is to state sharply the distinctive nature of these groups. A cycle of learning means that the whole group is involved in a process of thought-word-deed related to the faith. Although we are trained to think that thought precedes word, and that these two condition deed, we need to give that notion a radical review. In some cases though and word condition deed; in most cases the deed and the decisions that surround it are done apart from a guiding Christian principle.

This is due (1) to the fact that we simply are not trained to apply principles to action since we live in a pragmatic, rationally controlled culture; (2) to the complex problems of our modern industrial society which have outrun the morals formulated by the previous generations; and (3) to our training to separate the spiritual from other material, making it easy to be fiercely competitive and antagonistic in our economic life and assuaging the guilt thereby produced by good deeds or holy thoughts in the spiritual realm.

In our primary groups we want a cycle of Christian learning. If we can really foster the traditional thought-word-deed notion, then we should not hesitate in practicing that method; but we should not equate alertness to ideas with Christian faith. Perhaps we would more quickly establish the necessity of cycles of learning and give purpose to our program if we started with deed and worked back to Biblical material. The deed is real, the deed involves oneself, it commits us as thought and word do not. The deed presses every day; it cannot be postponed or held tentatively as a thought can. For this reason we need to give more attention to what men do, especially what they do when they are working. For most people, housewife as well as husband, work is the real world they cannot escape, and for many it is also their major creative effort.

One way to approach the matter would be a frank sharing of ethical choices which different people in the group have to face, and then development of a study of pertinent materials that would help shape a discussion in the light of the Christian faith. Another approach is to form groups on the basis of occupation and thereby assume a community of interest and a common background at the outset. There are difficulties in each of these approaches, but both assume the need to develop the Christian faith inductively, starting at the point of the person's involvement in the world.

12. *Is there a proper balance in the cycle of learning?* We assume that the cycle is thought-word-deed, and one cannot predict the amount of attention that should be given each element. There is also a necessity for seeing that various areas of concern are explored. The group may spend a long time on

race relations with great profit, but the whole of Christian enterprise is not contained within that concern. This means that someone in the group must take the initiative to introduce and show the significance of other areas of concern that are related to the one with which the group has been working.

Also, the group must consider somewhere in the cyle of learning Biblical material and the traditions of the church. Without an understanding of these materials we are cut off from our heritage. The case could probably be made for the notion that the Bible is not read nor studied by adults, not because it is dull or foreign to their thought forms but because of the non-rational attitude associating the Bible in their minds with the restricted code of their parents and other adults who trained them as children. An ambiguity arises at this point, because the parent and other adult socializers also left in their children a respect for the Bible. Perhaps "holy" is a correct description of what most adults feel about the Bible: holy in the sense that they respect it and associate, in a general way, what they consider valuable with its contents. They react to the Bible as they react to their conscience: with fear and respect.

We should not, therefore, assume that any one method of Bible teaching or study is preferred or contains a panacea for Biblical illiteracy. Rather, we must proceed on the basis of an attitudinal substructure that can be re-educated in a genuine way only at a slow pace and with great care. That attitudinal substructure must change before any significant Christian education can take place. The primary group must incubate a more mature relationship to God. Understanding the God of the Bible and how he acted and the way he was understood and misunderstood in the past provides us with our surest guide for our own response to him. We must help adults go beyond information about the Synoptic problem to such an understanding of the early church that the Synoptics are no longer a problem but a living testimony of men who experienced the love of God in Jesus Christ.

13. *Is there a way of helping adults become related to a group?* If our belief about the need for group experience in the church is sound, then we must have a plan for helping adults

become affiliated with a group. Even in smaller churches this can become a problem, for we forget people who do not regularly attend or who work on a time schedule that prohibits attendance on Sundays. Perhaps more important is the need for having a way to help adults shift to different groups when conditions change. Perhaps a good question to ask of our program is: "Can adults move from one group to another as the need requires?"

14. *Is there a regularized way of obtaining leaders for adult groups?* All of the foregoing questions hover about a conception of leadership. It is assumed that leadership, at least in the beginning of a group's life, is in a person. Later, when the group obtains cohesion, various leadership roles may be passed around. For example, a small team may prepare a report for specific discussion, another team may be making an on-the-spot investigation to report later to the group, etc. But to get the process started a person must have the training, vision, and verve necessary to lead a group of adults. Often a church will have one or two such persons or the professional leaders must consider this venture important enough to give it first priority. The basic question then becomes, "Is there a regularized way to duplicate leaders?"

By "regularized" we mean a deliberate effort to secure and prepare leaders for adult primary groups from the adults in the congregation itself. The word "prepare" should not be interpreted as a static norm, such as the taking of a course on leadership or formal educational attainment. Rather, "prepare" should be interpreted to mean alertness to growth, personal religious experience that is meaningful for life's encounters, intellectual alertness, devotion to the Lord of the church, and continuous stimulation to explore the relationship of faith to life.

15. *Is there a regularized way of obtaining leaders for church activities?* Almost all of the leadership of the local congregation must come from adults. Too often the various units of the church compete with each other for popular or well-known leaders. This is damaging in itself and fatal to the long-run

interests of the church. An adult program must assume responsibility for securing and preparing leaders for all the units of the church. Therefore, the adult program must contain not only a way of seeking out leaders but also ways of giving them special preparation for leadership tasks other than the general preparation they receive as active members of an adult primary group.

Home

16. *Is the home considered a Christian educational unit in itself?* American Protestantism has gone through several phases in its understanding of the role of the home in Christian nurture. One notion is that the home is an object of Christian education. In this view the adults are assembled in the church to study the home; materials are supplied to help them to be better parents or to mold the home into some ideal institution such as a microcosm of democracy. In this view the church promotes the ideal home and seeks to realize it. Another notion that has had wide acceptance is the view that the home and church are to work together in Christian nurture. This view necessitates common materials to be used by parents and teachers in Christian education. In actual practice this view uses the home to reinforce what the church wants taught, as the materials are shaped largely to the child's participation in formal classroom work of the church.

Another view is now emerging that gives promise of a more fruitful relation, namely, a frank recognition of the home as a unique institution with special and untransferable functions. In this view the church reinforces what the home should do and tries to make possible a better functioning of the home as a unit. To this end, materials are prepared to help the home: stories to be used at home, songs and activities that fit in the family festivals, etc. The family camp is an illustration of an activity that can be fostered by the church but is designed to help the family function as a unit. This view sees the parent as a teacher in the home, and therefore must prepare the parents to be teachers there.

An important part of this proposition is the Christian education of the parent in terms of his own need and at his level of competence. If the parent as a person is having a stimulating and helpful experience in the church at his point of need, his genuine affection for the affairs of God will be communicated to the child in hundreds of little ways.

17. *Are there therapeutic opportunities for family problems?* Family counseling is notoriously difficult because several people are involved and each has different needs. Competent family counseling is beyond the service that most churches can supply, unless they have ministers who are qualified to work in this area. But even if the minister is qualified, he probably could not handle the number of cases in the average church; and some way must be found to provide families with guidance when domestic crises develop. A well-rounded adult program must have a system of referral whereby families in crisis can get the help they need. Perhaps the minister should be the person to whom adults look for referrals to a family guidance agency or psychiatrist.

The Person

18. *What is the conception of the nature of the person?* This question seems so vague and abstract that it appears impossible to answer with any assurance. It will be useful, however, if it stirs up a puzzled brow and a perplexed counter-question such as, "What do you mean by the nature of the person?" With a little experience one can sense the way the leaders of the program understand the meaning of a person.

In many human organizations, including the church, persons are manipulated and used to the glory of the institution. Given life the way it is, a degree of manipulation is inevitable. That is, we must adjust our private wishes and feelings to the welfare of the group or anarchy will be the result. But the degree of manipulation is important. Do individuals feel that they have a chance to express themselves, to have a measure of control over the manner in which they will work in the church? Another way to ask the question is, "Do adults feel that the congregational leaders have a concern for persons in their work even though the institutional aspects of the church's life must sometimes overrule individual desires?"

19. *What is the conception of the role of the person in Christian education?* The conception we have of the person in the Christian education process influences decisively the way we shape our program. The mental image that guides much of our Protestant thought is that of the free individual capable of changing his life and the social institutions in which he participates. Such a notion simplifies tremendously the task of the church, for her energies can then be directed toward the redemption of the individual. It is assumed that this individual will in turn improve the institutions of society.

This idealism has native American roots related to our frontier mentality, our sheltered position from enemy attack, and our ever-increasing rate of economic growth based in large part on our abundance of various natural resources. But this attitude is not without its social liabilities; for as an ethic it releases the man of wealth and political power from responsibility for the poor, unemployed, or outcast. Individualism of this type can be a mask used sincerely, nevertheless used, to hide the structure of power that exploits individuals.

Probably no more effective strategy has ever been devised to control man than making him believe that as an individual he is capable of changing his system. Against the system the average man is powerless. We have moved into a day when the individual can find his economic and political strength only in groups, but many of our churches continue the line of interpretation that comes from our frontier-agrarian past which says that the individual is a free agent capable of changing social institutions. If we continue the line of interpretation which places the individual at the center of our attention, the goal of Christian education becomes a flowering and perfecting of individual gifts.

The centrality of the person as a concern of the Gospel must not be denied. The person is responsible to God for the character and conduct of his life. But the Biblical image of man never represents man apart from the community. The Old Testament is the story of a people in which the person's fate is inexorably interrelated with the destiny of the nation. In the New Testament the people of God are the church; without the society of believers there would be no Gospel of remembered acts of the Apostles. The letters of Paul were written to congregations about the common problems of the church. The corporateness of the Christian faith is celebrated in the Lord's Supper and demonstrated every time a person is baptized in the presence of the congregation. This is our way of recognizing that the person is a product of his interaction with social forces that surround him.

What effect does this image of the person have on Christian education? It first means that we must help educate people into a new kind of personhood. That is, the content of our Christian faith (Biblical, historical, etc.) should be explored to help us understand the perennial human conditions to which the Biblical message addresses itself regardless of cultural or historical epoch. This effort will not yield the glib individualism of popular American Protestantism, but it will represent a profound awareness of our human situation that will make the Biblical affirmation become true to us. It will cause us to ask the question, "Lord, what will thou have me do?" Second, having come to the place where that question is urgent, we will need to consider ourselves as under constraint to revise and reorder the corporate structure in which we live, yet not putting our faith in such activities as a substitute for the reality of God in our lives.

20. *Are there opportunities for personal counseling?* Any program that is effective will raise serious questions within adults as to their personal adequacy, guilt, frustrations, etc. Some of these inner disturbances are normal for anyone who is growing in self-understanding and are best healed by an understanding and supporting primary group. Some adults, however, will not find their way so naturally because their problems may be too deep and obscure. For these people there must be a

personal counseling service available either through the minister or some agency in the community. It is not ethical to
project a program for adults with exploration into personhood
as a goal without including a plan for effectively helping those
who begin to realize their need and who develop a desire for
professional counseling service.

Postscript

These twenty questions call attention to areas considered important for judging the quality of a Christian education program for adults. They are not, however, to be considered final
and definitive. They should be used by a local church committee as a first draft to start thinking and direct energy toward
the formulation of their own criteria. When that is done,
then the adults should be given an opportunity to express themselves regarding the value of the program in which they are
participating. In fact, adult primary groups could profitably
spend several months of their study time discussing the criteria
and in so doing determine for themselves their *raison d'être*.

17. Measurement and Evaluation in Christian Adult Education: Present Status and Future Possibilities

LEONARD A. SIBLEY, JR.
Secretary for Research, Board of Parish Education
United Lutheran Church in America

Suppose that you are told to go out and look for a treasure. No one gives you any clues about what the treasure is, where to look for it, whether you are getting closer to it; in fact, if you pick it up in your hand, no one will tell you that you have found it. Your chances of finding the treasure under those conditions would be slim indeed.

Contrast that with the more traditional treasure hunt, in which at every point you find clues pointing you toward your final goal. The clues may be cryptic, but with imagination and hard logic you can figure them out. You go from clue to clue always drawing nearer to the treasure and always seeing more and more clearly what the treasure is. In this kind of treasure hunt, you have no doubt when you have reached your objective.

These two types of treasure hunts provide an analogy for the difference between Christian education with and without evaluation. It has been customary in Christian education to go on from year to year setting up programs which are supposed to represent progress and improvement. But, if we do not evaluate to find out whether real progress has, in fact, been achieved, then we can go on changing things indefinitely without making any significant improvement. It has also been customary in Christian education to become dissatisfied with existing programs and to discard them completely in favor of the new. But, if we do not first evaluate to discover the values of existing programs, we are likely to discard any solid progress which we may have made in the past. Evaluation in Christian education provides the "clues" by which we can discover how well we are moving toward the "treasure"—Christian education which contributes in vital ways to each individual's growth toward greater Christian maturity.

Evaluation may be defined as any process by which we systematically gather and analyze objective evidence about an educational program, as the basis for objective judgments about the value and effectiveness of the program. Measurement is the process of applying some objective scale or standard to the evidence which we have collected. It is usually a part of any process of evaluation, but it does not involve the judgmental and decision-making aspects of evaluation.

Every curriculum, no matter how carefully planned and prepared, is a hypothesis. It represents the best guess of its creators as to what will produce effective Christian education. It may be a very promising hypothesis, built on solid foundations of educational theory, research, experience, and theology. But it is still a hypothesis and must be tested. The purpose of evaluation is to find out how much learning and what kinds of learning take place when the curriculum is used. When we have made such evaluations, then we are ready to move ahead confidently in revision of the program for greater effectiveness or development of a new program.

Types of Evaluation

Ralph W. Tyler has provided a useful framework in which to think about evaluation. Evaluation can be classified into three types, depending upon which aspects of the program are being studied in the evaluative process.

1. *Structure evaluation* deals with the conditions under which education takes place. It asks about the physical conditions: buildings, classroom facilities and equipment, teaching time available, size of class. It also asks about the qualifications of those who guide the educational process: the educational backgrounds, training, and attitudes of leaders. When we evaluate a program of Christian education on the basis of its structure, we are making the assumption that good results will occur when education takes place under good conditions. This is often a shaky assumption. All of us have seen poor education going on in the most lavish and up-to-date facilities, and most of us have seen good education taking place under very poor conditions.

Correctly used, structure evaluation can be very useful. At the national level, structure evaluation includes descriptive research designed to provide accurate information about the conditions under which curricula and programs of Christian education are used in local congregations. Without such information, it is difficult to provide materials which are adaptable to the variety of situations found across a denomination. At the local level, structure evaluation is represented by the survey of its Christian education program which a congregation makes before building a new educational unit.

2. *Process evaluation* deals with what teachers or pupils do in the educational process. It asks about class activities, pupil interest, participation and enthusiasm, teaching methods. This type of evaluation also involves an assumption—that good results will follow if certain activities take place in the educational process. This is sometimes a valid assumption. For example, carefully controlled studies have shown that individuals usually learn more when they participate in, and are actively involved in, the educational process. Therefore, we can evaluate an educational program on the basis of how much pupil involvement and participation it produces.

Such conclusions are not always valid, however. Research has shown that church school teachers tend to judge the success of a program on the basis of pupils' interest, attention, and participation. A teacher could tell jokes for thirty minutes, have good interest, attention, and even some participation. But it would not be likely to be a successful Christian learning experience. All of us have attended conferences which were successful in terms of interest, attendance, and involvement, but were unsuccessful in producing permanent changes in the understanding, attitudes, or behavior of those who attended.

Process evaluation also has important uses. At the national level, an important use of process evaluation is the study of teachers' reactions to, and use of, curriculum materials. It is often startling, and sometimes horrifying, to see how great a difference there is between what curriculum writers have in mind when they plan materials and what teachers actually do when they use materials. Curriculum materials have not been successfully prepared until they get themselves used in the way that they are supposed to be used. Process evaluation can give us information about how teachers use materials. This type of evaluation can also provide information about how teachers feel about materials. Materials which teachers do not like are less likely to be used effectively and, in the long run, are not likely to prove acceptable to the church.

3. *Product evaluation* deals with changes in the learner which result from the educational process. The purpose of education is to change the learner in some way—for example, to guide him toward deeper understandings, more wholesome attitudes, and more responsible patterns of action. Therefore we cannot say that the educational process has been successful until such changes have occurred.

In considering product evaluation, it is important to remember that we usually try to evaluate the extent to which the curriculum achieves its own objectives. The ultimate purpose of the whole process of Christian education is a total response of the personality in faith, commitment to God. In most cases we do not seek to evaluate this ultimate product. We rather seek to evaluate the extent to which the curriculum is successful in achieving its own, more proximate objectives—the extent to which it produces the changes in understanding, attitude, and behavior which it has been designed to produce.

Product evaluation is the most difficult type of evaluation, but it is the only kind of evaluation which can really tell us how effective our program has been. We may have the best possible educational facilities, and use the latest approved teaching methods; but if the learner does not change in the desired direction, the program is not successful.

Steps in Curriculum Evaluation

No matter what is to be evaluated, there are certain basic problems which must be dealt with. These problems also suggest the steps which have become generally accepted as basic procedures for most educational evaluation.

1. *Decide what is to be evaluated.* In education, these are usually objectives, statements of the changes which we hope will take place in learners as a result of the educational program. Stating objectives is one of the most difficult parts of curriculum and program development. A common tendency in Christian education is to be satisfied with objectives which are so vague and general that they give no adequate guidance either for program and curriculum development or for evaluation. It is helpful to remember that the same characteristics which make objectives suitable for evaluation also usually make objectives more helpful for curriculum development and teaching:

A. Good objectives are stated in terms of changes which take place in the learner rather than what the teacher does or the learner experiences in the learning process. "To provide an experience of Christian fellowship" is not a suitable objective, since it does not indicate why we want the learner to have this experience, or what we hope will happen to him as a result of it. "To help the learner to gain a deeper insight into the meaning of the communion of saints" is better. The fact that a teacher provides certain experiences for the learner is important only if those experiences change the learner in some way.

B. Good objectives are stated accurately and clearly. They should mean the same thing to every person who works with them. Vague words such as "understand," "enthusiasm," "appreciate," and "feel," should be clarified in terms of what the learner who achieves these objectives will say, do, think, or feel. Accurate objectives are related directly to the course or program. They include all important aspects of the course or program, and they do not include elements which are not specifically provided for in the course or program. Accurate objectives do not include terms or elements which are given only lip service or which are included only to make the objectives sound better. Religious terms such as the "will of God" and "the redemptive love of God," and life-involvement terms such as "daily-life problems," should be included in objectives only if the course or program provides specific means by which changes related to those terms might be achieved.

C. In so far as possible, good objectives are stated in terms of observable changes which take place in the learner. This is the basic standard. Objectives should give clear-cut and definite answers to such questions as these: "What changes or reactions would I look for in the learner that would make me feel that this course or program has been successful? What would he do, say, or think that would lead me to believe that he had made progress toward the purpose of this course or program?"

Sometimes it is not possible to state Christian education objectives in such behavioral terms. The changes we hope for may be inner and not directly observable. Or we may feel that the change we are seeking is too general to be summed up in a list of specific behavior characteristics. In that case, the curriculum builders and evaluators have the further responsibility to go on and state criteria for their objectives. This means that the answers to the questions listed in the previous paragraph are provided, not by the objectives themselves, but by a list of critical responses or criteria. In other words, we are saying, "Here is our general objective, which describes a kind of growth or learning which cannot be directly observed. So here is a list of responses or ways of behaving which can be observed, and which we feel would be reliable indicators that an individual is making progress toward the objective."

The definition of objectives is a difficult and frustrating procedure. It is not too difficult to get people to agree on very general statements of objectives. But when we try to interpret the general objectives in terms of what the learner would do if he had achieved the objective, then we find much less agreement. Good objectives are not only essential to good research, but they are also the foundation for effective curriculum and program. Writers can write better curriculum when they have thought out carefully what they hope their materials will accomplish. Teachers who know what they are trying to do for their pupils are better teachers. Learners who know what they are supposed to learn do more learning.

2. *Devise appropriate methods for gathering evidence about the curriculum or program.* A wide variety of evaluational devices has been developed. These include questionnaires, objective tests (true-false, multiple choice), essay-type tests, situational tests, sociograms, observational techniques, and many more. From this variety, we must select the types of devices which will provide the best evidence concerning our objectives and will be most practical in our situation. In making this selection several factors are involved.

A. Relevance. Appropriateness, or relevance, is an important quality of evaluational situations. That is, the evaluation device should call for, or bring out, the kinds of behavior envisioned in the objectives. For example, paper and pencil tests may be entirely appropriate for testing the learning or understanding of content material. Research has shown, however, that such tests are usually somewhat invalid as tests of behavior. There is usually a wide difference between what a person says he would do in a situation and what he actually does in the situation. Sometimes, of course, those are the only tests we can use. Then it is especially important to be aware of their limitations.

Evaluation devices should be based directly on the objectives of the curriculum or program. In developing devices, we ask,

"If I had taught this course myself, what would pupils do, say, feel or think which would make me feel that the course had achieved its objectives? What kinds of evaluation devices can I develop which will give evidence about the presence or absence of these reactions?"

B. Freedom of response. If evaluation is to provide guidance for curriculum revision and improvement, it must do more than simply provide a "Yes" or "No" answer to the question, "Have pupils learned?" Such an answer provides little guidance for improvement. Rather, evaluation must answer such questions as these: "What have pupils learned? How deep is their understanding? What are their misunderstandings?"

For this reason, evaluation devices are usually more fruitful when they provide freedom of response for the learner—when he can respond in his own words or act in a natural way. It is difficult to construct multiple-choice or true-false questions in which the correct answer is not obvious to all but the least sophisticated. Moreover, responses to such questions often give "Yes-No" answers which do not provide the differential analysis needed to guide curriculum development. Test situations, in so far as possible, should be natural parts of the educational process, and the learner should be free to respond in his own way, as much as possible in his own words.

C. Practicability. Sooner or later (preferably sooner) we must face the problem of the cost of evaluation. Some very valuable methods of data collection may be ruled out by their cost. For example, tape recordings may be a valuable method of collecting evidence about the teaching-learning process in the group. But it takes just as long to listen to a tape recording as it did to make it in the first place. Transcribing a tape recording of a group session is a difficult and time-consuming process. Therefore, in most cases, other methods of data collection must be substituted.

"For which of you, desiring to build a tower, does not first sit down and count the cost, whether he has enough to complete it?" All of the steps in evaluation should be carefully planned in advance, so that we do not devise methods of data collection which will prove impracticable, and so that we do not collect data which we later find ourselves unable to analyze.

D. Representativeness of sample. As we design devices for collecting data, we must also decide on the group (or sample) from which we plan to collect this data. A local congregation might test its entire "population"—all of its church school pupils. In most educational procedures, however, we cannot test everybody, so we must test a sample which is supposed to represent everybody. The most important aspect of a sample is not its size—public opinion polls use samples of 1,000 people to represent everybody in the United States. The most important aspect of a sample is its representativeness—the degree to which it is an accurate reflection or model of the total population. These same public opinion polls select their samples with the greatest care; and they consider a well-selected sample such a valuable asset that they guard their sample lists under top security.

A few general comments can be made about sampling. A volunteer sample is seldom a valid sample. If you send a questionnaire to 1,000 people and get 300 responses, you cannot draw valid conclusions from the responses of 300 volunteers. They may be those who are most enthusiastic about your program, or they may be those who are most critical of your program; but they are almost certain to differ in some way from the 700 people who did not respond.

For most evaluations, a random sample is the simplest and most useful. That is, you first decide how many groups or individuals you can include in your study. Then you select these from some list which contains every group or individual which could possibly be included in the study. This is usually done by picking a starting point at random, and then selecting every 5th, 10th, 35th or 60th name—whatever interval will produce the number you want in your final sample. Then it is important to try to get responses from every individual you have selected.

Good sampling is so important and so difficult that a qualified consultant can be used to good advantage in selecting a sample for an evaluation.

3. *Analyze the evidence provided by the people in your sample.* Masses of specific data must be reduced and summarized to show general trends, differences, and results. This analysis must be objective: just as much weight must be given to evidence which is critical of your program as is given to evidence which is favorable to the program. Selecting a few glowing testimonials may be helpful in promotion, but it is not objective evaluation.

Data analysis usually involves a combination of activities. Some of the most common types are:

A. Evaluation: judging the value of a piece of evidence—an essay, a report, an observation of behavior. The judgment usually involves asking such a question as, "To what extent does this piece of evidence show progress toward the objectives of the course or program or lack of such progress?" The judgment is usually put in some quantitative form: a rating, a ranking, or even a simple "present-absent" categorization. For reliability, it is usually best to have several people independently judge each piece of data, and then pool their judgments.

B. Counting or scoring: making frequency counts or scoring items to give a total score. Although counting is a simpler process than judging, it does not necessarily precede judging. More often than not, there is nothing to count until the data have been judged.

C. Description: telling what a person or group did, and how it was done. Description does not usually involve interpretative judgments, as does evaluation. The purpose of description is to transcend the specifics and to generalize from them. A case study is an example of descriptive analysis.

D. Statistical tests: a mathematical form of logic testing. These may be used at any point in data analysis to seek differences and relationships and to test whether these differences and relationships are large enough so that we can be confident they are not merely accidental or chance variations.

4. *Draw conclusions and make judgments about the value of the program or curriculum on the basis of the evidence.* Evaluation for its own sake is pointless. Evaluation has meaning only

as it points the way toward better educational techniques, more effective educational methods. For this reason, the final use to be made of the results of evaluation should be decided before any of the preceding steps are planned. The whole process of evaluation should be designed in the light of the purpose for which it is being done and the use to be made of the results. The final report of results should be planned and written to be as understandable and helpful as possible to those who are going to use it; and to be as relevant as possible to the use to which it is to be put.

The Place of Evaluation in Curriculum Development

As a result of denominational efforts at curriculum evaluation, we are beginning to see more clearly the place of research and evaluation in the process of curriculum development. Research has already made significant contributions at several stages.

1. *Evaluation of existing curriculum.* As has already been indicated, we often become dissatisfied with existing materials and discard them entirely in favor of the new. In this way, we lose most of the value achieved in the past. The first step in revising a curriculum or even in developing a new one is to evaluate existing materials, asking, "What are the strengths and weaknesses of this program or curriculum?" In this way, we can build the new on the value of the old, at the same time seeking to overcome the weaknesses and deficiencies of the old.

2. *Descriptive research.* The purpose of this kind of research is to provide accurate descriptions of the conditions under which the new materials will be used and the people who will use them. It would be unthinkable for a large manufacturing corporation to know little or nothing about the characteristics of its raw materials, to have little or no information about the production activities within the factory, to have even less information about what happens to the product after it leaves the plant. Christian education is not an assembly line procedure; but we cannot write usable materials unless we know something

about the people who will use them, the ways in which they will be used, and the conditions under which they will be used. Descriptive research guides curriculum development by providing such information.

3. *Pre-testing or field testing of new materials.* One hour of pre-test is worth ten hours of armchair discussion. It is impossible to predict infallibly how teachers and pupils will react to a program, how they will use it, and how much they will learn from it. Field testing means selecting a representative sample of classes which will use curriculum in preliminary form and report on the results. On the basis of objective analysis of these reports, the curriculum can be evaluated and revised before publication. Field testing is often an extensive and expensive process, but it usually results in materials which are more usable and have a longer life span. It is certainly less expensive than committing the curriculum to print and then evaluating to discover how usable and effective it is.

These forms of research and evaluation can, of course, become part of a continuing cycle of curriculum development. After new materials have been published and used for a while, it is time to begin evaluating them again as existing materials and to do a new descriptive study to discover whether conditions have changed. The insights from these activities then become a basis for future curriculum development and field-testing.

Evaluation of Adult Christian Education

We have devoted this much space to a general discussion of evaluation for two reasons: (1) Up to the present time very little has been done specifically in the evaluation of adult materials and programs. Conversations with adult editors in most of the major denominations reveal a strong felt need for evaluation, but little concrete effort in that direction. (2) The basic principles and methods of evaluation apply to Christian education at all levels, including the adult.

There are, however, special problems connected with the evaluation of adult Christian education. Teaching procedures for adult classes are sometimes less structured, and there is usually more individuality among leaders of adult classes. Experience has shown that most teachers of children tend to follow fairly directly the suggestions given in the Teacher's Guide. We can, therefore, base some important types of evaluation devices directly on those suggestions. We cannot make such an assumption about leaders of adult classes. This means that evaluation and reporting devices for these classes must be less structured, allowing more room for individuality and variation.

Many natural methods of collecting evaluation data are available in children's classes but not in adult classes. Children use workbooks in class, and these books can easily be designed so that they provide evaluation data as the children use them. Children are also more accustomed to doing written work, which can also provide evaluation data. Many adult classes, on the other hand, are based mainly on lecture and discussion; and class members are not accustomed, in the natural course of classroom procedures, to producing any kind of individual written materials which can serve as data for evaluation.

In both public school and church school, children are accustomed to taking tests. Adults, on the other hand, are likely to view with some suspicion any special effort to test their learning. On the other hand, there is one approach which can be used with adult classes to overcome some of these problems. Adults can be "let in" on the purposes and procedures of the evaluation process, so that they feel that by providing evaluation data they are making an important contribution to the future educational program of the church. Under these conditions, adults will gladly do many things which they would ordinarily resist as a part of the classroom procedure.

Let us now look in more detail at the types of data which might be collected for the evaluation of adult materials and program.

1. Information from Teachers

A. Questionnaires can be based on the Teacher's Guide. The first step is to divide the materials in the Teacher's Guide into elements, separate ideas or procedures which are suggested or described. Teachers can then be asked to report on each element: "Was it used? If used, how successful was it? What problems were encountered in using it?" Questionnaires can usually be worked out in check-list form, and teachers can be asked to complete a questionnaire each week. This type of data is used for process evaluation. It answers such questions as these: "What types of materials will teachers use, not use? What approaches are most successful, least successful, from the teacher's point of view?" This approach is best suited to materials which are highly structured.

B. General questionnaires can be used at the end of a term or course. Teachers can be asked to respond to such questions as these: "What parts of the material were most helpful, least helpful, and why? What were the high points of the unit for the class, the low points? What teaching methods did you find most successful, least successful?" This type of evaluation can be used with any kind of program, from the most structured to the most informal. It provides less specific guidance for the curriculum revision than does the preceding type, since it asks teachers to report on an entire unit or term, rather than on a specific session.

C. Teachers can also be asked to report on signs of learning or growth on the part of class members. Such reporting can be either on a session-by-session basis or on a unit basis. Questions on such report forms must be carefully worked out so that they spell out the objectives for the course in terms of specific behavior or reactions which teachers might observe.

If data can be collected for developing the instrument, the "critical incident" method can provide fruitful data. This method was developed by John Flanagan at the American Institute for Research, of the University of Pittsburgh. A number of incidents are collected and classified into reactions which show progress toward the objective for the program, or lack of progress. Teachers are asked simply to check which of these reactions they have observed in class members during the course.[1] This kind of data from teachers provides an approach

---

[1] Cf., Paul B. Diederich, "Methods of Studying Ethical Development," *Religious Education,* 50 (1955) , 162-66.

to product evaluation. It looks at the results or outcomes of the program through the eyes of the teacher, who may or may not be an unbiased observer, but who is at least available as a source of data.

2. Information from Class Members

A. The "post-meeting reaction form" has frequently been used. Specific forms and questions are usually designed in the light of the objectives for the course or session. The following is a simple example:

(1) How did you feel about this session (check along the line).

```
0                              50                          100
|___|___|___|___|___|___|___|___|___|___|
Terrible                                          Excellent
```

(2) Do you think you learned anything new?

```
0                              50                          100
|___|___|___|___|___|___|___|___|___|___|
Nothing                                        A great deal
```

(3) What were the three big ideas you got from this session?
(4) What did you like least about this session?

This kind of form can be used every week or once every unit. It provides data for both process and product evaluation, and can be filled out rapidly.

B. Before-and-after tests can be used in some situations. The same test is administered both before a course or unit is begun and after it has been completed. Again, the question should be based on the objectives of the course or unit. The type of test used is limited only by the time and ingenuity of the evaluator. It may include multiple choice questions on factual information, blanks to be filled in, attitude scales to be checked, problems to be completed in paragraph or essay form. This type of data is best suited for product evaluation when you wish to identify learning or changes resulting from the course or program.

Such tests can also be used on a "one shot" basis after a class session or unit to discover the meaning which class members have attached to the subjects taught or discussed. In this case, of course, it is difficult to be sure how much of what is produced has resulted from the session itself and how much the class members already had before the teaching went on. "One shot" testing cannot show change or movement.

C. One effective method of evaluation is to ask class members to set learning goals at the end of a session or series of sessions. A learning goal is a class member's statement of something specific which he intends to do during the next week to apply, or to learn more about, the subject which has been studied. Research has shown that such learning goals not only provide useful evaluation data, but also provide a powerful motivation for continued learning.

3. Information from Observers

Classroom observers can provide information about class sessions and some insight into the learning which has taken place. Observers can usually provide most of the kinds of data which have been described above as available from teachers. In addition, since they are not actively involved in the teaching process, they can provide more detailed information than teachers can give about the session itself.

Since observers, in most cases, will be relatively untrained, it is important to provide carefully planned report sheets which give specific indications of the types of information wanted from the observers. What this information is will depend upon the type of evaluation planned. Observers may be asked to describe group procedures and involvements as a basis for process evaluation. They may be asked to list all questions asked and all conclusions reached, as a basis for product evaluation. The objectives for a course or session may be carefully defined and observers asked to describe any happenings during the class session which seem to indicate progress or lack of progress toward these objectives.

4. *The "Pro-Con" Technique*

This useful technique can be used many different ways with class members, teachers, or observers. The subject is given a report form which contains two columns. In the first column he is asked to describe the "pro's"—all of the favorable points he can think of about the session, idea, book, or whatever is being evaluated. In the second column he is asked to describe the "con's"—all of the unfavorable aspects he can think of. The value of this technique lies in the fact that it produces more complete judgments and evidence on both sides. Most of us are prone to make a judgment about something and then to seek evidence to support our judgment. The pro-con technique encourages the individual to consider both sides of the question and to give both favorable and unfavorable judgments. It is widely useful in collecting evaluation data.

It is impossible in a paper of this scope to do more than indicate a sampling of the possibilities for evaluating adult Christian education. The first step in planning such an evaluation is to state the aims, objectives, or desired outcomes in terms of observable behavior or assessable reactions. Then one is ready to plan how to collect the kinds of evaluation data which will produce evidence about these outcomes and to plan how to analyze and summarize these data when they have been collected. At this point, the advice of evaluation specialists, consultants, and experienced research workers can be most helpful.

A Look at the Future

It seems obvious that the quantity of Christian education evaluation and research will increase rapidly during the next few years. There is more interest in this field now than ever before in the history of Christian education. There is now available a growing repertoire of techniques especially suited to this kind of evaluation. As the quantity of evaluation increases, it is important that the quality also increase. This means that competent Christian education research workers must be recruited and trained, and that adequate facilities, personnel, and financing be made available for research work.

It is possible that in the near future primary responsibility for curriculum evaluation will be given to the editors who are responsible for producing the materials, rather than to outside specialists. Editors can easily learn to use a few basic evaluation techniques. It is a good deal easier to give such training to an editor than it is to give an outside specialist the complete background of the curriculum which he needs if he is to produce the most useful results.

We have only begun to explore the possibilities for basic research in Christian education. Research may be defined as a systematic effort to understand complex phenomena which are of more than immediate concern. In contrast, evaluation deals with a more limited, immediate concern (program, curriculum). Evaluation can usually lead only to improvement of existing materials and methods; it takes basic research to provide the striking breakthroughs which result in new and far more effective educational methods.[2]

It is likely that research and evaluation can become more deeply integrated into the whole process of curriculum development and thus make a more useful contribution toward improvement of curriculum. For example, research and evaluation now usually begin after curriculum objectives have been set, but research should make a valuable contribution to the statement of such objectives.

As interest develops in Christian education research and evaluation, it will be necessary to become more selective about the projects which are undertaken. Even a small research project can consume a surprising amount of time and money. Some questions are not worth the time and money required to answer them. One critical test is, "How much difference will these answers make after we have found them? Can this study

---

[2] Examples of the kinds of basic research needed are listed in Herman E. Wornom, ed., "Highlights of Recommendations for Research," *Religious Education,* 55 (1960) , 49-67.

lead to any important change or improvement?" In addition, there are some important questions which cannot be answered by research, or at least cannot be answered by anything short of a long-term, full-scale research effort. It is vital that we do not waste time, money, and effort in trying to answer questions which are not worth answering or which cannot be answered.

Evaluation and Research—A Quest for the Will of God

In our programs of research and evaluation, we seek to pray, "Thy will, not mine, be done." We believe that the Holy Spirit guides us as we develop objectives and plan curriculum. We believe that the Holy Spirit guides the teacher as he teaches and the learner as he learns.

Just so, we believe that the Holy Spirit guides us as we seek to evaluate what has happened when the curriculum was used. Our own prejudices, biases, and opinions can be powerful blocks to the work of the Spirit. When we set out openmindedly to gather evidence and to analyze it objectively, then we are opening our minds to the guidance of the Spirit, who may lead us into all truth.

18. Adult Education in the Church of Tomorrow: A Study Outline

LAWRENCE C. LITTLE
Chairman, Department of Religious Education
University of Pittsburgh

THE FOLLOWING Study Outline was circulated in advance of the Workshop to aid its members in their preparation for effective participation. The Workshop could not have dealt directly with all the elements included in this outline, and it was not intended as a "program" for the daily sessions. All these elements, however, are related to the problem of understanding modern adults and providing curricula designed to serve them adequately. Participants in the workshop were urged to acquire the necessary preliminary orientation by reading as widely as possible in literature dealing with the problems of adult education and by discussing the issues raised with friends and colleagues in advance of the Workshop sessions.

The Study Outline is reproduced in its original form.

I. The Cultural Context of Christian Adult Education

What are some of the factors and forces which constitute "our problem" as producers and users of the curriculum of Christian education for adults?

1. As we view the American society and culture of today:
   a. What trends and tendencies seem to encourage and support the development of wholesome and mature personality and lead to creative living among adults?
   b. Which tend to hinder and inhibit these outcomes?
   c. How are adults being affected by the pressures and tensions in our changing American culture? How well are adults generally meeting the demands being made upon them by modern culture?
   d. What elements in "the American way of life" seem to be in conflict with Christian standards and values? What elements contribute to Christian living?

2. Several terms are used frequently in casual conversation to designate certain aspects of American culture and types of personality. What is the significance of these for Christian adult education? For example:

"affluent society"	"beatnik"
"celebrity gods"	"man in the gray flannel suit"
"credit-card society"	"organization man"
"hidden persuaders"	"saint on Main Street"
"Madison Avenue"	"status seekers"
"megalopolis"	"thief in the white collar"
"planned obsolescence"	"ugly Americans"
"street corner society"	"waste makers"
"waist-high culture"	

3. What problems are created for Christian adult education by such features of American culture as:

   racial tensions, discrimination, segregation
   unemployment, rising taxes, inflation
   crime and juvenile delinquency
   deterioration of our "inner cities"
   changing patterns of home life, increasing divorce rate
   vast agricultural surpluses
   declining private support of benevolent causes
   increasing need of public support of education and welfare
   use of alcohol and "tranquilizers" to escape tensions
   rising proportion of "senior citizens" in the total population
   increasing mobility
   trends toward conformity
   threats to freedom
   others?

4. What problems are created by such features of the world situation as:
   international tensions, the cold war
   exploding world population

impoverishment, disease, and ignorance among great masses

economic, political and social revolutions; the "tide of rising expectations" in many of the merging and newly independent nations

rapid spread of Marxism and communist imperialism

threats of nuclear warfare

dilemmas of American foreign policy

others?

5. What is the "new shape" of American religion? How adequate is this religion for transforming people and producing an effective alternative to atheism and materialism? Why have some formerly "Christian" societies turned communist? What kind of religion do we need in times like these? How can we get it? What does this signify for Christian adult education?

6. What new opportunities and problems are created by the modern ecumenical movement? What forces seem likely to retard the surge toward unity among the various denominations and divisions of Christendom? How can Christian adult education help to advance the cause of Christian unity and stem the world-wide drift toward secularism?

7. How shall we evaluate both renewal and current directions in Christian theology? What are some implications of these tendencies for Christian adult education? In what directions do we need to make further advances (for example, in understanding the Bible, the Gospel, the church, the ministry) ?

8. What are the criteria by which the church may determine its effectiveness? How well is the church meeting its responsibilities in our modern era? How could it meet them better?

9. What should be the relation of the church to modern culture? What, specifically, is the responsibility of the church in the field of adult education? What is the significance of the "spectator role," the problem of non-involvement in many of the major concerns of contemporary life? (What bearing does Christian commitment have here?)

10. What are some other questions and problems that should be faced by the churches as they seek to provide a more adequate curriculum of Christian education for adults?

II. Foundations

What are some requirements of an adequate curriculum of Christian education for adults? What are some of the factors (psychological, social, theological) that must influence its development? What are some of the basic assumptions involved?

1. What have modern knowledge and research contributed to our understanding of adults and adult education?
   a. The nature of man
   b. The relation of the individual to his environment
   c. The cultural transmission of values
   d. Human growth and learning
   e. The significance of interpersonal relationships
   f. Adult needs, potentialities, motivation
   g. Moral and religious development in adulthood
2. How is understanding of these affected by the Christian perspective? What are some of the assumptions necessarily involved in Christian education?
   a. Regarding persons
   b. The nature and conditions of Christian growth
   c. The role of the church in adult education
3. What are the criteria for judging the quality of Christian education for adults? What behavioral outcomes should be expected?
4. What should be the content of a Christian education curriculum for adults? Can we have "content" and still avoid legalism, moralism, indoctrination?
5. On what bases should the methodology of Christian education for adults be determined?

III. Current Status

What is the present status of the curriculum of Christian education for adults?

1. What does the Survey of Current Curricula of Christian Education for Adults, as reported by the study committees of the various denominational boards and other educational agencies, reveal regarding:
   a. Objectives of Christian education for adults
   b. Relation of stated objectives to published materials
   c. Procedures followed in producing materials
   d. Types of curricula available
   e. Efforts to adapt curricula to various types and levels of experience
   f. Use of present curricula
   g. Provision for guiding local church leaders in the selection and use of curricula
   h. Feedback for purposes of evaluation and revision
   i. Results obtained from use of present curricula
   j. Significant recent developments
   k. Unmet needs and problems

2. What do an analysis and critique of the total existing curriculum of Christian education for adults reveal regarding:

    a. Concepts of the curriculum

    b. Relationship to contemporary adult life and needs

    c. Theories of learning presupposed

    d. Methods of teaching recommended

    e. Relation of these to recent insights regarding effective adult learning

    f. Common emphases and major divergencies

    g. Areas of strength and obvious weaknesses in current curricula

    h. Adult needs still unmet

    i. Developments that show promise for possible future advance

IV. Needed Changes

What changes, improvements, and additions are needed in order to meet the requirements of an adequate curriculum?

1. Concept of the church

How can a more adequate doctrine of the church and its mission be formulated and become more widely accepted? How can the confusion regarding the moral and spiritual implications of Christian commitment be overcome? What is the unique role of the church in modern society?

What is the place of the laity in the church? How should the "priesthood of believers" be interpreted today? How can we better relate the "inchurch" and the "outchurch" phases of the total program of the church? What are the implications of recent studies of the nature of the ministry? How are the images of the ministry and the laity related?

How can the essentials of Christian ideals and faith be presented so that they seem more valid and real to members of the church? How can church members be helped to understand that the essence of Christianity is not sitting in pews and listening to music and a sermon, but that it is personal and small-group search for faith and skills in changing individual life and human society? How can the unchristian character of so much of modern life both at home and abroad be presented so that the Christian task becomes clearer? How can the church become a vital community of persons who have enough conviction and skill to "clean up the social dirt in our own backyards while making a more effective impact upon conditions in other parts of the world?"

How can all the ministries of the church, including such aspects as preaching, worship, stewardship, evangelism, missions, and education be so inter-related that we overcome the present fragmented organization and program of the church and develop an image of the whole church?

2. Theology

How can the meaning of the Christian faith be interpreted in terms that are relevant to the thought and experience of modern adults? How can the discrepancy between theological and Biblical thinking on the professional level and the general level of church membership be remedied? How can the insights of theology be related to those of the "secular" disciplines in ways that will enrich Christian education? Is it correct to say that there is a "recent trend" in Christian theology? Christian theology seems to be moving in several different directions. For example, theologies of the "word of God," "personal encounter," "existentialism," and "Biblical theology" connote divergent approaches to Christian truth.

Obviously, different systems of theology imply differences in concepts of Christian education theory and practice. How important is it that we critically examine the anthropologies in current statements of theology? What are the possibilities of the enrichment of Christian theology by dialogue with the behavioral sciences?

Within the context of Christian adult education are included leaders who subscribe to several theological positions. How can this problem be dealt with constructively in future designs of the curriculum?

3. Christian education of adults

What makes "Christian education for adults" different from "adult education"? How can leaders in both fields take advantage of insights from the other field? How can we determine what particular areas each can cover best and how their work can be related most effectively and usefully?

What distinguishes Christian *adult* education from the Christian education of children and youth? Is the concept of a "vertical curriculum" valid? Is the "graded curriculum" outmoded? Can the study of the same concepts by persons of all ages be justified from the standpoint of an adequate theory of learning?

How can we help adults to realize their continuing need to learn, to unlearn, and to relearn, particularly in the areas of moral and spiritual growth?

Most adults live in several Gestalts at once. They are individuals first and live in a society of peers. They may be married and must behave in the unique relationship of man and wife. If they are parents, the behavior problem is more complex. Church membership is another dimension—and so on. How can Christian education aid them in meeting these multiple responsibilities?

How can we overcome the disrepute into which the adult Bible class has fallen in recent years and give Christian adult education the stature it deserves in the total life and work of the church? What new proposals can we make for Christian adult education over and beyond the church school hour? Do we need a new approach to the organization of adult education in the church? How can we gain the support of the present church leadership in providing a more adequate total program of Christian education for adults?

4. Theory of the curriculum

How can we change the present restricted view that the curriculum consists only of printed materials to one that includes the use of all activities and resources of the church? How overcome the dichotomy between "curriculum" and "program"? How develop a co-ordinated approach to adults rather than segmented approaches through departments of Christian education, men's and women's work, social action, etc.? How can we help church leaders to see that education is the functional aspect of all the activities of the church and requires the co-ordinated effort of all the various organizations and agencies?

5. Objectives

Can we restate the objectives of Christian education for adults so that proper reference is made both to (1) the abiding values of the Christian experience and heritage (or, as one member of the workshop suggested, "confrontation of the grace of God as it is revealed in Jesus Christ") ; and (2) the interests, needs, and responsibilities of adults in the world of today?

6. Learning theory

How can we develop a better understanding of the learning process: how adults learn; the types of experience and relationships in which effective learning and growth take place; the significance of motivation and participation in meaningful activities; the role of "images" and of non-verbal communication; the bearing of the "self-image" upon learning; the problems of fixation, "embeddedness," "dated emotions," repressions, and inhibitions to learning; the importance of measurement and evaluation, etc.?

7. Teaching methods

What methods of teaching are more likely to bring about desired changes in the attitudes, knowledge, and skills of adults? How can we utilize the dynamics of adult growth? What resources for Christian

adult education are to be found in the newer media of mass communication? How can we make better use of motivation and communication research?

How can the values of the Christian faith and heritage be related
more effectively to the interests and needs of adults in the world of
today? How can knowledge and action be more effectively related?
How can leaders of Christian study groups be aided in the use of
better methodology and group procedures?

8. Insights from other patterns of adult education

How can Christian adult education make effective use of the experience of certain creative lay movements in American Protestantism that lie outside the usual church school channels? What can we
learn from Catholic and Jewish forms of adult education? From
significant adult movements abroad? From general adult education?
From the work of libraries, labor unions, the National Training
Laboratories, etc.?

High schools, colleges, and universities are greatly expanding their
programs of "continuing education" and are reaching millions of
adults. What are the results of these efforts, positively and negatively,
from the standpoint of the churches?

What use can the churches make of patterns followed by such
organizations as Alcoholics Anonymous, Camp Farthest Out, Christian Business Men's League, Fellowship of Christian Athletes, Moral
Rearmament, Yokefellows, etc.?

9. Measurement and evaluation

How can we measure the cognitive, attitudinal, and motivational
changes that take place in members of adult groups? How judge the
relative effectiveness of various types of learning experiences and
teaching situations? What use can be made of the types of measurement and evaluation that have been developed in experimental
laboratories like the Character Research Project, University Testing
Service, etc.? How can the results of measurement be utilized in the
evaluation and revision of curricula for the Christian education of
adults? How can measurement and evaluation become built-in features of curriculum construction?

10. Procedures in the production and use of curricula

What are valid organizing principles for a curriculum of Christian
education for adults?

How can curriculum materials be prepared so as to provide for the
flexibility in use which our changing culture demands?

How can the flow of curriculum production be improved? How can we insure the relevance of published materials to the needs and interests of users? How can users have a more responsible part in the identification of needs? How can they be aided in the selection of proper curriculum materials in the light of their needs?

How should the curriculum of Christian education for adults be related to the Co-operative Curriculum Project of the National Council of Churches?

Any considerable modification of present patterns will meet with strong resistance. How can we deal constructively with the problem of preparing for and guiding change?

11. New types of curricula

What are some areas in which new curricula should be developed:
Family life and parent education?
Older youth-young adults?
Aging, "senior citizens"?
Christian vocations?
The implications of the gospel for (whatever) vocation?
The handicapped?
Intergroup tensions?
International affairs?
Theology for laymen?
WHAT ELSE?

12. New resources for leaders

As compared with the Christian education of children and youth, the literature in Christian adult education is relatively meager and limited. What do we need in the way of research and experimentation, study outlines, texts, and other publications, that will provide more adequate resources for leaders in the Christian education of adults?

What additional provision can be made for the in-service training of voluntary church school leadership? For potential leadership beyond the church school? How can theological seminaries and universities help here? Denominational boards and councils of churches?

V. How Can These Needed Changes Be Effected?

(Consideration of this area was one of the main concerns of the workshop.)

19. A Selected Bibliography

Compiled by LAWRENCE C. LITTLE

Abrahamson, Julia. *A Neighborhood Finds Itself.* New York: Harper and Brothers, 1959.

Adams, Walter, and John A. Garraty. *Is the World Our Campus?* East Lansing: Michigan State University Press, 1960.

Adler, Mortimer J., and Milton Mayer. *The Revolution in Education.* Chicago: The University of Chicago Press, 1958.

Adorno, Theodor W., *et al. The Authoritarian Personality.* New York: Harper and Brothers, 1950.

Adult Education Association of the U. S. A. *Adult Education Issues in Dispute.* Chicago, 1960.

———. *Creating a Climate for Adult Learning.* Chicago, 1959.

———. *Education for Aging.* Chicago, 1960.

Abrecht, Paul. *The Churches in Rapid Social Change.* Garden City, N. Y.: Doubleday and Company, 1961.

Albrecht, Ruth Esther. *The Social Roles of Old People.* Unpublished doctoral dissertation, University of Chicago, 1952.

Alcorn, Marvin D., and J. M. Linley. *Issues in Curriculum Development.* Tarrytown-on-Hudson, New York: World Book Company, 1959.

Alexander, Frederick. *Adult Education in Australia.* Melbourne: F. W. Cheshire, 1959.

Allport, Gordon W. *The Individual and His Religion.* New York: The Macmillan Company, 1950.

———. *Personality: A Psychological Interpretation.* New York: Henry Holt and Company, 1937.

American Library Association, Library-Community Project Headquarters Staff. *Studying the Community: A Basis for Planning Library Adult Education Services*. Chicago, 1960.

Anderson, George C. *Man's Right to be Human*. New York: William Morrow and Company, 1959.

Anderson, John E., ed. *Psychological Aspects of Aging*. Washington: American Psychological Association, 1956.

Angell, Robert C. *Free Society and Moral Crisis*. Ann Arbor: University of Michigan Press, 1958.

Arendt, Hannah. *The Human Condition*. Chicago: The University of Chicago Press, 1958.

Argyle, Michael. *Religious Behavior*. Glencoe, Ill.: The Free Press, 1959.

Augsburger, Myron S. *Called to Maturity*. Scottdale, Pa.: Herald Press, 1960.

Bainbridge, John. *The Super-Americans*. Garden City, N. Y.: Doubleday and Company, 1961.

Bainton, Roland H. *Christian Attitudes Toward War and Peace*. Nashville: Abingdon Press, 1960.

Barnes, Roswell P. *Under Orders: The Churches and Public Affairs*. Garden City, N. Y.: Doubleday and Company, 1961.

Barron, Milton L. *The Aging American: An Introduction to Social Gerontology and Geriatrics*. New York: Thomas Y. Crowell Company, 1960.

Barth, Karl. *Church Dogmatics*. Edinburgh: T. & T. Clark, 1936.

―――. *The Humanity of God*. Richmond, Va.: John Knox Press, 1960.

Bateson, Gregory, and Jurgen Ruesch. *Communication: The Social Matrix of Society*. New York: W. W. Norton and Company, 1951.

Bell, Daniel. *Work and Its Discontent*. Boston: Beacon Press, 1958.

Benedict, Ruth. *Patterns of Culture*. Boston: Houghton Mifflin Company, 1934.

Bennett, John C., et. al. *Ethics and the Arms Race*. New York: Charles Scribner's Sons, 1961.

Benson, Purnell H. *The Interests and Activities of Engaged and Married Couples in Relation to Their Personal Adjustment*. Unpublished doctoral dissertation, University of Chicago, 1953.

―――. *Religion in Contemporary Culture*. New York: Harper and Brothers, 1960.

Bentwich, Norman D. *The Religious Foundations of Internationalism*. New York: Bloch Publishing Company, 1960.

Berelson, Bernard. *Graduate Education in the United States*. New York: McGraw-Hill Book Company, 1960.

Berger, Peter L. *The Noise of Solemn Assemblies*. Garden City, N. Y.: Doubleday and Company, 1961.

―――. *The Precarious Vision*. Garden City, N. Y.: Doubleday and Company, 1961.

Bergevin, Paul, and John McKinley. *Design for Adult Education in the Church.* Greenwich, Conn.: The Seabury Press, 1958.

Berkowitz, Howard. *A Study of Psychological Attributes in the Second Half of Life.* Unpublished doctoral dissertation, University of Texas, 1957.

Berthold, Fred, Jr. *The Fear of God: The Role of Anxiety in Contemporary Thought.* New York: Harper and Brothers, 1959.

Betts, George Herbert. *The Curriculum of Religious Education.* New York: Abingdon Press, 1924.

Birren, James E., ed. *Handbook of Aging and the Individual.* Chicago: The University of Chicago Press, 1960.

Blakely, R. J. *Adult Education in a Free Society.* Toronto: Garden Bird Publications, 1958.

Bonnell, John S. *No Escape from Life.* New York: Harper and Brothers, 1958.

Booth, Alan. *Christians and Power Politics.* New York: Association Press, 1961.

Bossard, James H. S., and Eleanor S. Boll. *Ritual in Family Living.* Philadelphia: University of Pennsylvania Press, 1950.

Bower, William C., and Percy R. Hayward. *Protestantism Faces Its Educational Task Together.* Appleton, Wis.: C. C. Nelson Publishing Company, 1949.

Bowles, Chester. *Ideas, People and Peace.* New York: Harper and Brothers, 1958.

Boyd, Malcolm. *Christ and Celebrity Gods.* Greenwich, Conn.: The Seabury Press, 1958.

————. *Crisis in Communication.* Garden City, N. Y.: Doubleday and Company, 1957.

Brogan, D. W. *Citizenship Today.* Chapel Hill: University of North Carolina Press, 1960.

Brown, Norman O. *Life Against Death.* Middletown, Conn.: Wesleyan University Press, 1959.

Browne, Benjamin P., ed. *Techniques of Christian Writing.* Philadelphia: Judson Press, 1960.

Brunner, Edmund deS., *et al. An Overview of Adult Education Research.* Chicago: Adult Education Association of the U. S. A., 1959.

Brunner, Emil. *The Divine Imperative.* Philadelphia: The Westminster Press, 1947.

Burman, Arthur C. *Aspirational Fulfillment Among Adults on Lower Socioeconomic Levels with Implications for Adult Education.* Unpublished doctoral dissertation, Indiana University, 1959.

Butterfield, Herbert. *International Conflict in the Twentieth Century.* New York: Harper and Brothers, 1960.

Buttrick, George A. *Biblical Thought and the Secular University.* Baton Rouge: Louisiana State University Press, 1960.

Caliman, Alvis W. *Personality Adjustment of Aging Women.* Unpublished doctoral dissertation, Michigan State University, 1951.

Canadian Association for Adult Education. *Adult Education in Canada.* Toronto: University of Toronto Press, 1960.

Carey, James J. *Forms and Forces in University Adult Education.* Chicago: Center for the Study of Liberal Education for Adults, 1961.

Carnegie Endowment for International Peace. *The United States Public and the United Nations: Report on a Study of American Attitudes on the U. N. and the Communication of Information to the U. S. Public.* New York: The Endowment, 1958.

Carnell, Edward J. *The Case for Orthodox Theology.* Philadelphia: The Westminster Press, 1959.

Carrier, Blanche. *Integrity for Tomorrow's Adults.* New York: Thomas Y. Crowell, 1959.

Carrington, W. L. *Psychology, Religion and Human Need.* Great Neck, N. Y.: Channel Press, 1957.

Casteel, John. *Spiritual Renewal through Personal Groups.* New York: Association Press, 1957.

Cattell, Raymond B. *Description and Measurement of Personality.* Yonkers-on-Hudson, N. Y.: World Book Company, 1946.

Cavan, Ruth, *et al. Personal Adjustment in Old Age.* Chicago: Science Research Associates, 1949.

Cavanagh, J. R. *Fundamental Marriage Counseling: A Catholic View.* Milwaukee: Bruce Publishing Company, 1957.

Chamberlin, J. Gordon. *Parents and Religion.* Philadelphia: The Westminster Press, 1961.

Chandler, Edgar H. S. *The High Tower of Refuge.* New York: Frederick A. Praeger, 1959.

Chapple, Eliot D., and Leonard R. Sayles. *The Measurement of Management.* New York: The Macmillan Company, 1961.

Character Research Project, Union College. *Attitude Measurement and Growth.* Schenectady, 1960.

———. *Powerful Learning Tools in Religion.* Schenectady, 1958, 1959.

Christensen, Glen A. *An Analysis of Selected Issues in Family Life Education.* Unpublished doctoral dissertation, Michigan State University, 1958.

Clark, Burton R. *Adult Education in Transition.* Berkeley: University of California Press, 1956.

Clark F. LeG., and Agnes C. Dunne. *Aging in Industry.* New York: Philosophical Library, 1956.

Clemmons, Robert S. *Dynamics of Christian Adult Education.* Nashville: Abingdon Press, 1958.

———. *Young Adult Work in the Church.* Nashville: Abingdon Press, 1959.

Cleveland, Harlan, Gerald J. Mangone, and John Clark Adams. *The Overseas Americans.* New York: McGraw-Hill Book Company, 1960.

Clough, Shepard B. *Basic Values of Western Civilization.* New York: Columbia University Press, 1960.

Cogley, John, ed. *Religion in America.* New York: Meridian Books, 1958.

Collins, Thomas. *The Golden Years.* New York: John Day Company, 1956.

Comings, Carolyn C. *Satisfaction of Wife with Husband's Job.* Unpublished doctoral dissertation, Ohio State University, 1959.

Council on Human Relations. *Resource Handbook in Human Relations.* Cleveland, 1960.

Cousins, Norman. *In Place of Folly.* New York: Harper and Brothers, 1961.

Cox, Christine. *A Study of the Religious Practices, Values and Attitudes in a Selected Group of Families.* Unpublished doctoral dissertation, Cornell University, 1957.

Crook, Roger H. *The Changing American Family.* St. Louis: The Bethany Press, 1960.

Cully, Kendig B. *Basic Writings in Christian Education.* Philadelphia: The Westminster Press, 1960.

Culver, Elsie T. *New Church Programs With the Aging.* New York: Association Press, 1961.

Cuninggim, Merrimon, ed. *Christianity and Communism.* Dallas: Southern Methodist University Press, 1958.

Dawson, Christopher. *The Crisis of Western Education.* New York: Sheed and Ward, 1961.

Deffner, Donald Louis. *The Church's Role in Adult Education.* Unpublished doctoral dissertation, University of California, 1957.

Deutscher, Irwin. *Married Life in the Middle Years: A Study of the Middle Class Urban Postparental Couple.* Unpublished doctoral dissertation, University of Missouri, 1959.

de Unamuno, Miguel. *The Tragic Sense of Life.* Gloucester, Mass.: Peter Smith, Publisher, 1931.

de Vries, Egbert. *Man in Rapid Social Change.* Garden City, N. Y.: Doubleday and Company, 1961.

Dewey, John. *A Common Faith.* New Haven: Yale University Press, 1934.

De Wire, Harry A. *The Christian as Communicator.* Philadelphia: The Westminster Press, 1961.

DeWolf, L. Harold. *The Case for Theology in Liberal Perspective.* Philadelphia: The Westminster Press, 1959.

Dicks, Russell L. *Toward Health and Wholeness.* New York: The Macmillan Company, 1960.

Dillenberger, John. *Protestant Thought and Natural Science.* Garden City, N. Y.: Doubleday and Company, 1960.

Dimmitt, J. Sterling. *The Congruence of Past and Ideal Self Concepts in the Aging Male.* Unpublished doctoral dissertation, University of Florida, 1959.

Donahue, Wilma, comp. *Education for Later Maturity.* New York: Whiteside, Inc., and William Morrow and Company, 1955.

————, and Clark Tibbitts, eds. *The New Frontiers of Aging.* Ann Arbor: University of Michigan Press, 1957.

Dumont, Christophe Jean. *Approaches to Christian Unity.* Baltimore: Helicon Press, 1959.

Duncan, Otis D., and Albert J. Reiss, Jr. *Social Characteristics of Urban and Rural Communities.* New York: John Wiley and Sons, 1956.

Eklund, John M. *Tools for Peace.* Denver: National Farmers Union, 1960.

Eldsdon, K. T. *Reality and Purpose: A Visitor's Reflections on Some Aspects of American Adult Education.* Chicago: Center for the Study of Liberal Education for Adults, 1957.

Elkin, Harry. *Adult Jewish Education in the United States.* Unpublished doctoral dissertation, Dropsie College, 1954.

Eliot, Thomas Stearns. *Complete Poems and Plays.* New York: Harcourt, Brace and Company, 1952.

Ellis, Evelyn E. *A Study of the Correlates of Upward Social Mobility Among Unmarried Career Women.* Unpublished doctoral dissertation, Ohio State University, 1951.

Elmen, Paul. *The Restoration of Meaning to Contemporary Life.* Garden City, N. Y.: Doubleday and Company, 1958.

Ely, Mary L., ed. *Handbook of Adult Education in the United States.* New York: Institute of Adult Education, Teachers College, Columbia University, 1948.

Ensley, F. Gerald, *The Marks of Christian Education.* Nashville: Methodist Publishing House, 1958.

Erikson, Erik H. *Childhood and Society.* New York: W. W. Norton and Company, 1950.

————. *Identity and the Life Cycle.* New York: International Universities Press, 1959.

Ernsberger, David J. *A Philosophy of Adult Christian Education.* Philadelphia: The Westminster Press, 1959.

Evaluation and Christian Education. New York: Office of Publication and Distribution, National Council of Churches, 1960.

Fagley, Richard M. *The Population Explosion and Christian Responsibility.* New York: Oxford University Press, 1960.

Fairchild, Roy W., and John C. Wynn. *Families in the Church: A Protestant Survey.* New York: Association Press, 1961.

Fallaw, Wesner. *Church Education for Tomorrow.* Philadelphia: The Westminster Press, 1960.

Federal Council on Aging. *Programs, Resources for Older People: Report to the President.* Washington, 1959.

Feldman, Francis L. *The Family in a Money World.* New York: Family Service Association, 1957.

Feucht, Oscar E. *Helping Families Through the Church.* St. Louis: Concordia Publishing House, 1957.

——, ed. *Sex and the Church.* St. Louis: Concordia Publishing House, 1961.

Fichter, Joseph. *Social Patterns in the Urban Parish.* Chicago: The University of Chicago Press, 1954.

Fletcher, C. Scott. *The Battle of the Curriculum.* White Plains, N. Y.: Fund for Adult Education, 1958.

——, ed. *Education for Public Responsibility.* New York: W. W. Norton and Company, 1961.

Fortune, Editors of. *America in the Sixties: The Economy and the Society.* New York: Harper and Brothers, 1960.

——. *The Exploding Metropolis.* Garden City, N. Y.: Doubleday and Company, 1958.

Frakes, Margaret. *Bridges to Understanding.* Philadelphia: The Muhlenberg Press, 1960.

Freeman, Samuel D. *Adult Education in the Jewish Community Center.* Unpublished doctoral dissertation, Columbia University, 1953.

Friday, Wallace. *Adults at Worship.* Nashville: Abingdon Press, 1959.

Friedmann, Georges. *Industrial Society: The Emergence of the Human Problems of Automation.* Glencoe, Ill.: The Free Press, 1955.

Fromm, Erich. *Escape from Freedom.* New York: Farrar and Rinehart, 1941.

Fry, John R. *A Hard Look at Adult Christian Education.* Philadelphia: The Westminster Press, 1961.

Fuller, C. Dale. *Training of Specialists in International Relations.* Washington: American Council on Education, 1957.

Fuller, Edmund. *Man in Modern Fiction.* New York: Random House, 1958.

Gable, Lee J. *Encyclopedia for Church Group Leaders.* New York: Association Press, 1959.

Galbraith, John K. *The Affluent Society.* Boston: Houghton Mifflin Company, 1958.

Gardner, John W. *Excellence.* New York: Harper and Brothers, 1961.

Garrett, Charles W. *A Curriculum Structure for Older Persons in the Church Based Upon a Study of the Opinions of Ministers and Older Persons.* Unpublished doctoral dissertation, New York University, 1954.

Garthoff, Raymond L. *Soviet Strategy in the Nuclear Age.* New York: Frederick A. Praeger, 1958.

Gassner, John. *Theatre at the Crossroads.* New York: Holt, Rinehart and Winston, 1960.

Geaney, Dennis. *Christians in a Changing World.* Notre Dame, Indiana: Fides Publishers, 1959.

Gibb, Jack. *Applied Group Dynamics.* Boulder, Colo.: Department of Psychology, University of Colorado, 1956.

Ginzberg, Eli, ed. *The Nation's Children.* Published for the Golden Anniversary, White House Conference on Children and Youth. 3 vols. New York: Columbia University Press, 1960.

Glick, Paul C. *American Families.* New York: John Wiley and Sons, 1957.

Gordon, Milton M. *Social Class in American Sociology.* Durham, N. C.: Duke University Press, 1958.

Gorham, Donald R. *Understanding Adults.* Philadelphia: The Judson Press, 1958.

Grattan, C. H., ed. *American Ideas about Adult Education.* New York: Bureau of Publications, Teachers College, Columbia University, 1959.

Gray, Robert M. *A Study of the Older Person in the Church.* Unpublished doctoral dissertation, University of Chicago, 1954.

Greeley, Andrew W. *The Church and the Suburbs.* New York: Sheed and Ward, 1959.

Green, J. Carleton. *Patterns of Adjustment in Character Research Project Families.* Unpublished doctoral dissertation, Boston University, 1954.

Greene, John Thomas. *The Role of Religiosity in Marital Success.* Unpublished doctoral dissertation, University of North Carolina, 1955.

Griffith, Thomas. *The Waist-High Culture.* New York: Harper and Brothers, 1959.

Gurin, Gerald, Joseph Beroff, and Sheila Feld. *Americans View Their Mental Health.* New York: Basic Books, 1960.

Gwynn, John M. *Curriculum Principles and Social Trends.* New York: The Macmillan Company, 1960.

Hadsell, John Sidney. *Some Principles and Methods for Teaching the Christian Faith to Adults Through the Use of the Bible.* Unpublished Ed. D. thesis, Teachers College, Columbia University, 1957.

Hahn, Walter F., and John C. Neff, eds. *American Strategy for the Nuclear Age.* Garden City, N. Y.: Doubleday and Company, 1960.

Haimowitz, Morris L., and Natalie Reader Haimowitz. *Human Development: Selected Readings.* New York: Thomas Y. Crowell Company, 1960.

Hall, Calvin S., and Gardner Lindzey. *Theories of Personality.* New York: John Wiley and Sons, 1957.

Hall, G. Stanley. *Adolescence: Its Psychology and Its Relations to Physiology. Anthropology. Sociology, Sex, Crime, Religion, and Education.* New York: D. Appleton and Company, 1904.

Halzel, Lawrence. *An Analysis of the Problems of Older People According to Sex, Age, Income and Marital Status.* Unpublished Ed. D. thesis, Boston University, 1959.

Harkness, Georgia. *The Church and Its Laity.* Nashville: Abingdon Press, 1962.

Haselden, Kyle. *The Racial Problem in Christian Perspective.* New York: Harper and Brothers, 1959.

Havighurst, Robert J. *Human Development and Education.* New York: Longmans, Green and Company, 1953.

———. *The Social Competence of Middle-Aged People.* Chicago: Committee on Human Development, University of Chicago, 1957.

———, and Ruth Albrecht. *Older People.* New York: Longmans, Green and Company, 1953.

———, and Betty Orr. *Adult Education and Adult Needs.* Chicago: Center for the Study of Liberal Education for Adults, 1956.

Hazelton, Roger. *God's Way With Man.* Nashville: Abingdon Press, 1956.

———. *New Accents in Contemporary Theology.* New York: Harper and Brothers, 1960.

Healy, Daniel J. *Selecting the Adult Educator.* Unpublished doctoral dissertation, New York University, 1959.

Herberg, Will. *Protestant—Catholic—Jew.* New York: Doubleday and Company, 1955.

Hero, Alfred O. *Americans in World Affairs.* Boston: World Peace Foundation, 1959.

———. *Opinion Leaders in American Communities.* Boston: World Peace Foundation, 1959.

Herschberger, Guy F. *The Way of the Cross in Human Relations.* Scottdale, Pa.: Herald Press, 1958.

Hillman, Arthur. *Neighborhood Centers Today.* New York: National Federation of Settlements and Neighborhood Centers, 1960.

Himwich, H. E., ed. *Tranquilizing Drugs.* Washington: American Association for the Advancement of Science (Publication No. 46), 1957.

Hollander, Sophie S. *Impressions of the American.* Berkeley: California Book Company, 1961.

Hollingshead, August B., and Frederick C. Redlich. *Social Class and Mental Illness.* New York: John Wiley and Sons, 1958.

Hook, Sidney. *Political Power and Personal Freedom: Critical Studies in Democracy, Communism, and Civil Rights.* New York: Criterion Books, 1959.

Hordern, William. *The Case for a New Reformation Theology.* Philadelphia: The Westminster Press, 1959.

———. *A Layman's Guide to Protestant Theology.* New York: The Macmillan Company, 1955.

Horney, Karen. *Neurosis and Human Growth.* New York: W. W. Norton and Company, 1950.

————. *Our Inner Conflicts.* New York: W. W. Norton and Company, 1945.

Houle, Cyril O. *Adult Education in the British West Indies.* Chicago: Center for the Study of Liberal Education for Adults, 1960.

————. *The Inquiring Mind.* Madison: University of Wisconsin Press, 1961.

Hoult, Thomas H. *The Sociology of Religion.* New York: The Dryden Press, 1958.

Howe, Reuel L. *The Creative Years.* Greenwich, Conn.: The Seabury Press, 1959.

————. *Man's Need and God's Action.* Greenwich, Conn.: The Seabury Press, 1953.

Hunsaker, Herbert C., and Richard Pierce. *Creating a Climate for Adult Learning.* Chicago: Adult Education Association of the U. S. A., 1959.

Hurlock, Elizabeth B. *Developmental Psychology.* New York: McGraw-Hill Book Company, 1959.

Hunter, Floyd. *Top Leadership, U. S. A.* Chapel Hill: The University of North Carolina Press, 1959.

Hurwitz, Nathan. *Marital Roles and Adjustment in Marriage in a Middle-class Group.* Unpublished doctoral dissertation, University of Southern California, 1958.

James, Edwin O. *Marriage and Society.* New York: John de Graff, 1955.

James, William. *The Varieties of Religious Experience.* New York: Longmans, Green and Company, 1902.

Jaspan, Norman, and Hillet Black. *The Thief in the White Collar.* Philadelphia: E. P. Lippincott Company, 1960.

Jaspers, Karl. *The Future of Mankind.* Chicago: The University of Chicago Press, 1961.

Johnson, F. Ernest, ed. *Patterns of Ethics in America Today.* New York: Harper and Brothers, 1960.

————, ed. *Patterns of Faith in America Today.* New York: Harper and Brothers, 1957.

Johnson, Robert Clyde. *Authority in Protestant Theology.* Philadelphia: The Westminster Press, 1959.

Joint Section of Education and Cultivation, Board of Missions of the Methodist Church. *The Christian Mission Today.* Nashville: Abingdon Press, 1960.

Jones, Donald C. *An Investigation of the Influence of Work Experience in the Formulation of Life Goals of Young Adults.* Unpublished doctoral dissertation, Teachers College, Columbia University, 1951.

Judy, Martin T. *The Larger Parish and Group Ministry.* Nashville: Abingdon Press, 1959.

Kaplan, Abbott. *Study-Discussion in the Liberal Arts.* White Plains, N. Y.: Fund for Adult Education, 1960.

Kaplan, Max. *Leisure in America.* New York: John Wiley and Sons, 1960.

Kaplan, O. J., ed. *Mental Disorders in Later Life.* Stanford, Cal.: Stanford University Press, 2nd edition, 1956.

Katz, Elihu, and Paul F. Lazarsfeld. *Personal Influence.* Glencoe, Ill.: The Free Press, 1959.

Kean, Charles D. *The Christian Gospel and the Parish Church.* Greenwich, Conn.: The Seabury Press, 1953.

Keeler, Sister Mary Jerome, ed. *Handbook of Catholic Adult Education.* Milwaukee: Bruce Publishing Company, 1959.

Keith, Robert A. *Some Attitudes Toward the Older Worker and His Role.* Unpublished doctoral dissertation, University of California at Los Angeles, 1954.

Kelso, Louis O., and Mortimer J. Adler. *The Capitalist Manifesto.* New York: Random House, 1958.

Kempfer, Homer. *Adult Education.* New York: McGraw-Hill Book Company, 1955.

Kidd, James R. *How Adults Learn.* New York: Association Press, 1959.

Kierkegaard, Sören. *Purity of Heart.* New York: Harper and Brothers, 1956.

King-Hall, Sir Stephen. *Defence in the Nuclear Age.* Garden City, N. Y.: Doubleday and Company, 1958.

Kissinger, Henry A. *Nuclear Weapons and Foreign Policy.* New York: Harper and Brothers, 1957.

Klapper, Joseph T. *The Effects of Mass Communication.* Glencoe, Ill.: The Free Press, 1960.

Klein, Alan F. *Role Playing in Leadership Training and Group Problem Solving.* New York: Association Press, 1956.

Kligler, Deborah S. *The Effects of the Employment of Married Women on Husband and Wife Roles.* Unpublished doctoral dissertation, Yale University, 1954.

Kluckhohn, Clyde, Henry A. Murray, and David M. Schneider, eds., *Personality in Nature, Society, and Culture.* New York: Alfred A. Knopf, Inc., 1953.

Knoles, George H. *The New United States.* New York: Henry Holt and Company, 1959.

Knowles, Malcolm S. *Informal Adult Education.* New York: Association Press, 1956.

———, and Hulda Knowles. *How to Develop Better Leaders.* New York: Association Press, 1955.

———, and Hulda Knowles. *Introduction to Group Dynamics.* New York: Association Press, 1959.

———, ed. *Handbook of Adult Education in the United States.* Chicago: Adult Education Association of the U. S. A., 1960.

Koenig, Robert E. *The Use of the Bible with Adults.* Philadelphia: The Christian Education Press, 1959.

Konvitz, Milton R. *Fundamental Liberties of a Free People.* Ithaca, N. Y.: Cornell University Press, 1957.

Kraemer, Hendrick. *The Theology of the Laity.* London: Lutterworth Press, 1958.

Krech, David, and Richard S. Crutchfield. *Theory and Problems of Social Psychology.* New York: McGraw-Hill Book Company, 1948.

Krim, Seymour, ed., *The Beats.* Greenwich, Conn.: The Seabury Press, 1960.

Krutch, Joseph W. *Human Nature and the Human Condition.* New York: Random House, 1959.

Kubie, Susan H., and Gertrude Landau. *Group Work With the Aged.* New York: International Universities Press, 1953.

Laidlaw, Alexander Fraser. *The Campus and the Community.* Montreal: Harvest House, 1961.

Lambert, Richard D., ed. *Religion in American Society.* Philadelphia: The American Academy of Political and Social Science. Special Issue of *The Annals,* Nov. 1960.

Langer, Marion. *Learning to Live as a Widow.* New York: Julian Messner, 1957.

Larrabee, Eric, and Rolf Meyersohn, eds. *Mass Leisure.* Glencoe, Ill.: The Free Press, 1958.

Larsen, Dorothy H. *A Survey of Older Church Members as a Basis for Developing New Activities.* Unpublished Ed. D. thesis, Teachers College, Columbia University, 1958.

Lavine, Eileen M. *Learning to Work with the Aged.* The Bronx 57, New York: William Hodson Community Center for Older Persons, 1960.

Lawler, Marcella R. *Curriculum Consultants at Work.* New York: Bureau of Publications, Teachers College, Columbia University, 1958.

Lazarsfeld, Paul F., and Patricia L. Kendall. *Radio Listening in America.* New York: Prentice-Hall, 1948.

Leach, Max. *Christianity and Mental Health.* Dubuque, Iowa: William C. Brown, 1957.

Leavenworth, Lynn, ed. *Great Themes in Theology.* Philadelphia: The Judson Press, 1958.

Lee, Dorothy. *Freedom and Culture.* Englewood Cliffs, N. J.: Prentice-Hall, 1959.

Lee, Robert. *The Social Sources of Church Unity.* Nashville: Abingdon Press, 1960.

LeFever, Ernest W. *Ethics and United States Foreign Policy.* New York: Meridian Books, 1957.

Leff, Ada G. *Initiating a Program of In-service Education for Teaching*

Parent Education. Unpublished Ed. D. thesis, Teachers College, Columbia University, 1959.

Leibrecht, Walter, ed. *Religion and Culture: Essays in Honor of Paul Tillich.* New York: Harper and Brothers, 1959.

Leighton, Alexander H., John A. Clausen and Robert N. Wilson, eds. *Explorations in Social Psychiatry.* New York: Basic Books, 1957.

Lentz, Richard E. *Making the Adult Class Vital.* St. Louis: The Bethany Press, 1954.

Lerner, Max. *America as a Civilization.* New York: Simon and Schuster, 1957.

Lifton, Walter. *Working With Groups: Group Processes and Individual Growth.* New York: John Wiley and Sons, 1961.

Ligon, Ernest M. *Dimensions of Character.* New York: The Macmillan Company, 1956.

————. *Let Husbands Be Men and Wives Be Women.* Schenectady, New York: Character Research Project, Union College, 1960.

————. *Parent Roles, His and Hers.* Schenectady, New York: Character Research Project, Union College, 1959.

————. *The Psychology of Christian Personality.* New York: The Macmillan Company, 1935.

————, and Leona J. Smith. *Dynamic Luxuries for Great Homes.* Schenectady, New York: Character Research Project, Union College, 1960.

Lindhorst, Frank A. *Teaching Adults.* New York: Abingdon-Cokesbury Press, 1951.

Linton, Ralph. *The Study of Man.* New York: D. Appleton-Century Company, 1936.

————. *Culture and Mental Disorders.* Springfield, Ill.: Charles C. Thomas, 1956.

Lipset, Seymour Martin. *Political Man; The Social Bases of Politics.* Garden City, N. Y.: Doubleday and Company, 1959.

————, and Reinhard Bendix. *Social Mobility in Industrial Society.* Berkeley: University of California Press, 1959.

Littell, Franklin H. *The German Phoenix.* Garden City, N. Y.: Doubleday and Company, 1960.

Little, Lawrence C. *A Bibliography of Doctoral Dissertations on Adults and Adult Education.* Pittsburgh: The Department of Religious Education, University of Pittsburgh, 1962.

————, ed. *Formulating the Objectives of Christian Adult Education.* Pittsburgh: The Department of Religious Education, University of Pittsburgh, 1958.

————. *Foundations for a Philosophy of Christian Education.* Nashville: Abingdon Press, 1962.

————, ed. *The Future Course of Christian Adult Education.* Pittsburgh: University of Pittsburgh Press, 1959.

————, ed. *Guidelines for the Development of Christian Education Curricula for Adults*. Pittsburgh: Department of Religious Education, University of Pittsburgh, 1961.

————. *Researches in Personality, Character, and Religious Education: A Bibliography of American Doctoral Dissertations, 1885 to 1959*. Pittsburgh: University of Pittsburgh Press, 1962.

Little, Sara. *Learning Together in the Christian Fellowship*. Richmond, Va.: John Knox Press, 1956.

Liveright, A. A. *Strategies of Leadership in Conducting Adult Education Programs*. New York: Harper and Brothers, 1959.

Loomis, Earl A., Jr. *The Self in Pilgrimage*. New York: Harper and Brothers, 1960.

Lowry, Louis. *Adult Education and Group Work*. New York: Whiteside, Inc., and William Morrow, 1955.

Luckey, Eleanor Braun. *An Investigation of the Concepts of the Self, Mate, Parents, and Ideal in Relation to the Degree of Marital Satisfaction*. Unpublished doctoral dissertation, University of Minnesota, 1959.

Lynd, Helen M. *On Shame and the Search for Identity*. New York: Harcourt, Brace and Company, 1958.

Lynn, Ercell V. *Parents as Religious Educators*. Unpublished doctoral dissertation, Teachers College, Columbia University, 1953.

McCoy, Lee H. *The Church at Work in Adult Education*. Unpublished D. R. E. thesis, Southwestern Baptist Theological Seminary, 1957.

McHose, Elizabeth. *Family Life Education in School and Community*. New York: Bureau of Publications, Teachers College, Columbia University, 1952.

Macmurray, John. *The Self as Agent*. New York: Harper and Brothers, 1957.

McDougall, William. *An Introduction to Social Psychology*. London: Methuen and Company, 1908.

McKinley, John. *Creative Methods for Adult Classes*. St. Louis: Bethany Press, 1960.

MacLellan, Malcolm. *The Catholic Church and Adult Education*. Unpublished doctoral dissertation, Catholic University of America, 1935.

McNulty, John P. *The Superior Old Person: Case Studies and Furthering Conditions*. Unpublished doctoral dissertation, Ohio State University, 1954.

Mace, David R., and Vera Mace. *Marriage: East and West*. Garden City, N. Y.: Doubleday and Company, 1959.

Malcolm, Donald J. *Interaction Problems of Adults in a New England Town*. Unpublished doctoral dissertation, Harvard University, 1951.

Marlowe, David. *Some Personality and Behavioral Correlates of Conformity*. Unpublished doctoral dissertation, Ohio State University, 1959.

Marney, Carlyle. *Structures of Prejudice.* Nashville: Abingdon Press, 1961.

Marty, Martin E. *The New Shape of American Religion.* New York: Harper and Brothers, 1959.

Maslow, Abraham H. *Motivation and Personality.* New York: Harper and Brothers, 1954.

————, ed. *New Knowledge in Human Values.* New York: Harper and Brothers, 1959.

Mason, Joseph G. *How to Be a More Creative Executive.* New York: McGraw-Hill Book Company, 1960.

Mastej, Mary Martina. *A Study of the Influence of Religious Life on the Personality Adjustment of Religious Women as Measured by a Modified Form of the Minnesota Multiphasic Personality Inventory.* Unpublished doctoral dissertation, Fordham University, 1954.

Maston, Thomas B. *Segregation and Desegration.* New York: The Macmillan Company, 1959.

Maves, Paul B. *The Best Is Yet to Be.* Philadelphia: The Westminster Press, 1951.

————. *The Christian Religious Education of Older People.* Unpublished doctoral dissertation, Drew University, 1949.

————. *Understanding Ourselves as Adults.* Nashville: Abingdon Press, 1959.

————, and J. Lennart Cedarleaf. *Older People and the Church.* New York: Abingdon-Cokesbury Press, 1949.

————, ed. *The Church and Mental Health.* New York: Charles Scribner's Sons, 1953.

Mayer, Martin. *Madison Avenue, U. S. A.* New York: Harper and Brothers, 1958.

Mead, Margaret, ed. *Cultural Patterns and Technical Change.* New York: New American Library, 1955.

Meehl, Paul, *et al. What, Then, Is Man?* St. Louis: Concordia Publishing House, 1958.

Mercer, Blaine E., and Edwin R. Carr. *Education and the Social Order.* New York: Rinehart and Company, 1957.

Mezirow, Jack D., and Dorothea Berry. *The Literature of Liberal Adult Education.* New York: Scarecrow Press, 1960.

Michalson, Carl. *Faith for Personal Crises.* New York: Charles Scribner's Sons, 1958.

Michigan Department of Public Instruction. *Planning for Public School Adult Education.* Bulletin No. 428, 1960. Lansing, Michigan, 1960.

Miklas, Sebastian, ed. *Principles and Problems of Catholic Adult Education.* Washington: The Catholic University of America Press, 1959.

Miles, Matthew B. *Learning to Work in Groups.* New York: Bureau of Publications, Teachers College, Columbia University, 1959.

Miller, Alexander. *The Man in the Mirror*. Garden City, N. Y.: Doubleday and Company, 1958.

Miller, Daniel R., and Guy E. Swanson. *The Changing American Parent*. New York: John Wiley and Sons, 1958.

Miller, Donald G. *The Nature and Mission of the Church*. Richmond, Va.: John Knox Press, 1957.

Miller, Haskell. *Compassion and Community*. New York: Association Press, 1961.

Miller, Marilyn V., ed. *On Teaching Adults: An Anthology*. Chicago: Center for the Study of Liberal Education for Adults, 1960.

Miller, Randolph C. *Be Not Anxious*. Greenwich, Conn.: The Seabury Press, 1957.

————. *Biblical Theology and Christian Education*. New York: Charles Scribner's Sons, 1956.

————. *Christian Nurture and the Church*. New York: Charles Scribner's Sons, 1961.

————. *Education for Christian Living*. Englewood Cliffs, N. J.: Prentice-Hall, 1956.

Miller, T. Franklin. *The Growing Christian: A Guidebook on Personal Religious Living*. Anderson, Ind.: Gospel Trumpet Company, 1960.

Miller, William. *The Protestant and Politics*. Philadelphia: The Westminster Press, 1960.

Millis, Walter. *Permanent Peace*. Santa Barbara, Cal.: Center for the Study of Democratic Institutions, 1961.

————. *A World Without War*. Santa Barbara, Cal.: Center for the Study of Democratic Institutions, 1961.

Mills, C. Wright. *The Causes of World War III*. New York: Simon and Schuster, 1958.

Minear, Paul S. *Horizons of Christian Community*. St. Louis: Bethany Press, 1959.

————, ed. *The Nature of the Unity We Seek*. St. Louis: The Bethany Press, 1958.

Mishkin, Rosalie. *Relationship Between Personality Needs of Men and Women and Occupational Choice*. Unpublished Ed. D. thesis, Teachers College, Columbia University, 1959.

Missenard, Andra. *In Search of Man*. Translated from the French by Lawrence B. Blochman. New York: Hawthorne Books, 1957.

Moberg, David O. *Religion and Personal Adjustment in Old Age; A Study of Some Aspects of the Christian Religion to Personal Adjustment of the Aged in Institutions*. Unpublished doctoral dissertation, University of Minnesota, 1952.

Mohan, Robert Paul, ed. *Technology and Christian Culture*. Washington: The Catholic University of America Press, 1960.

Mollegen, Albert T. *Christianity and Modern Man: The Crisis of Secularism.* New York: Bobbs-Merrill, 1961.

Monsma, John O., ed. *The Evidence of God in an Expanding Universe.* New York: G. P. Putnam's Sons, 1958.

Montagu, M. F. Ashley. *Anthropology and Human Nature.* Boston: Porter Sargent, 1957.

Moreau, Jules L. *Language and Religious Language.* Philadelphia: The Westminster Press, 1961.

Morris, Charles. *Varieties of Human Value.* Chicago: The University of Chicago Press, 1956.

Mottershead, Noel F. *A Comparative Study of World Movements in Adult Education.* Unpublished doctoral dissertation, University of California, 1949.

Moustakas, Clark E., ed. *The Self: Explorations in Personal Growth.* New York: Harper and Brothers, 1956.

Mowrer, O. Hobart. *The Crisis in Psychiatry and Religion.* Princeton, N. J.: Van Nostrand Company, 1961.

———. *Learning Theory and Behavior.* New York: John Wiley and Sons, 1960.

Muelder, Walter G. *Foundations of the Responsible Society.* Nashville: Abingdon Press, 1959.

———. *Religion and Economic Responsibility.* New York: Charles Scribner's Sons, 1953.

Mueller, Kate H. *Educating Women for a Changing World.* Minneapolis: The University of Minnesota Press, 1954.

Munro, Harry C. *Protestant Nurture.* Englewood Cliffs, N. J.: Prentice-Hall, 1956.

Murphy, Gardner. *Human Potentialities.* New York: Basic Books, 1958.

Murray, A. Victor. *Natural Religion and Christian Theology.* New York: Harper and Brothers, 1956.

Myers, Francis M. *The Warfare of Democratic Ideals.* Yellow Springs, Ohio: The Antioch Press, 1956.

National Council of Churches of Christ in the U. S. A., Division of Christian Education. *A Guide for Curriculum in Christian Education.* Chicago, 1955.

National Recreation Association. *Recreation Activities for Adults.* New York: Association Press, 1950.

Neill, Stephen. *The Christian Character.* New York: Association Press, 1955.

———. *A Genuinely Human Existence.* Garden City, N. Y.: Doubleday and Company, 1959.

Nelson, Erland N. P. *Patterns of Religious Attitudes Shifts from College to Fourteen Years Later.* Psychological Monographs No. 424. Washington: The American Psychological Association, 1956.

Nelson, Robert G. *Congo Crisis and Christian Mission*. St. Louis: The Bethany Press, 1961.

Niblett, William R. *Christian Education in a Secular Society*. Fair Lawn, N. J.: Oxford University Press, 1960.

Neubeck, Gerhard. *Factors Affecting Group Psychotherapy with Married Couples*. Unpublished Ed. D. thesis, Teachers College, Columbia University, 1953.

Nichols, Roy F. *Religion and American Democracy*. Baton Rouge: Louisiana State University Press, 1959.

Nida, Eugene A. *Message and Mission: The Communication of the Christian Faith*. New York: Harper and Brothers, 1960.

Niebuhr, H. Richard. *Christ and Culture*. New York: Harper and Brothers, 1951.

———. *The Purpose of the Church and Its Ministry*. New York: Harper and Brothers, 1956.

———. *Radical Monotheism and Western Culture*. New York: Harper and Brothers, 1960.

Niebuhr, Reinhold. *Pious and Secular America*. New York: Charles Scribner's Sons, 1958.

Northridge, W. L. *Disorders of the Emotional and Spiritual Life*. Great Neck, N. Y.: Channel Press, 1961.

Noss, David S. *Some Proposed Criteria for Selection of Motion Picture Materials to be Used in the Religious Education of Adults*. Unpublished doctoral dissertation, University of Chicago, 1952.

Nottingham, Ruth D. *A Psychological Study of Forty Unmarried Mothers*. Unpublished doctoral dissertation, Ohio State University, 1935.

Oates, Wayne E. *Christ and Selfhood*. New York: Association Press, 1961.

———. *Religious Dimensions of Personality*. New York: Association Press, 1957.

Obenhaus, Victor. *The Responsible Christian*. Chicago: The University of Chicago Press, 1957.

Osborn, Alex F. *Applied Imagination*. New York: Charles Scribner's Sons, 1957.

Outler, Albert. *Psychotherapy and the Christian Message*. New York: Harper and Brothers, 1954.

Owen, Margaret Frances Richards. *A Philosophy for Christian Family Life*. Unpublished Ed. D. thesis, Teachers College, Columbia University, 1952.

Packard, Vance. *The Hidden Persuaders*. New York: David McKay Company, 1957.

———. *The Status Seekers*. New York: David McKay Company, 1959.

———. *The Waste Makers*. New York: David McKay Company, 1960.

Pearl, Lester S. *The Dynamics of Education for Marriage in the United*

States. Unpublished doctoral dissertation, University of North Carolina, 1951.

Peck, Robert F., et al. *The Psychology of Character Development.* New York: John Wiley and Sons, 1960.

Pederson, John N. *The Meaning and Implications of Family Life Education.* Unpublished Pe. D. thesis, Indiana University, 1952.

Peet, Harriet E. *The Creative Individual.* New York: The Ronald Press, 1960.

Perla, Leo. *Can We End the Cold War?* New York: The Macmillan Company, 1960.

Perlman, Helen H. *Social Casework: A Problem Solving Process.* Chicago: The University of Chicago Press, 1957.

Petersen, Renee, and William Petersen. *University Adult Education: A Guide to Policy.* New York: Harper and Brothers, 1960.

Phelps, Harold A., and David Henderson. *Population in Its Human Aspects.* New York: Appleton-Century-Crofts, 1958.

Phenix, P. H. *Religious Concerns in Contemporary Education.* New York: Bureau of Publications, Teachers College, Columbia University, 1959.

Phillips, William, ed. *Art and Psychoanalysis.* New York: Criterion Books, 1957.

Phipps, Lloyd J. *Successful Practices in Adult Farmer Education.* Danville, Ill.: Interstate Printers and Publishers, 1954.

Pierson, Frank C. *The Education of American Businessmen.* New York: McGraw-Hill Book Company, 1959.

Piper, Otto A. *The Biblical View of Sex and Marriage.* New York: Charles Scribner's Sons, 1960.

Pittenger, W. Norman. *Theology and Reality.* Greenwich, Conn.: The Seabury Press, 1955.

Poteat, Edwin M. *Jesus' Belief in Man.* Nashville: Abingdon Press, 1956.

Potts, Robert E. *Effect of Childhood Punishment and Reward Upon Observable Personality Characteristics of the Adult.* Unpublished doctoral dissertation, Ohio State University, 1952.

Poupko, Bernard A. *Forms of Jewish Adult Education in America.* Unpublished doctoral dissertation, University of Pittsburgh, 1952.

Powell, John W. *Learning Comes of Age.* New York: Association Press, 1956.

Pressey, Sidney L., and Raymond G. Kuhlen. *Psychological Development Through the Life Span.* New York: Harper and Brothers, 1957.

Pritzkau, Philo T. *The Dynamics of Curriculum Improvement.* Englewood Cliffs, N. J.: Prentice-Hall, 1959.

Progoff, Ira. *Depth Psychology and Modern Man.* New York: Julian Press, 1959.

Raines, Robert A. *New Life in the Church.* New York: Harper and Brothers, 1961.

Ramsey, Paul. *Basic Christian Ethics*. New York: Charles Scribner's Sons, 1950.

———. *War and the Christian Conscience*. Durham, N. C.: Duke University Press, 1961.

Ranck, J. Allan. *Education for Mission*. New York: Friendship Press, 1961.

Rasmussen, Albert T. *Christian Social Ethics*. Englewood Cliffs, N. J.: Prentice-Hall, 1956.

Raybould, S. G., ed. *Trends in English Adult Education*. London: Heinemann Publishers, Ltd., 1959.

Redfield, Robert. *The Educational Experience*. Pasadena Cal.: Fund for Adult Education, 1955.

Reissman, Leonard. *Class in American Society*. Glencoe, Ill.: The Free Press, 1959.

Religious Education Association. *What Is the Nature of Man? Images of Man in Our American Culture*. Philadelphia: The Christian Education Press, 1959.

Rhodes, Arnold B., ed. *The Church Faces the Isms*. Nashville: Abingdon Press, 1958.

Richardson, Harold W. *A Study of the Readiness of American Baptist Theological Students Holding Opposing "Fundamentalist" and "Modernist" Theological Views to Associate in Religious Groups with Those Differing from Themselves*. Unpublished doctoral dissertation, University of Michigan, 1952.

Riesman, David. *Constraint and Variety in American Education*. Garden City, N. Y.: Doubleday and Company, 1958.

———, et al. *The Lonely Crowd*. New Haven: Yale University Press, 1950.

Roberts, David E. *Psychotherapy and the Christian View of Man*. New York: Charles Scribner's Sons, 1954.

Robertson, E. H. *Man's Estimate of Man*. Richmond, Va.: John Knox Press, 1958.

Rockwood, Catherine A. *The Personal and Family Life Needs of College Women with Implications for Education*. Unpublished doctoral dissertation, University of Chicago, 1952.

Rogers, Carl R. *On Becoming a Person*. Boston: Houghton Mifflin Company, 1961.

Rogers, William C. *Community Education in World Affairs*. Minneapolis: The University of Minnesota Press, 1956.

Rokeach, Milton. *The Open and Closed Mind*. New York: Basic Books, 1960.

Ross, Murray G., and Charles E. Hendry. *New Understandings of Leadership*. New York: Association Press, 1957.

Sadler, James B. *Attitudes toward the Church as a Helping Agency*. Unpublished Ed. D. thesis, University of Pennsylvania, 1959.

Samenfink, Jacob Anthony. *A Study of Some Aspects of Marital Behavior as Related to Religious Control.* Unpublished Ed. D. thesis, Florida State University, 1956.

Sanders, Irwin. *The Community: An Introduction to a Social System.* New York: The Ronald Press, 1958.

Sarnoff, David, *et al. The Fabulous Future.* New York: E. P. Dutton Company, 1956.

Schachtel, Ernest G. *Metamorphosis.* New York: Basic Books, 1959.

Schaie, Klaus K. *Rigidity-flexibility and Intelligence.* Washington: American Psychological Association, 1958.

Schilling, S. Paul. *Methodism and Society in Theological Perspective.* New York: Abingdon Press, 1960.

Schindler, John A. *How to Live 365 Days a Year.* Englewood Cliffs, N. J.: Prentice-Hall, 1953.

Schmidt, John F. *Patterns of Poor Adjustment in Persons of Later Maturity.* Unpublished doctoral dissertation, University of Chicago, 1950.

Schneider, Herbert W. *Morals for Mankind.* Columbia: University of Missouri Press, 1960.

Schramm, Wilbur. *The Impact of Educational Television.* Urbana: University of Illinois Press, 1960.

———. *Responsibility in Mass Communication.* New York: Harper and Brothers, 1957.

Scott, John. *Democracy Is Not Enough.* New York: Harcourt, Brace and Company, 1960.

Scott, Marshal L. *A Proposal for Strengthening Presbyterian Churches of Industrial Communities Through the Use of Adult Education.* Unpublished Ed. D. thesis, Teachers College, Columbia University, 1953.

Scott, Nathan A., ed. *The Tragic Vision and the Christian Faith.* New York: Association Press, 1957.

Seeley, John R., Alexander Sim and Elizabeth W. Loosley. *Crestwood Heights: A Study of the Culture of Suburban Life.* New York: Basic Books, 1956.

Sellers, James Earl. *The Church and Mass Communication.* Unpublished doctoral dissertation, Vanderbilt University, 1958.

Seton-Watson, Hugh. *Neither War Nor Peace.* New York: Frederick A. Praeger, 1960.

Seward, Georgene. *Psychotherapy and Culture Conflict.* New York: The Ronald Press, 1957.

Shartle, Carol L. *Executive Performance and Leadership.* Englewood Cliffs, N. J.: Prentice-Hall, 1956.

Sheats, Paul, Clarence Jayne and Ralph Spence. *Adult Education: A Community Approach.* New York: The Dryden Press, 1953.

Sherrill, Lewis J. *The Gift of Power.* New York: The Macmillan Company, 1955.

Shock, N. W. *Trends in Gerontology*. Stanford, Cal.: Stanford University Press, 2nd edition, 1957.

Shuster, George N. *Education and Moral Wisdom*. New York: Harper and Brothers, 1960.

Siegle, Peter E. *New Directions in Liberal Education for Executives*. White Plains, N. Y.: Fund for Adult Education, 1958.

Sillars, Robertson. *Seeking Common Ground in Adult Education*. Chicago: Adult Education Association of the U. S. A., 1958.

Simon, H. A. *Models of Man: Social and Rational*. New York: John Wiley and Sons, 1957.

Simos, Jack. *Social Growth Through Play Production*. New York: Association Press, 1957.

Sisemore, John T. *The Sunday School Ministry to Adults*. Nashville: Convention Press, 1959.

Sloyan, Gerard S., ed. *Shaping the Christian Message*. New York: The Macmillan Company, 1958.

Smith, Ethel S. *The Dynamics of Aging*. New York: W. W. Norton, 1956.

Smith, Eugene L. *God's Mission and Ours*. New York: Abingdon Press, 1961.

Sorokin, Pitirim. *Social and Cultural Dynamics*. Boston: Porter Sargent, 1957.

————. *The Ways and Power of Love*. Boston: The Beacon Press, 1954.

Southard, Samuel. *The Family and Mental Illness*. Philadelphia: The Westminster Press, 1957.

Southern Conference on Gerontology. *Aging: A Current Appraisal*. Gainesville: University of Florida Press, 1956.

Spike, Robert W. *In But Not Of the World*. New York: Association Press, 1957.

————. *To Be a Man*. New York: Association Press, 1961.

Spindler, George D. *The Transmission of American Culture*. Cambridge, Mass.: Harvard University Press, 1959.

Staley, Eugene. *The Future of Undeveloped Countries*. New York: Harper and Brothers, 1954.

Stanford, Stephen S. *Changing Ideologies of the American Home*. Unpublished doctoral dissertation, University of Colorado, 1959.

Starbuck, Edwin D. *The Psychology of Religion*. New York: Charles Scribner's Sons, 1901.

Staton, Thomas F. *How to Instruct Successfully*. New York: McGraw-Hill Book Company, 1960.

Stein, Maurice R. *The Eclipse of Community*. Princeton: Princeton University Press, 1960.

Steiner, Peter C., and Robert Dorfman. *The Economic Status of the Aged*. Berkeley: The University of California Press, 1957.

Sternberg, Fritz. *The Military and Industrial Revolution of Our Time.* New York: Frederick A. Praeger, 1959.

Stevens, Phillipa. *A Social Psychological Study of Pregnant Women.* Unpublished doctoral dissertation, University of Texas, 1954.

Stieber, Jack, Walter E. Oberer and Michael Harrington. *Democracy and Public Review.* Santa Barbara, Cal.: Center for the Study of Democratic Institutions, 1960.

Stinnette, Charles R. *Anxiety and Faith.* Greenwich, Conn.: The Seabury Press, 1955.

―――. *Faith, Freedom and Selfhood.* Greenwich, Conn.: The Seabury Press, 1959.

Stirling, Nora. *Family Life Plays.* New York: Association Press, 1961.

Strodtbeck, Fred L. *A Study of Husband-Wife Interaction in Three Cultures.* Unpublished doctoral dissertation, Harvard University, 1950.

Sullivan, Harry Stack. *Conceptions of Modern Psychiatry.* Washington: William Alanson White Psychiatric Foundation, 1947.

Syracuse University. *New Directions for Adult Education.* Syracuse: Syracuse University Press, 1959.

Sztankay, Zoltan. *Christianity, Democracy and Technology.* New York: Philosophical Library, 1957.

Taeuber, Conrad, and Irene B. Taeuber. *The Changing Population of the United States.* New York: John Wiley and Sons, 1958.

Tasch, Ruth Jacobson. *The Role of the Father in the Family.* Unpublished doctoral dissertation, Teachers College, Columbia University, 1950.

Tavard, H. G. *The Church, the Layman and the Modern World.* New York: The Macmillan Company, 1959.

Taylor, Marvin J., ed. *Religious Education; A Comprehensive Survey.* Nashville: Abingdon Press, 1960.

Thelen, Herbert A. *Dynamics of Groups at Work.* Chicago: The University of Chicago Press, 1954.

―――. *Education and the Human Quest.* New York: Harper and Brothers, 1960.

Theobald, Robert. *The Rich and the Poor.* New York: The New American Library, 1961.

Thibaut, John W., and Harold H. Kelley. *The Social Psychology of Groups.* New York: John Wiley and Sons, 1959.

Thomas, George F. *Christian Ethics and Moral Philosophy.* New York: Charles Scribner's Sons, 1955.

Thompkins, Dorothy C. *The Senile Aged Problem in the United States.* Berkeley: Bureau of Public Administration, University of California, 1955.

Thompson, Kenneth W. *Christian Ethics and the Dilemmas of Foreign Policy.* Durham, N. C.: Duke University Press, 1959.

Thouless, Robert H. *Authority and Freedom: Some Psychological Problems of Religious Belief.* Greenwich, Conn.: The Seabury Press, 1954.

Tibbitts, Clark, ed., *Handbook of Social Gerontology.* Chicago: The University of Chicago Press, 1960.

———, and Wilma Donahue, eds. *Aging in the Modern World.* Ann Arbor: University of Michigan Press, 1957.

———, eds. *Aging in the Modern World: A Study Discussion Series for Adults.* Ann Arbor: University of Michigan Press, 1957.

———, eds. *Aging in Today's Society.* Englewood Cliffs, N. J.: Prentice-Hall, 1960.

Tillich, Paul. *Dynamics of Faith.* New York: Harper and Brothers, 1957.

———. *Systematic Theology.* Chicago: The University of Chicago Press, 1951.

———. *Theology of Culture.* New York: Oxford University Press, 1959.

Tizard, Leslie J., and Harry J. S. Guntrip. *Middle Age.* New York: Crown Publishers, 1959.

Torrance, T. F. *Conflict and Agreement in the Church.* 2 vols. London: Lutterworth Press, 1959.

Toynbee, Arnold. *Christianity Among the Religions of the World.* New York: Charles Scribner's Sons, 1957.

Trueblood, Elton, and Pauline Trueblood. *The Recovery of Family Life.* New York: Harper and Brothers, 1953.

Turrell, Ruth E. Barrett. *Protestantism in Family Life Education.* Unpublished Ed. D. thesis, Teachers College, Columbia University, 1955.

Underwood, Kenneth W. *Protestant and Catholic: Religious and Social Interaction in an Industrial Community.* Boston: The Beacon Press, 1957.

Union College Character Research Project. *Powerful Learning Tools in Religion.* Schenectady, N. Y., 1958.

Vahanian, Tilla. *How Women Feel About Being Women.* Unpublished Ed. D. thesis, Teachers College, Columbia University, 1954.

Vidich, A. J., and J. Bensman. *Small Town in Mass Society.* Princeton, N. J.: Princeton University Press, 1958.

Vidler, A. Alex R. *Christian Belief and This World.* Greenwich, Conn.: The Seabury Press, 1957.

Visser t' Hooft, William Adolph. *The Pressure of Our Common Calling.* New York: Doubleday and Company, 1959.

von Hildebrand, Dietrich, and Alice Jourdain. *Graven Images: Substitutes for True Morality.* New York: David McKay Company, 1957.

Wadler, Nathan H. *Adult Jewish Education in New York City.* Unpublished Ed. D. thesis, Teachers College, Columbia University, 1952.

Warburg, James P. *The West in Crisis.* Garden City, N. Y.: Doubleday and Company, 1959.

Ward, A. Dudley, ed. *Goals of Economic Life.* New York: Harper and Brothers, 1953.

Ward, Leo R. *Catholic Life USA.* St. Louis: B. Herder Book Company, 1959.

————. *The Living Parish.* Notre Dame, Ind.: Fides Publishers, 1959.

Warner, W. Lloyd. *American Life: Dream and Reality.* Chicago: The University of Chicago Press, 1953.

————. *The Living and the Dead.* New Haven: Yale University Press, 1959.

Weatherford, Willis D., Jr., ed. *The Goals of Higher Education.* Cambridge, Mass.: Harvard University Press, 1960.

Webber, George W. *God's Colony in Man's World.* Nashville: Abingdon Press, 1960.

Weigel, Gustave. *Faith and Understanding in America.* New York: The Macmillan Company, 1959.

West, Charles C. *Outside the Camp.* Garden City, N. Y.: Doubleday and Company, 1959.

Wheelis, Allan. *The Quest for Identity.* New York: W. W. Norton and Company, 1958.

White, Claude W. *A Denominational Program for the Aging.* Unpublished D. R. E. thesis, Southwestern Baptist Theological Seminary, 1956.

White, Ralph K., and Ronald O. Lippit. *Autocracy and Democracy: An Essay in Experimental Inquiry.* New York: Harper and Brothers, 1960.

Whitehead, Alfred North. *Adventures of Ideas.* New York: The Macmillan Company, 1933.

Whyte, William H., Jr. *The Organization Man.* Garden City, N. Y.: Doubleday and Company, 1957.

Widmer, Frederick W. *Christian Education and the Family; a Philosophy and a Program of Christian Education for Home and Church.* Unpublished Th. D. thesis, Union Theological Seminary (Richmond, Va.), 1958.

Wieman, Henry Nelson. *Intellectual Foundations of Faith.* New York: Philosophical Library, 1961.

Wiggins, James W., and Helmut Schoeck, eds. *Foreign Aid Re-examined: A Critical Appraisal.* Washington: Public Affairs Press, 1958.

Williams, Arthur. *Recreation for the Aging.* New York: Association Press, 1953.

Williams, Daniel Day. *What Present-Day Theologians Are Thinking.* New York: Harper and Brothers, Revised Edition, 1959.

Willkens, Fred H. *A History of Protestant Adult Religious Education, 1900–1938.* Unpublished doctoral dissertation, University of Pittsburgh, 1939.

Willkens, William H. R. *A History of the Adult Education Programs and*

Agencies of the American Baptist Convention. Unpublished doctoral dissertation, University of Pittsburgh, 1958.

Winch, Robert F. *Mate Selection.* New York: Harper and Brothers, 1958.

Winter, Gibson. *Love and Conflict: New Patterns in Family Life.* Garden City, N. Y.: Doubleday and Company, 1958.

————. *The Suburban Captivity of the Churches.* Garden City, N. Y.: Doubleday and Company, 1961.

Wise, Carroll A. *Psychiatry and the Bible.* New York: Harper and Brothers, 1956.

Wood, Hugh B. *Foundations of Curriculum Planning and Development.* Seattle: Cascade Pacific Books, 1960.

Wood, Robert C. *Suburbia: Its People and Their Politics.* Boston: Houghton Mifflin Company, 1959.

Worth, Howard A. *A Concept of Maturity with Implications for Religious Education.* Unpublished D. R. E. thesis, Hartford Theological Foundation, 1951.

Wyckoff, D. Campbell. *The Gospel and Christian Education.* Philadelphia: The Westminster Press, 1959.

————. *Theory and Design of Christian Education Curriculum.* Philadelphia: The Westminster Press, 1961.

Wynn, John C. *How Christian Parents Face Family Problems.* Philadelphia: The Westminster Press, 1955.

Yarnold, Greville D. *The Spiritual Crisis of the Scientific Age.* New York: The Macmillan Company, 1959.

Yinger, J. Milton. *Religion, Society and the Individual.* New York: The Macmillan Company, 1957.

Ziegler, Earl F. *Christian Education of Adults.* Philadelphia: The Westminster Press, 1958.

Zunich, Michael. *Relationships between Maternal Behavior and Attitudes toward Family Life.* Unpublished doctoral dissertation, University of Florida, 1959.

Index

Adult Bible Class: and Uniform Lesson Series, 205
Adult Bible Course. See Methodist Church
Adult Christian education: unique characteristics of, 127; principles leading to improvement, 128-31
Aging: and adult education, 131; growing conservatism during, 145
Albrecht, R., 96
Alcoholics Anonymous, 266
Allport, Gordon, 13, 95, 241, 246, 247
Allport-Vernon Scale of Values, 8, 19-20
American Institute for Research, 291
Anti-Semitism, 13
Apostles' Creed, 189
Aquinas, Thomas, 44
Argyle, M., 2
Aristotle, 44, 75
Arnold, Martha, 3-4
Aspiration: levels of, 100-02
Attitudes: changes in adult years, 96-97
Augustine, 44, 47
Authoritarianism, 12, 54-55
Ayad, J. M., 95

Bacon, Francis, 75
Baptist, 218
Barth, Karl, 111, 172, 235-38
Barzun, Jacques, 63
Basic Christian Books. See Methodist Church
Bayley, N., 97
Behavior: views of Barth, 235-38; Brunner, 238; Ramsey, 238-39; Thomas, 239-40; relationship to character, 242-44; role-relationship, 251-54; proper outcome of faith, 255-56; stating objectives in terms of, 282-83
Behavioral change: and adult learning, 124; Christian and secular concepts, 124; a goal of Christian adult education programs, 129-30
Behaviorism, 45
Benedict, Ruth, 39
Bergevin, Paul, 94
Betts, George Herbert, 219-20
Bible study, 64
Biblical theology: and the revival of interest in contemporary theology, 172-73; and the reading of the Bible, 174; and the church, 174-75
Björkquist, Manfred, 111
B'nai B'rith, 134
Bodet, Torres, 192
Bonhoeffer, Dietrich, 111
Broadcasting and Film Commission, 71
Broen, W. E. Jr., 5-6
Brown, Norman O., 48
Brunner, Edmund deS., 89, 91, 101
Brunner, Emil, 238, 242, 244, 252
Buber, Martin, 40
Busse, E. W., 96

Camp Farthest Out, 117
Camus, Albert, 43, 50, 114
Cana Movement, 110
Canadian Council of Churches: lay movements of, 116
Catholic Church. *See* Roman Catholic Church
Cattell, Raymond B., 241, 248
Chandler, A. R., 96

Change: role in societal progress, 136-37

Character: varying definitions, 241-42; empirical dimensions, 242-44; types of, 244-45; trait theories, 245-49, 250-51

Character Research Project, 89, 90, 93, 94, 97, 99, 101, 102

Christian Churches. See Disciples of Christ

Christian Discipleship Series. See Disciples of Christ

Christian education: and human reason, 37

Christian Faith and Life Series. See United Presbyterian Church

Christian Family Movement, 110

Christian Fellowship Foundation, 117

Christianity: definition of, 233; relation to behavior, 233-35

Church: and culture, 28-33; theological orientation, 28-31; sociological orientation, 31-33; and Biblical theology, 174-75; definition of, 234; as a community of persons, 234-35; as the people of God, 235; role of conceptualization in its membership procedures, 263-64

Church and Home Series. See United Church of Christ

Cocktail Party, The, 40-41

Cofer, Charles N., 91-92

Columbus Group, 231

Comenius, Johann Amos, 75

Communicant classes, 263-64

Communication: contemporary hindrances to, 58-59; Christian education and, 59-60; and feeling, 60-62; and religious faith, 60-61; and ideas, 62-67; and images, 67-69.

Communism, 144

Conceptualization: definition, 48-50; formation in childhood, 52

Confraternity of Christian Doctrine, 110

Congregational Church, 218

Congregational Institutes of Jewish Studies, 134

Cooperative Curriculum Project. See National Council of Churches

Cornell, George W., 109

Counseling, 276-77

Crutchfield, R. S., 95

Culture: and the church, 28-33; and motivation, 91; the local church's relation to, 264-66; coordination of the church's adult program with community, 266-67; study outline, 297-99

Curriculum: varieties of theoretical orientation, 46-47; based on interpersonal relationships, 161; current status, 199-215; 300-01; confusion about definition, 199-200; elective materials, 211-13; relationship with the home, 213-14; needed research on status, 214-15; definition, 217; merging of program and printed materials, 217; increased need for elective materials, 226-27; foundational elements of an adequate curriculum, 299-300; needed changes, 301-05. See also Uniform Lesson Series and Graded Lesson Series

Dartmouth College, 8, 20

Decision-making: and motivation, 93, 94; and dialogical communication, 163-66

Dewey, John, 36, 75

Diagnostic technique for improving Christian adult education, 130-31

Dialogue: errors in monological method of communication, 153-54; principle of, 154-55; nature of, 155-58; Incarnation and, 159-61; curriculum and, 161-63; Word of God and word of man, 162; purposes of education and, 163-68; and decision making, 165-66; in theology, 172

Dickens, Charles, 50

Dipboye, W. J., 10

Disciples of Christ, 6; Christian Discipleship Series, 211, 213

Dissenter churches, 104

Donahue, Wilma, 251

Douglass, Truman, 171

Earlham College, 117

Eastern Orthodoxy, 175

Ecumenical movement and Christian education: definition, 185-86; ecumenical education, 186-87; evidences of ecumenicity, 188-89; growth in the world community, 193-95; work of the World Council of Christian Education, 195-98

Edelman, Lily, 134
Education: philosophy of, 75-77; person-centered vs. content-centered,
75-76
Eichmann, Adolf, 61
Eliot, T. S., 40-41
Erikson, Erik, 35, 39, 245
Evaluation: standards required for,
125; feasibility of, 205-06; definition
of criteria, 257-58; purpose of, 258-
59; list of criteria for adult program,
260-77; need for, 278-79; definition
of, 279; types of, 279-82; steps in,
282-88; role in curriculum development, 288-89; place in Christian
adult education, 289-94; future pros-
pects, 294-96
Evangelical academies: in Germany,
112; Holland, 112-13; France, 113
Evangelical Church, 112
Evanston Ecumenical Institute, 116-17,
231

Faith: operating definitions, 260; role
in evaluation, 260-61
Faith and Life Community (Texas),
230-31
Faith and Life Institutes, 117
Faith for Life Series. See Graded
Lesson Series
Family: role in Christian education,
143-44; curriculum for, 213-14; as an
educational agency, 273-74; in
evaluation of the educational pro-
gram, 273
Farnsworth, P. R., 95
Ferraro, C. D., 23
Fichter, J. H., 15, 18
Five Oaks Christian Workers Center,
117
Flanagan, John, 291
Foreign Policy Association, 71
Frakes, Margaret, 106-07, 112
Freud, Sigmund, 45-46
Friendship Press, 217
Fromm, Erich, 39
Fund for Adult Education, 66

Gentile, Giovanni, 47
Gillespie, J. W., 95
Gillin, John, 253
Graded Lesson Series: patterns of
publication, 210-11; committee on,

221-22; relationship to adult Chris-
tian education, 221; Older Youth-
Young Adult committee on, 221;
"Faith for Life" series, 221-22
Grail Movement, 110
Great Books series, 70
Group dynamics: 54-55, 79; research
on, 66; discussion groups in the
church, 121; role of group process
theory in evaluation, 267-70

Havighurst, Robert J., 96, 99, 100,
241-42, 244
Hegel, George F., 36
Herbart, Johann Friedrich, 75
Herberg, Will, 28, 30, 170
Highbaugh, Irma, 197
Holmes, Jack Clellon, 28
Holy Spirit: role in adult learning,
262-63
Home. See Family
Hordern, William, 211
Horney, Karen, 39, 41-42, 243
Howe, Reuel, 90
Humanitarianism: and religion, 12-13
Hurlock, E. B., 96
Huxley, Julian, 36

Impersonalization, 39-40
Incarnation: and dialogical communi-
cation, 159-61; role in the relation-
ship with God and neighbor, 254
Inner Mission Movement, 114-15
Institutes of Judaism, 134
International Christian Leadership
Movement, 148
International Council of Religious
Education, 218
International Graded Lesson Series.
See Graded Lesson Series
International Lesson Committee. See
Uniform Lesson Series
International Missionary Council, 189-
90, 197
International Sunday School Associa-
tion, 218
International Uniform Lesson Series.
See Uniform Lesson Series
Iona Community, 111

James, William, 1
Jesus Christ: ground of Christian selfhood, 42-43; teachings of, 48

Jewish education: insights from, 133-35

Jones, E. Stanley, 117

Jones, Mary C., 3-4

Kansas City Study of Adult Life, 252

Kaplan, Abbott, 66

Kay, Harry, 67

Keeler, Sister Jerome, 131

Kelly, E. L., 19-20

Kerouac, Jack, 28

Kierkegaard, Sören, 40

Kingsbury, Forrest A., 10-12

Kingsley, Charles, 50

Kirchentag, 114-16, 230

Kirkridge, 117

Knowles, Malcolm S., 102, 203

Kraemer, Hendrik, 104, 106, 111, 230

Krech, David, 95

Kuhlen, Raymond G., 3-4, 10, 96

Laity: theology of, 178-81

Laymen: influential role in churches, 104-07; estrangement from institutional church, 106-07; denominational efforts at renewal, 107-10; preaching and renewal, 107-08; men's and women's groups, 108-09; in the Roman Catholic Church, 109-10; ecumenical efforts at renewal, 110-16; European emphases, 110-16; evangelical academies, 112-14; American lay movements, 116-20; areas of current need, 120-21

Laymen's Missionary Movement, 105

Laymen's Movement for a Christian World, 117

Laymen's Theological Library, 70

Lazerwitz, J., 15, 18

Leadership: need for increased development programs, 227-28; role in evaluation, 272-73; development of, 273

Leadership Education Curriculum, 227-28

Learning: definition of, 48-50; and communication skills, 61; and Christian adult education's methodology, 77-80; and changes in behavior, 78-79; characteristics of adult learning, 80-81; personal goals, 90; effect of sex differences among teachers on, 92; results with children compared to parents' viewpoints, 97; and dialogical communication, 153-68; theory of adult learning, 203; concept in Uniform Lesson series, 204-05; cycles of learning and evaluation, 268-71

Lee, J. William, 61

Lewin, Kurt, 100

Liebrecht, Walter, 117

Ligon, Ernest, 89-90, 98, 245

Linton, Ralph, 251

Littell, Franklin H., 111, 230

Living Room Learning, 134

Love: New Testament definition, 233-34; expressed in the church, 235; chief characteristic of the Christian, 240; obedient love, 249-51, 254

Luther, Martin, 173

Lutherans, 6, 12

Mace, David, 197

MacLeod, George, 111

Marx, Karl, 45

Maslow, A. H., 2

Maturity: and Christian education objectives, 82

McCann, R. V., 95-96

McCluskey, Howard, 67-68

McDougall, William, 249

Mead, Margaret, 39, 66, 72, 193

Meaning: lack of, 33-39

Men's clubs in the church, 108-09

Mergers: among denominations, 175-76

Methodist Church: Basic Christian Books, 70; Adult Bible Course, 70; Board of Social and Economic Relations, 118-19; Adult Fellowship Series, 211; Advanced Studies Series, 211

Methodists, 70, 105

Methodist Episcopal Church, 218

Methods: and content, 53-55; lecture vs. discussion, 63; a theory for adult Christian education, 73-87; purposes of a theory, 73-75; and a concept of education, 75-77; and the nature of learning, 77-80; and characteristics of learners, 80-81; and objectives, 81-86; types of, 84; and evaluation, 86-87; dangers involved in use of secular methods, 123-26

Middle Ages, 27

Moral law: relationship to public issues, 138; dangers resulting from ignoring, 139-41

Moreau, Jules, 63

Motivation: in religious development, 25; insights for Christian adult education, 88; definition of, 88-92; in learners, 92-93; in educators, 92; and decision making, 94; and personal beliefs, 94-98; and life situations, 98-100; and levels of aspiration, 100-02

Mott, John R., 105

Muelder, Walter, 32

Mumford, Lewis, 195

National Council of Catholic Men, 109, 110

National Council of Catholic Women, 110

National Council of Churches of Christ: lay movements, 116; Commission on General Christian Education, 202, 217-18, 229; Division of Christian Life and Work, 217; Division of Home Missions, 217; Division of Foreign Missions, 217; United Church Women, 217; United Church Men, 217; Division of Christian Education, 217; Department of Administration and Leadership, 217; Department of Children's Work, 217; Department of Youth Work, 217; Department of Family Life, 217; Department of Audio-Visual and Broadcast Education, 217; Friendship Press, 217; Commission on Missionary Education, 217, 229; Department of Curriculum Development, 217-18; Cooperative Publication Association, 222; Steering Committee for Curriculum Study, 222; Cooperative Curriculum Project, 223-25, 226, 229; future goals for cooperative adult curriculum ventures, 225-32; Leadership Education Curriculum, 227-28; Committee on Adult Work, 228

Needs: psychological, 91; normative, 91

Nicene Creed, 189

Niebuhr, H. Richard, 235, 243, 250

Niemöller, Martin, 111

Niles, D. T., 182

Objectives: and methodology, 81-86; and needs, 81-84; and evaluation, 86-87, 261-63, 282-84; and dialogical communication, 163-68; erroneous ideas about, 163-64

Observers: role in evaluation, 293

Orbach, Harold L., 15, 251

Oxford Group Movement, 105

Pace, C. R., 10

Packard Manse, 117

Parishfield, Michigan, 230

Peck, Robert F., 241-42, 244

Pelikan, Jaroslav, 211

Person: conception of, 274-75, role in Christian education, 275-76

Pestalozzi, Johann Heinrich, 75

Pollak, Otto, 251

Positive Potential Study of the Character Research Project, 99

Powell, M., 23

Pre-Cana Movement, 110

Prejudice: and religion, 13

Presbyterian Church in Canada, 117

Presbyterians, 70, 218. See also United Presbyterian Church

Pre-Testing, 289

Priesthood of all believers, 179

Pro-Con technique of evaluation, 294

Progoff, Ira, 191

Protestant Episcopal Church: 117, 218; Seabury Series, 70

Psychology of religion, 1-2

Quakers, 105, 117

Ramsey, Paul, 238-39

Rassemblements Protestant, 116

Reaction tests, 292

Reformation, 65, 179

Religion: varieties of definition, 2-7, 24-25; influence of the cultural context, 7-9, 25, 27; psychological factors, 9-14; and church attendance, 11, 15, 16, 18, 19-20, 22; trends in adult years, 14-18; and prayer, 17; and radio listening, 17; college students' attitudes toward, 18-19, 51-52; and beliefs, 18-21; and attitude changes, 20-22; increased interest

with aging, 23-24, 25; and motivational patterns, 25; need for research, 25-26; and the Beat Generation, 28; humanistic varieties, 36-37
Remmers Scale of Values, 19-20
Renaissance, 50
Research: need for in adult education, 231-32; descriptive type, 288-89
Riesman, David, 35-36, 39, 243
Rocco, Alfredo, 47
Rogers, Carl, 250-51
Roman Catholic Church: 12, 14, 15, 16, 18, 105, 176; lay activity and church renewal, 109-10, 178; Christian Family Movement, 110, 132; Pre-Cana and Cana Movements, 110, 131; Grail Movement, 110; adult education programs, 131; Institutes of Industrial Relations, 131; adult education centers in Chicago, 131-32; and Biblical theology, 174-75; Ecumenical Council, 190; Pope John XXIII, 190

Schand, J., 6-7
Schilling, S. Paul, 119-20
Seabury Series. See Protestant Episcopal Church
Selfhood and Christian education, 41-43
Sermon on the Mount, 48
Sigtura Foundation, 111
Smith, Adam, 45
Socrates, 75
Spencer, Herbert, 75
Spiegel, John, 252
Starbuck, Edwin D., 1
State Department, 71
Steinbeck, John, 50
Stern, G. G., 10
Still, J. W., 96-97
Strong, E. K., 96
Student Volunteer Movement, 105
Study Outline for Workshop participants, 297-305
Stuttgart Declaration of Guilt, 112, 121
Sullivan, Harry Stack, 39, 243

Talk Back, 71
Television, Radio and Film Commission of the Methodist Church, 71
Thadden-Trieglaff. See von Thadden
Theology and Christian adult education: revival of interest in, 169-72; local church isolation from theology, 170; Biblical theology, 172-75; ecumenical theology, 175-78; accents on laity, 178-81; the world in theological perspective, 181-84
Thomas, George, 239-40
Thomism. See Aquinas
Thurian, Max, 189
Tillich, Paul, 27, 37-38, 60
Troeltsch, Ernst, 183
Tyler, Ralph W., 279-82

Unamuno, Miguel de, 47
UNESCO, 192-93
Uniform Lesson Series: equated with adult curriculum, 200; questionable status of, 200, 209-10; definition of, 200-01; extent of use, 201, 210, 219-21; varieties of publication format, 201; purpose of, 202; Bible centrality, 202-03; relation to contemporary life, 203; concept of learning theory, 203-05; evaluation practices in, 205-07; role of stated objectives in, 206; comparisons among various sets of, 207-10; possibilities of more inter-denominational publishing efforts, 208-09; lack of relationship to the home, 213; committee on, 218-21; International Lesson Committee, 218; Handbook of Principles and Procedures, 219; objectives of, 219; Cycle committee, 220; quarterly committee, 220; age group committee, 220; future projections of, 220-21, 225-26
United Church of Canada: Five Oaks Christian Workers Center, 117
United Church of Christ, 208; Church and Home Series, 212, 213
United Lutheran Church Faith and Life Institutes, 117
United Presbyterian Church, 35, 208; Christian Faith and Life Series, 210-11
Unitarians, 6, 12

Values: and religion, 18-21; relative stability in adulthood, 96-98; factors influencing changes within adult values, 97-98
Visser t'Hooft, W., 186

Vocation: education's role in the choice of, 145-46; public service and Christian vocation, 146-47; values applied to one's vocation, 147-49; international relations and Christian vocation, 149-52
von Thadden-Trieglaff, Reinhold, 115

Ward, Leo R., 109-10
West, Charles, 30
Whitehead, Alfred North, 105, 183
Wichern, Johann Hinrich, 114
Williams, Daniel Day, 177
Wilson, W. Cody, 13
Winch, R. F., 10
Women's Society, 108
Workshop at Pittsburgh (1958), 203, 216
World Council of Christian Education: cooperation with the World Council of Churches, 190; emerging role of adult education, 196; work in various countries, 196-97

World Council of Churches: 1954 Assembly at Evanston, 116-17, 118, 186; 1961 New Delhi Assembly, 175, 186; Central Committee, 186; merger with the International Missionary Council, 189-90; Department on the Cooperation of Men and Women in Church and Society, 197; Department on Laity, 197
World Institute on Christian Education (Tokyo, 1958), 196
World Student Christian Federation, 105, 190
Wright, Herbert F., 91
Wyckoff, D. Campbell, 223

Yokefellow Movement, 117
Young, J., 95
Young Men's Christian Association, 105, 113, 116, 190
Young Women's Christian Association, 105, 116, 190

Zola, Émile, 45